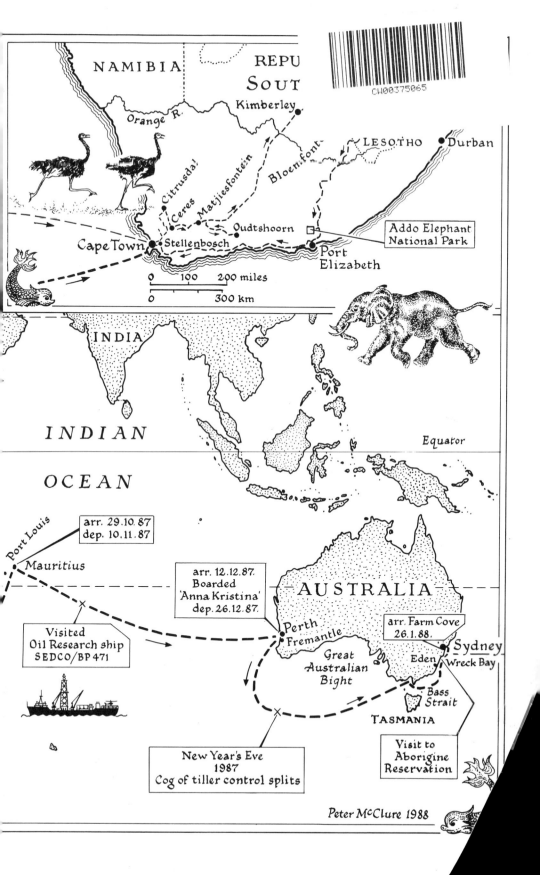

NAMIBIA

REPU
SOUT

Orange R.

Kimberley

LESOTHO Durban

Citrusdal

Ceres

Matjiesfontein

Bloemfont

Cape Town Stellenbosch Oudtshoorn

Addo Elephant
National Park

Port
Elizabeth

| 0 | 100 | 200 miles |
| 0 | | 300 km |

INDIA

INDIAN

OCEAN

Equator

Port Louis

arr. 29.10.87
dep. 10.11.87

Mauritius

arr. 12.12.87.
Boarded
'Anna Kristina'
dep. 26.12.87.

AUSTRALIA

Visited
Oil Research ship
SEDCO/BP 471

arr. Farm Cove
26.1.88.

Perth
Fremantle

Sydney

Eden Wreck Bay

Great
Australian
Bight

Bass
Strait

TASMANIA

New Year's Eve
1987
Cog of tiller control splits

Visit to
Aborigine
Reservation

Peter McClure 1988

MARCUS MAINWARING

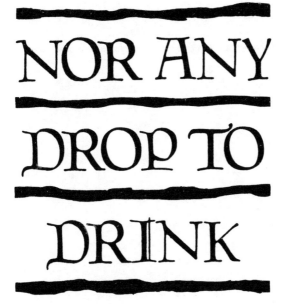

NOR ANY DROP TO DRINK

**ENGLAND TO AUSTRALIA
MAY 1987-JANUARY 1988**

BLOOMSBURY

First published 1988
Copyright © 1988 by Marcus Mainwaring

Bloomsbury Publishing Ltd, 2 Soho Square, London W1V 5DE

British Library Cataloguing in Publication Data

Mainwaring, Marcus
Nor any drop to drink.
1. Voyages from Great Britain to Australia
by sailing ships, 1987–1988
1. Title
910.4′5

ISBN 0–7475–0235–8

Typeset by Cambrian Typesetters, Frimley, Surrey
Printed in Great Britain by
Butler & Tanner Ltd, Frome, Somerset

To my wife
with whom this book could not have been written

Contents

Illustrations

MAPS

DRAWING

Acknowledgements

I would like to thank the following people for their help and support: Brian Rosen; Virginia Allan; Wally Franklin; Gerry Weingarth; Mark Crittle. Mark Hopkinson gave me the use of a beautiful flat at Palm Beach; Rank Xerox provided me with a portable electric 575 typewriter which survived the perils of the sea. John Sorensen, Sven Strömberg and Walther Roth put up with me throughout the voyage. Mark Lucas set up the deal and advised me, and, finally, Rory, my wife (Rosamund in the book), read and typed the manuscript.

Picture Credits

The author and publishers are grateful to the following for permission to reproduce photographs: Malcolm Clarke, nos 1, 4, 7, 8, 29 (reproduced in *Sailing Home*, a pictorial record of the First Fleet Re-enactment published by Angus & Robertson in 1988); Sigge Gustafsson, nos 10, 27; Rosamund Mainwaring, nos 2, 3, 5, 6, 9, 11, 12, 13, 14, 15, 16, 17, 18, 19, 20, 21, 22, 25, 26, 28; Glen Short, nos 23, 24.

1

The Press-Gang

The phone rang. It was Mark, my literary agent. We exchanged the usual pleasantries. I began to feel tense. Any moment now, I thought, he was going to start badgering me for a certain manuscript which was some weeks overdue.

'Are you free for the next nine months?' he asked.

'Yes,' I replied without thinking. I felt annoyed with myself. He had caught me off guard. I usually excel in the art of spontaneous prevarication. 'Well . . . er . . . more or less free,' I continued vaguely. 'My doctor . . . I have certain commitments.'

'Such as?'

'Well it depends on what you mean by the word "free",' I retaliated. There's nothing like a touch of semantics to obfuscate the clearest of issues and dislocate the process of coherent, linear thought.

'Would you like to go on a cruise to Australia?'

'For nine months?' Even I knew it didn't take nine months to get to Australia.

'It doesn't go direct,' he explained. 'It calls in at Tenerife, Rio de Janeiro, Cape Town, Mauritius – a few weeks in each port.'

'What's the snag?'

'There's no snag. Well . . . it stops off at Portsmouth for two weeks.'

'I thought there must be something.'

'We want you to write a book about it. It's a trip to commemorate the sailing of the First Fleet of settlers for Botany Bay, two hundred years ago this month.'

'Why me?'

'We couldn't find anyone else da ... dynamic enough. Besides, you used to teach history and we want a travelogue that juxtaposes the past with the present.'

'Yes, I remember teaching some scrofulous adolescents about the original voyage. It was a major achievement which, in my opinion, hasn't received the accolade it deserves. Eleven square rigged ships carrying nearly a thousand convicts set sail – '

'Save it for the book,' Mark interrupted.

'When do I leave?'

'Next week,' he said.

'But that's next week,' I protested.

'Spot on. I don't know how you do it.'

'But I'll need more than a week to get ready. Arrangements will have to be made.'

'Now listen,' he said. 'I'll handle most of the paperwork. All you've got to do is fill in a few forms which I'll bring over tomorrow. I'll take you to the docks on Saturday 25th April, and see you on board. Meanwhile you go shopping. Buy yourself some suntan oil.'

'What's the name of the ship? What line? P&O?'

'Oh, I nearly forgot. I'll probably be able to get you a hefty advance but it won't come through till you're on the high seas. Take some spending money for drinks and trips ashore. Everything else is paid for. And one last thing. You'll need a visa for Australia. That shouldn't be too much of a problem. You haven't got a criminal record, have you?'

'I didn't think it was still necessary.'

'Oh, by the way. They'll pay for Rosamund to fly out for the two middle legs – Rio to Cape Town and Cape Town to Mauritius.'

This sounded like a good deal to me. Already I had visions of myself sitting in a deckchair clutching a massive gin and tonic, so I went to the drinks cabinet and made myself one.

I sat down to compose a shopping list. I'd need a matching set of pigskin suitcases, a couple of safari suits, a portable brass peppermill and a new dinner jacket. This last item made me stop and think. Mark had been evasive when I'd enquired about the shipping line. He had been very quick to change the subject to money, in which he knew I had more than a passing interest. I like to receive it first and then pass it on to purveyors of perishable goods. Mark, on the strength of our acquaintance, had invested heavily in shares in Distillers and Imperial Tobacco.

I pondered over his reluctance to supply details and his unusually accommodating attitude towards the financing of the trip. Eventually I came to the conclusion that he'd probably booked me on one of those cheap Russian cruises. I wasn't too bothered. I'd heard that, although they lacked refinement, the caviare was first class. And I could save on the expense of a dinner jacket. Besides, Rio would be Rio whatever the shipping line.

I picked up the newspaper and idly turned the pages. A heading caught my eye:

THE FIRST FLEET RE-ENACTMENT VOYAGE.

As I read the article, certain phrases etched themselves into that part of the cerebrum which governs the faculty for self-preservation: 'Great maritime adventure . . . a fleet of square riggers will replicate the original voyage . . . passengers will act as trainee crew . . . a voyage of nine months braving forty-foot South Atlantic waves.'

What the hell was all this about? A sudden increase in electrical activity in the cranial cavity made me feel dizzy. They say that intelligence is simply the ability to relate one thing to another and then reach a conclusion. I was relating so many things so fast that I could feel my software beginning to overheat. And when I saw the accompanying illustration, it began to melt. I stared in horror at a photo of a square rigger moored at St Katharine's Dock. Suicidal maniacs hung from spars a hundred feet above the deck. It made me feel seasick just to look at it.

I decided to phone Mark – no easy task. It's easier to get through to Waterloo Station.

I got through to his assistant. She took pity on me. After years of working for Mark she can recognise genuine anguish even over crossed lines.

'You've seen the newspapers,' he said, getting in first and taking some of the wind out of my sails. The following conversation has been heavily censored. All Anglo-Saxon expletives which lent rhythm and emphasis have been left out to save paper and printing costs.

'I wouldn't go on the Serpentine on one of those,' I squawked.

'They've got diesel engines,' he countered.

'I don't care if they've got jet engines.'

'They've all been subjected to a rigorous inspection by the Board of Trade.'

'So had the *Titanic*,' I shrieked. 'And what's all this about passengers being trainee crew? Have you seen those masts? You know I have trouble travelling upstairs on a double-decker bus. Have you read about the *Tucker Thompson*? Sixty feet long indeed! Do you know how long sixty feet is? It's short. I could get the bloody thing in my sitting-room. And what kind of name is *Tucker Thompson*? It sounds like a picnic hamper from one of the less fashionable stores.'

'You don't have to go on the *Tucker Thompson*,' he said soothingly. 'There's the *Søren Larsen*. She's a hundred and forty feet long.'

'Short!' I corrected him. 'That's the one in the photo. These . . . these . . . these ships . . . boats . . . coracles . . . should be in a dry dock like the *Cutty Sark*, propped up on reinforced girders.'

'Some of them have got cabins,' he said.

'I don't care if some of them have got bowling alleys.' He let me ramble on for a while. Every now and then his calm, hypnotic voice interjected. His remorseless logic began to wear me down. I finally capitulated when he offered to treat me to an expense account meal at *my* favourite restaurant, after which he would drive me to St Katharine's Dock to inspect the fleet. This was privileged treatment. Mark usually insisted on his favourite Greek restaurant, knowing that most people, even hardened dipsomaniacs like myself, can only drink so much Retsina. My revenge would have an excellent bouquet. The particular claret I had in mind cost £120 a bottle.

We arrived at St Katharine's Dock at about four o'clock and made our way to the *Søren Larsen*. I fell up the gangplank. By the time I had found my bearings Mark was deep in conversation with a craggy-faced man. This was the Captain, Anthony Davies. I had seen his photo in the brochure. Mark beckoned to me. I stumbled over a rope.

'It's a bit ropy,' I said. Everybody winced; but the ghastly pun was absolutely unintentional. The Captain held out his hand. I reciprocated and grasped thin air. He moved his hand to meet mine. Our palms crossed. Once again I grasped thin air.

'I haven't found my sea legs yet,' I explained.

Eventually a firm grip enclosed my hand. His pale blue eyes betrayed no emotion. Then I was introduced to Andy, the medical officer. His fingers were as thick as my wrists. He had muscles on his feet – this was something I hadn't seen before. The rest of the crew were of similar physical construction. I began to feel more confident. They all looked so tough and professional. I was in good hands.

'So you're a writer,' said the Captain, 'and I gather you don't know much about the sea.' He was right. To me the English Channel was simply an inconvenience which generated long queues at ferry terminals. It was an obstacle between me and the vineyards and restaurants of France. I had seen it clearly once from Brighton Pier. My other sightings had been somewhat blurred by the duty-free gin and the condensation streaming down the windows of cross-channel ferries. My general impression of it was one of uniform greyness, occasionally streaked with slivers of gangrenous green.

For five minutes the Captain talked eloquently and passionately about the sea's ever-changing face; about its transient
moods; and about how I would find it a constant source of
inspiration.

'Perhaps *you* should write the book,' I said and looked
hopefully at my agent.

'And *you* run the ship?' he said.

'Can I have a look downstairs?' I asked. The Captain's glare
bored through me. Andy wandered off, whistling.

'That won't be necessary,' said Mark. 'I'm afraid the *Søren
Larsen* is fully booked for the first leg, from here to Portsmouth.
We'll have to try another ship. I think there's a vacancy on the
Amorina. It's moored at Tower Pier. Let's wander over and
check it out.'

The Captain drew me aside. He stared hard into my eyes.

'Don't worry, you'll soon learn the ropes.' He waved at what
seemed to me to be a hopelessly complex tangle of rigging. I
suddenly realised that he was speaking literally. My interest was
aroused. What to me had always been a cliché to be studiously
avoided was now imbued with new life. Never before had I
questioned the origin of the expression.

'This,' he said, tugging at the nearest one, 'is a halyard. And
this is a bunt line. This is a clew line. You'll find it confusing at
first, but you'll soon learn. And by the way, there's really only
one rope on a ship like this and that's the bell rope.' He pulled
it. The bell rang. There was a stampede to the mess table.

'We eat early at sea,' he said. 'We rise early and turn in early –
that is unless you are on watch. Good luck on the *Amorina*.'

As we set off for the *Amorina* we passed the *Tucker Thompson*
which was moored just behind the *Søren Larsen*.

'That thing hasn't got room for engines,' I said. 'There's
barely a space in the bilges for somebody to pedal.'

Mark hurried me past. We fought our way along the
Embankment through hordes of Japanese tourists to Tower

Pier. To get to the *Amorina* we had to cross the decks of the *Kaskelot* – a square rigger that had starred in such films as *Return to Treasure Island* and *The Last Place on Earth*. It looked a bit too authentic for my liking.

I wasn't too inspired by the *Amorina* either, although I took some comfort from the fact that it had a steel hull. Apparently it had once been a light ship. The rigging was swarming with people with underdeveloped nervous systems.

A young Swedish girl showed us a cabin – a double berth. It was about seven feet by five, with a toilet and shower en suite. I was suddenly somewhat mollified to realise that, by the standards of the other ships, this was the height of luxury.

'You will have a friend,' she said. I looked at Mark.

'What if my wife finds out?'

'That's a euphemism for the bloke you'll be sharing the cabin with, you idiot.'

'Christ! What if he turns out to be an eighteen-stone slob with halitosis, festering feet and a snore like a chainsaw?'

'Well, it's better than sharing with the anchor chain,' he said.

'It's all right for you,' I grumbled. 'You'll be sitting in your office in Regent Street while I'm tossing about for nine months on forty-foot waves, surrounded by lunatics who actually enjoy risking their lives. Who do you think I am? Shackleton? Sir Francis Chichester?'

I was beginning to have second thoughts. My courage was seeping away now that my liver had come to grips with the claret. Post-prandial depression was setting in. Mark recognised the danger signals.

'They'll be open soon,' he said, looking at his watch.

'I'm not going,' I said firmly.

'I'll get your poetry published,' he said.

'In one of those slim volumes on antique laid paper?'

'Very slim,' he said.

'This is just another form of press-ganging,' I said.

'Welcome aboard,' he replied.

2
The Cocktail Party

I felt no apprehension when we set sail from London at two-thirty p.m. on Monday 27 April 1987. This first leg to Portsmouth was to be more of an occasion than an adventure – a mere aperitif. Most of the passengers, or rather trainee crew, were only going on the first leg. A lot of them were businessmen or highly paid professionals who had the money but not the time to go any further. The real voyagers were joining at Portsmouth or Rio. About ten of us were going the whole way to Sydney, and we had been split up among the various ships.

I stood at the rail with Gordon, an Australian pastry cook, watching the proceedings. We took a long time to get under way. The *Amorina* went north up the Thames, describing a figure of eight. I felt I ought to go to the bridge and tell them that the sea was the other way.

'We're doing all this to get in line,' said Gordon as if he could read my thoughts. 'The *Søren Larsen*'s got to lead. She's the flagship.'

He flicked a cigarette in the Thames and lit another. I decided to conduct an informal interview.

'What made you decide to embark on this momentous voyage?'

'What?'

'Why are you going on this trip?'

'Oh – just fancied it. That's all.' This fellow would be the ruin of Terry Wogan. We stood in silence, watching Tower Bridge slowly open. Gordon yawned.

'That's a fine bridge,' I said. 'Neo-Gothic.'

'Yeah!'

'You smoke a lot, Gordon?'

'Yeah – I do.'

'Been smoking long, Gordon?'

'Given up for the last ten years. Or so my wife thinks. Spent the last ten years smoking at the bottom of the garden. Now I can smoke in peace for the next nine months.' He looked ecstatic. Some people have the strangest reasons for travelling. This was a new one on me. Gordon wandered off coughing.

As we passed under Tower Bridge the *Amorina*'s masts seemed dangerously close to the walkway that connects the tops of the two towers. She really was a Tall Ship.

The wind was against us so we were under power. A few minutes later the trainee crew started to put up a few token sails to keep the BBC happy, directed by Walther, the first mate.

I stood and watched. This was not out of laziness or fear of becoming horny-handed. Walther had taken me aside earlier. He had explained that since most of this crowd were only going as far as Portsmouth, it would be better if Gordon and I kept in the background to let the rest of them have an opportunity to pull a rope or two. After all, we had nearly nine months to learn the ropes. Gordon hadn't understood Walther's eccentric English and was in the midst of the mêlée. It was the first time I had seen him without a cigarette.

It was an entertaining spectacle. About half the trainee crew, having the wherewithal to grease the axle around which the world revolves, owned small yachts, so they thought they knew a bit about sailing. The remainder, like me, were ignorant landlubbers. The zest of the amateur yachtsmen combined with the ignorance of the others was a recipe which did not make a good cocktail. Walther's fractured English was the Mickey Finn it did not need.

Walther would shout an order to the forty-odd people milling about and mayhem would ensue.

'*Ease the bunt lines,*' Walther shrieked. The landlubbers charged up the deck in one direction and the amateur yachtsmen in the other. The landlubbers, realising that they were going the wrong way, then set off in hot pursuit of those who thought they knew where the bunt lines were. They didn't. It was like watching a rugger match played by the Gadarene swine.

One character, who had been more than usually boastful about his sailing prowess, seized a rope and clung to it possessively. Immediately four others hurled themselves at it. It was lucky they all had potbellies. They bounced off each other.

Walther then made a mistake. He had obviously forgotten that this mob, and that is exactly what they were by now, had paid real money for the privilege of pulling a few ropes on this jaunt down the English Channel.

'*Zese are ze bunt lines,*' he shouted above the uproar, and placed himself in front of them. He disappeared under about 140 stone of expense-account lard. Some of them, in their eagerness to get a hand round a rope, were now climbing up and over the backs of the others. It reminded me of the Eton Wall Game. All I could see of Walther was one foot protruding from under a wobbling pyramid that heaved and grunted. After five minutes of this, half of them dropped out to give their pacemakers a chance to cool down.

I was in a bad way too. I'd laughed until I got a stitch in my side. Gordon had had the sense to drop out early and have a cigarette. It was safer. Christ knows what would happen in the mid-Atlantic or in the Roaring Forties.

The 'know-it-all' character, who'd come to grief earlier, had now recovered. He stood on somebody's head to begin his assault on the pyramid. It's a pity Eddie Waring's dead. He should have been there – not me – shouting, 'That fellow's due for an early bath.'

Walther was, in fact, an excellent and experienced seaman. He just hadn't been prepared for such blind enthusiasm. Later, on the Portsmouth to Tenerife leg, he brought the watch system into operation. This meant that about eight trainee crew were on duty at any one time, supervised by two professional crew. The rest were then theoretically off-duty. Things calmed down a bit, but not entirely. As I was to discover to my cost, there was always some hyperactive rope addict around who couldn't go ten minutes without a feel of the hemp. One chap in particular, who didn't join the *Amorina* until Portsmouth, seemed to be in need of a permanent fix. It was never safe to stand near a rope when he was in the vicinity – but more of him later.

I couldn't take any more of this, so I went to the stern to watch the scenery. We were now 'sailing' down the sweet and softly flowing Thames in a stately procession. The *Søren Larsen* led, followed by the *Kaskelot*, the *Trade Wind*, the *Amorina* and the *Tucker Thompson*. The *Bounty*, the *Anna Kristina* and other ships would be joining the fleet at Portsmouth. Crowds lined the Embankment and the office block windows were full of people waving us farewell. I began to feel quite important. There were only a few on the south bank, apart from workmen leaning on their shovels. They were probably worried that if Maggie got to hear about this trip they'd end up with one-way tickets to Australia – like the first lot. Such is the social divide of the Thames.

We passed Butler's Wharf and I could see through the gaping windows of the once great warehouse the new steel girders that propped up what was now merely a façade. Soon it would be converted into expensive flats for Yuppies. Some people aboard were tut-tutting. Far better to let these redundant warehouses rot.

On down the Thames we sailed, passing a Bovis Housing project – more tut-tutting – and acres and acres of industrial dereliction. Hardly any small cargo ships come up this far now. Container ships have killed the London docks.

We passed the spot where some misguided American wanted to build a replica of the Elizabethan theatre in which some of Shakespeare's plays were first performed. Unfortunately the original theatre had been on the site of what was now a council depot. I don't know how many years he had been fighting for planning permission, but apparently there was now a weak amber light at the end of the bureaucratic tunnel.

Such a shortage of land around here. On and on we went, passing rotting wharves, empty warehouses and gaunt, rusting cranes.

Jack Bingham announced his presence with a whiff of cigar smoke. He was another who had given up smoking. He had made a last-minute dash ashore to buy a crate of cigars. Jolly Jack, I called him. He seemed uncharacteristically subdued. He owned a hotel in Folkestone and I knew that he was a keen yachtsman.

'Why aren't you up there with the rest of them?' I asked, jerking my thumb in the direction of the boat deck which ran the length of the roof of the mess, galley and bridge, and from which still emanated quite a hullabaloo.

'It's my leg,' he complained. 'I injured it two weeks ago. It got worse yesterday. My foot swelled up. The nurse gave me antibiotics and told me to keep it above my head. Spent the whole night on the bunk with it jammed against the ceiling. Didn't sleep much.'

'Why did you come then?'

'Paid for the trip before I had the accident.'

'Accident? What happened? Tell me about it.'

'No. You might put it in the book.' He looked embarrassed.

'I promise I won't.'

'All right then. I've got these flagpoles in front of the hotel. I think they give the place a nautical flavour. Anyway, every Saturday night, after throwing-out time, the local brigands think it good sport to shin up them and steal the flags.'

'Yeah?'

'Yeah! I lost twenty-three flags last year. It was getting a bit expensive, so I decided to put a stop to it.'

'Yeah?'

'Yeah. Well, I went out and bought a big tin of grease. I put a ladder against one of them and started to grease the pole.' He paused. He looked embarrassed.

'Carry on.'

'I did very well at first. I managed to grease it right to the top. Then the ladder skewed off the pole. I suppose I was very lucky in a way. I managed to grab the pole and wrap my arms and legs round it. For a microsecond I knew what it was like to be a koala bear. Then gravity took over and I descended, accelerating at so many feet per second per second. Picked up a nasty big splinter on the way down, as well as a few other injuries.'

I looked at Jack with admiration. Most people limit themselves to the sort of accidents that cause traffic jams and loss of their no-claims bonus.

We were in the Thames Estuary now. The gravel pits of Thurrock receded in our wake. A haze obscured the land which for the last hour had been dreary and monotonous. Earlier I had seen a man walking his dog along the treeless flats. He had seemed the last man on earth.

The sea mists were rising. I stared down at the water hissing along the hull. It was grey and cold. The mists thickened. It was like being at the centre of a vast pearl. The sun, though low in the sky, was out there somewhere, its rays filtered and refracted by eerie, swirling vapour.

I looked down at the rushing water. Now and again its sinuous flight was pocked with whirlpools, like catherine wheels burning out. A buoy as big as a house burst out of the mist and careered by, not ten feet from our port side.

I wondered if we were supposed to pass that close. Two minutes later my question was answered. We ran aground on a sandbank. It wasn't a very dramatic experience. The *Amorina* simply stopped with a mild shudder.

The Swedish crew were more irritated than alarmed by the incident. There didn't seem to be any attempt to apportion blame. Thank God they weren't Italian. They would have beaten each other over the head with sextants and rolled-up charts. They did, however, revert to their own language. That took me back a few years. It sounded like a mild argument between Bill and Ben the Flowerpot Men.

Then somebody got out a chart of the Thames Estuary and put away the one of the Severn Estuary. The *Amorina* was thrown into *reverse* and we were off again.

This time it was the turn of the amateur yachtsmen to start tut-tutting as they disappeared below to check their insurance policies.

I was confused. What were these Swedes up to? As a nation they have a reputation for efficiency. Perhaps they were trying to pack in the accidents early and get them over with. I would have dismissed the matter had it not been for an earlier incident which I had thought nothing of at the time. They had anchored briefly off Gravesend to take aboard diesel and, in the process, rammed the fuel lighter. The authorities seemed more annoyed by the fact that they had dropped anchor opposite a huge sign that stated: 'DANGER. SUBMARINE CABLES.'

Later I stood alone on the deck. The mist insinuated itself in milky coils through the shrouds and lines and hung in dripping layers along the spars. I could hardly see the night light on top of the main mast. It seemed as remote as a star.

There's something infinitely melancholy about estuaries. Neither river nor sea, they conjure up in one a feeling of limbo. Perhaps it is because they suggest the sadness of departure, yet tempt one with a final glimpse of land. Estuaries make you look back and think of the person you have left behind.

The rigging creaked and the tidal brine slapped against the sides of the ship. Then I heard it. A funereal 'clong' rolled over the waters – a single desolate note that tolled in time to the motion of the ship as it rose and sank on the gentle swell. I have never heard a more mournful sound than this invisible bell. I strained to see through the mist.

'It's a buoy,' said Jack, materialising out of the darkness. 'It must be a very old one. The modern ones usually have sirens and sound like dying cows. Come and have a drink. We're all in the bar.'

'I thought I would try to cut back on the drinking this trip. I was only going to drink in sight of land.'

'See that light over there?' I thought I could just detect an amber glow in the seething mist. 'That's the lamp on the buoy.'

'But that's not land.'

'It's attached to land by a chain.'

'But that doesn't count,' I protested.

'Let's just say that it's very wet land. Come on. Don't stand here looking back.'

'All right, Jack.'

I've spent all my life looking back and, at the same time, following the pipes of Pan.

I settled down in the bar with Walther – Valter, as he pronounced it – Jack, and a mixed bag of Australians and Americans. The Americans, I noticed, had brought their own whisky.

Walther was exercising his ecological conscience. He had, as I had already discovered, a political conscience, a social conscience, and an environmental conscience as well. I don't know where he found room for them all.

'Sailing once, I met zis vale . . .'

'Whale.'

'Ya, a vale. It vas ze most – how you say it – it vas ze most moving, emotional moment of my life. It vas besides ze ship. I looked down upon it.'

'What did God say to the aborigines?'

'I looked down at zis vale. Ze vale looked back. Ze vale looked deep in mine eyes.'

'Don't do anything till I get back.'

'And this vale knew. Ze vale *knew*.'

'What did ze vale know, Walther?' Walther's eyes were wild.

15

For a moment I thought he'd taken offence at my flippant parody of his accent.

'*Ze vale knew*,' shrieked Walther, and paused for dramatic effect. The Americans started edging away.

'Ze vale knew,' he said, lowering his voice, 'dat he had made ze right decision. Oh ya.' The Americans fled.

'How – cough – do you rate – cough – Maggie's – cough – chances – Marcough?' asked Jack.

'Decision?'

'Ya. Decision. Ze vale knew dat ze great-great grandfathers of his origins had made ze vise decision.'

'You'd better humour him,' said Jack out of the corner of his mouth.

'Vat is dat?'

'Very interesting, Walther. But we don't quite follow your drift . . .'

'Vales are mammals. Ya. So are dolphins and porpoi. Vell, millions of years behind us, zey haf a choice – to live on ze land or to live in ze sea and ve choose ze land. Evolution. Ve haf evolved hands. *Hands.*'

Walther waved his hands. Jack bit through the end of his cigar and swallowed it.

'Ya! Hands vith vich to smoke ze cancer sticks. Hands vith vich to count ze money. Hands vich commit all manner of evils. Ze vale, he choose ze purity of ze sea. Ze vale knew dat ze land vould lead to ze veeping and ze gnashing of teeth.'

'He eschewed the vale of tears, eh Walther?' I said. Jack was looking at his hands, aghast.

'Chewed? Ze vale chews nothing. Ze vale filters his food. Ze vale lives in brotherhood. Ze vale . . .'

There was a commotion at the bar. There were cries of anguish and amazement.

'What? No beer left?' bleated a voice above the din. I led the stampede to the bar. It was true. Petra, the barmaid, looked smug (we were going to have trouble with her later).

THE COCKTAIL PARTY

The fleet had been open to the public at St Katharine's Dock. The *Amorina*, with a proper bar, had been especially popular. The public had made a determined attempt to drink her dry. They had nearly succeeded. The Swedes had either been oblivious of our childish licensing laws or had considered the Thames to be international waters. Walther came to Petra's aid.

'Ya. Ze Cockneys. Zey invade us. Zey trink till zey are vithout legs. Some of them ve haf to carry ashore.'

We settled down again with gin and tonics.

'This is the bitter end,' I said. Everyone groaned except Jack.

'A very appropriate pun, Marcus. Very nautical.' We all looked puzzled. 'A bitter,' continued Jack, 'is the rope at the end of an anchor chain – the ship's end. If the anchor gets caught on the sea bed and the ship needs to make a quick getaway, you simply cut through a chain link. But it's only done in an emergency – with great reluctance. Anchors are expensive. Hence the bitter end.'

'Ya. I look down at zis vale and his eye is knowing and sad. Wery sad. Vat are you doing to ze sea? it asks. All zis plastic bobbing about. Ze beer cans. Ze oil. Ze . . . hey, take it easy vith ze gin. Zey are trinking zat on ze bridge.'

The *Amorina* shuddered. The engine protested. Then she ploughed on again. We all looked at Walther.

'Ya, another sandbank. No problem. Ve biff our vay over. I tink maybe ve anchor for ze night. I go to ze bridge.'

'What's the Captain up to?'

'There is no Captain. He doesn't join us till we get to Portsmouth.'

'Who's the handsome, swashbuckling fellow with silver hair? I thought he was the Captain.'

'Oh him. He's just one of the part-owners. When we get to Portsmouth, he's flying back to Sweden.'

'Thank Christ for that.'

'Now that we've had our ration of sandbanks, we'll probably anchor in a deepwater channel for supertankers,' said Jack.

Somebody was passing round big glossy postcards of the *Amorina*.

'Two pounds each.'

The grey-haired part-owner was obviously planning on flying back first class.

One showed the *Amorina* in half profile, heeling over at a twenty-degree angle – tall, white, elegant – her bow adorned with mustachios of foam as she cut through a turquoise sea. Very cavalier. She looked splendid, the curved blades of her jib sails straining above the bowsprit; and behind them, the great white pagoda of her five square sails.

The other postcard revealed an aspect of the *Amorina* hidden by her majestic sails. Her rakish lines, which began with the tip of her bowsprit and followed the line of the deck, were abruptly terminated by a lump, a massive carbuncle, that rose uncompromisingly out of her stern. This was the bar, welded on, like the hood of a pram, above the natural line of the deck.

'Makes her look like a hip bath,' Jack grumbled.

'She's a converted lightship,' I said. 'That's her there.' I pointed at a faded framed photo hanging on the wall behind us. This got the amateur yachtsmen sniggering and sneering.

'The *Trade Wind* and the *Tucker Thompson* could sail rings round this thing,' said one.

'Wait till you see the *Anna Kristina*,' said another.

'*Anna Kristina*?'

'Yeah. She's joining us at Portsmouth. She's sailing down from Bergen. Saw her once off the coast of Norway. Excellent sailing ship. Close to the water.'

'What do you mean, close to the water?' I asked.

'Just that. Only a couple of feet between the deck and the sea. No boat deck on the roof of the galley like this tub. Crests of the waves at eyebrow level, even in moderate seas. Great fun putting up sails knee-deep in water. You really have to hang on.'

'Hang on?'

'Yeah. One hand for yourself, one for the ship. Easy to get swept overboard.'

'I really envy you, Marcus,' said Jack.

'Why?'

'People going the whole way can change ships each leg. The *Anna Kristina*'s yours, any time you like. Then you'll know what sailing's all about.'

I considered this a dubious privilege and made a mental note to cross the *Anna Kristina* off my list. Close to the water indeed. What was wrong with these people?

'It'll be good for the book,' said another idiot. 'You can't go the whole way on this.'

'I can. Besides I need a cabin to write in. Space for an electric typewriter,' I said, to howls of derision.

'They're already calling this the hospital ship. Get yourself on the *Anna Kristina* for an Atlantic crossing. You'll get lots of material for the book,' he persisted. I wished he'd shut up. He was putting me in a spot.

'Besides, this literary agent fellow of yours, he's bound to suggest it.'

'Suggest what?'

'Suggest that you change ships. Go on a real sailing ship.'

'Do you want a p . . .' He looked strong and fit. 'Another gin and tonic?'

Walther returned. I was relieved. I was fed up with all this talk of hauling on sheets knee-deep in brine.

'You've got a German accent. I thought you were Swedish,' I said to change the subject.

'Ya. I am a Svedish national. I vas spending my childhood in a refugee camp. My parents, zey are from a German sect living in ze Carpathian Mountains. Ve vere displaced. Some years after ze var ze authorities giff us two choices – Sweden or Australia. My mother she haff heard zat ze Australians are a ver rough people who are eating snakes for dinner. So to Sveden ve go.'

Petra closed the bar at two a.m. I lingered until it was empty and then decided to take a walk on the deck. Now that we were at anchor the mist no longer writhed and swirled but draped itself over the ship in a white mantle of silence. My vision was restricted to no more than six feet. I groped my way towards the bow. Although I was virtually sightless and encapsulated in silence, my other senses became curiously alert. I could smell the salt tang of the estuary; and as I passed the bosun's locker its powerful reek broke down into the almost palpable constituents of tarred rope, oiled string, waxed sail thread, paint thinner and linseed oil.

The wheelhouse gradually materialised in a yellow nimbus of diffused light. I peered in the starboard window. Walther was studying a chart. The scar at the corner of his left eye pulled it into a squint. The usual expression of amused disdain played around his mouth. I waved to him feeling rather foolish. He stared through me. With a slight shock I suddenly realised he couldn't see me. I felt like a voyeur. I moved away to the rail. There I could sense but not see the tidal current sluicing along the hull. I heard footsteps and the bark of a cough. It was Gordon.

'Came up for a fag,' he explained. 'Can't sleep. Spent nearly every night for the last twenty years baking bread and cakes. Didn't go to bed till my wife opened the shop in the morning.'

He flicked his cigarette end over the side. Its trajectory burnt a red vein in the opalescence. He lit another. For a moment his face was illuminated by the cupped orange glow.

'Why don't you . . .?'

'That would be chain-smoking. See you later.' He stepped into the mist and disappeared like a ghost passing through a wall. I took another peep in the wheelhouse. Walther, like a Rodin sculpture, was hunched over a chart. He was asleep. Somewhere in the mist Gordon coughed. I went below.

The next three days were uneventful. Forbidden to touch a sheet, clew or bunt line until after Portsmouth, I loafed around on deck and studied the English Channel. It was as flat as a Welsh miners' choir. It was like a canal without any scenery, the banks two trembling cliffs of heat haze. Perfidious Albion was giving us a brief sample of summer (a purely notional season) before spring dissolved into the long grey days of rain preceding an autumnal hurricane that destroyed a million trees. The Americans and Australians were seduced by the weather.

'What's all this about old England being a rain-slashed swamp?' they cried in unison.

'You wait,' I replied with the smug finality of a professional pessimist.

We sailed along the coast of Kent, Sussex and Hampshire without a glimpse of the green and pleasant land. It was like travelling down a deep railway cutting.

'Ve are opposite Shoreham-by-Sea,' Walther announced on the second day, pointing at the tall curtain of haze. We glared, willing it to part.

'I got married there,' I said.

'It doesn't say so on ze chart,' Walther grunted.

The nights were no better. Somebody had installed a portable electric keyboard in the bar. It had a synthesiser programmed to provide the player with a background accompaniment. It was a Japanese atrocity. It had a repertoire a cut above a Swiss cuckoo clock. It went 'tum-tiddle-boom-boom, tum-tiddle-boom-boom' with a 'beep-beep' every twenty seconds by way of variety. It destroyed conversation. The hearty hail-fellow-well-met brigade took over. Each evening became the trailer to a nightmare; a blur of red faces and gaping mouths. Each night I sank into a fitful sleep with 'Oh dem golden slippers' ringing in my ears.

On the evening of the third day we entered Portsmouth waters. The fleet anchored in St Helens Roads off the Isle of Wight, a grey smear under crepuscular skies. By now I was worried.

'What am I going to write about?' I complained to Jack.

'Listen,' he replied. 'You've got two Atlantic crossings ahead of you. After that the southern latitudes of the Indian Ocean and then the Great Australian Bight. This was just a cocktail party.'

3

The Lull Before the Storm

The fleet was scheduled to leave Portsmouth for Tenerife on 13 May. I was under orders to report back on the 11th. This gave me just over a week to settle my affairs in London, see to visas and inoculations and make the necessary purchases. I gave priority, however, to the disposal of my Monday morning, British Leyland, gremlin-infested automobile and its replacement with something new, small and reliable. My wife Rosamund had an adult job that ensured a steady income. She hadn't the time to spend three days a week loitering without intent in garage forecourts.

I went to a Fiat dealer. I told the salesman I needed a Panda on the road, taxed and registered, in six days. This was a mistake. He knew then I hadn't the time to shop around for a good part-exchange deal.

'Hmm. One of them,' he said eloquently, viewing my sulphur yellow monster from the other side of the street as if the boot contained a ticking parcel.

'Don't you want a closer look?' I pleaded. I crossed the road. He followed reluctantly.

'I'll give you something for the AA badges,' he said.

'It's got a re-conditioned engine,' I said. 'Pass anything.'

'Pass anything except a petrol station,' he countered, trying to disguise his laughter under a coughing fit.

'No rust,' I lied. 'It's got an aluminium bonnet and boot.'

'Puts up the scrap value a bit,' he conceded. 'But we will pass it on, must pass it on. I've got shares in Uni-Parts. Don't want to see the bottom drop out of them. I'll give you the list price – £250.'

'Done,' I said rather too quickly. I'd been considering abandoning it in Chalk Farm Road with a full tank and the keys in the ignition.

I went to a camping equipment shop in Victoria Street to purchase some of the items deemed necessary for survival on the high seas. I tried on some orange heavy-weather gear which made me look and feel like a traffic cone. I couldn't bend my arms and legs. I extricated myself with difficulty. I decided to do without it. I took a sleeping bag, a balaclava, some thick socks and a pair of green wellies to the counter. The proprietor suggested I buy a waterproof torch.

'If you fall in the sea, sir, it will remain lit. It will be a beacon for you. It will save you. It will withstand the pressure of two thousand feet of water.'

I gave in. It didn't occur to me at the time that I, myself, would not be able to withstand the weight of 2,000 feet of water. (A few weeks later it succumbed to atmospheric pressure. I threw it overboard in mid-Atlantic in 5,000 feet of water.)

I went to Oxford Street. There I bought a wax jacket in lieu of the heavy-weather gear. More elegant, I thought. Such a garment is fine for shopping in Knightsbridge or taking the corgis for a walk around the stable block but it provided, as I was to discover, no protection against the wind-driven rain of the Bay of Biscay.

The day before I left for Portsmouth I made the usual obligatory phone calls. I rang my mother first.

'Whatever you do, don't get your feet wet,' she exhorted. 'I'm off to bridge now. Don't get your feet wet.'

'If I fall in the sea I'll endeavour to keep my feet above water,' I replied, but the line was dead.

My mother has this theory that the state of one's feet dictates the state of one's general health. Wet feet, in her medical lore, are the cause of all illness – acute, chronic and terminal. This belief, however erroneous, can be traced back to our agricultural forebears. Much of my grandmother's farm in South Wales consisted of marshland intersected with narrow but tantalisingly leapable drainage dykes. Thus wet feet (or a wet foot) were a constant hazard. To be thrown from a horse, run over by a tractor, processed through a chaffing machine, trampled by a herd of irate heifers or tangled up in a baler were considered minor mishaps. But to suffer a wet foot – a 'bootful' as they put it – was a calamity. When such a calamity occurred the victim immediately squelched back to the farmhouse. There he would be set upon (it was a male-oriented society) by my grandmother. Wellies and socks would be torn off and the feet roasted before a roaring fire of Rhondda Valley coal and half a telegraph pole stuck up the chimney, while hot whisky and fresh orange juice were in the making.

I telephoned the farm. My Uncle David answered.

'Those bloody things are death traps,' he said. 'One capsized in the Caribbean not long back. Nineteen drowned. Grab as many life jackets as you can and sleep on them. Here's Bransby.'

'So you won't be down for hay-making this year,' he said. 'Here's Godfrey.'

'Just make friends with the ship's cook,' he said. 'And you'll be all right. Here's your grandmother.'

'Look after your feet,' she advised. 'See you next year.'

I had decided to catch the six-fifty-five on 12 May – the earliest train to Portsmouth – on the supposition that it would be uncrowded. I was partly right. I traversed the platform four times before I found standing room in the one and only smokers' carriage which seemed to have been tacked on to the back as an afterthought. The rest of the train was virtually empty. Thus eleven coachloads of fresh air and one of carcinogenic gases wove their way to the southwest coast.

THE LULL BEFORE THE STORM

I got off feeling like a kipper. By the time I arrived at the *Amorina*, with both shoulders almost dislocated by the weight of maritime accessories, I was beginning to have serious doubts again about the wisdom of the venture. Once on board I cheered up a bit. Everyone said, 'Hi Marcus, nice to see you!' Well, nearly everyone. They'd probably worked at McDonald's at one time or another.

I went below to my cabin. Before I'd unpacked less than half my gear, the wardrobe and drawers were full. I usually travel light – hipflask, toothbrush and credit card. However, this time I was encumbered. The instruction booklet had made it clear that oilskins, wellies, waterproof trousers, souwesters and various other nautical accoutrements were *de rigueur* on such a voyage. I had a quarter of a hundredweight of dried figs as an antidote to constipation, one of the side effects of the Swedish diet, and enough typing paper for a sequence of historical novels. Where would it all go? When confronted with a problem, I usually give up. I gave up and went ashore to procure essential supplies.

The first street I came to had more pubs than the Rhondda Valley, but no off-licence. After asking for directions from the usual crowd of strangers to the area, deaf-mutes and mental patients out on day release, I found one up a side street. When the churl in charge refused to accept a cheque, even with a VISA card, I realised just how far from civilisation I had come. What other hazards lay ahead?

All I wanted to do was buy a few bottles of whisky and gin. Every other building was a pub but they were all closed. It seemed I could buy anything else from a harpoon to a cement mixer. Why is life so complicated?

I was beginning to feel fractious when I noticed a swing sign that stated in elegant lettering:

HARVEYS
Purveyors of Fine Wines.

I pushed open the door beneath and was confronted by a staircase. What kind of off-licence was this? My curiosity was aroused. Summoning up my strength, I ascended.

I found myself in a dignified, oak-panelled room that reminded me of one of the more traditional London clubs. There was a faint aroma of beeswax and lavender. The walls were adorned with oil paintings and marine memorabilia, and shelf after shelf of bottles stood in neat lines, as if on parade.

I was fascinated by the labels! *Reina Victoria, Club Amontillado, Copper Beach, Bristol Cream, Isabelita.* As I read, my excitement increased. *Bual, Verdelho, Sercial, Malmsey. MALMSEY!* Buzzers buzzed and bleepers bleeped in the deeper recesses of my memory bank. Surely Malmsey, highly praised by Shakespeare and once the favourite tipple of English aristocrats, was from the Canary Islands? And that was where I should be in three weeks' time if somebody could keep one foot on the plug of the Swedish bathtub into which Mark had so recklessly consigned me.

Malmsey! I was inspired. Why travel? Why go to the Canary Islands at all? I could sit here, drink a distillation of their sun and earth, contemplate marine paintings of square riggers battling through savage seas and use my imagination. The result would probably be more interesting than the real thing. And safer.

'Can I help you?' asked a melodious female voice, rousing me from my reverie. I turned and there before me stood the source of that sweet yet astringent scent of lavender. Here was a rare species indeed: an English rose of the type one usually only comes across in romantic novels.

'Yes, I'd like to buy three bottles of whisky and three of gin. I'm going on one of those square riggers. You've probably heard about it. There's been a lot of fuss. Storage space is something of a problem. Polish Pure Spirit, if you've got it. The higher the proof the better.'

'I'm sorry, but we only deal in port, sherry and wine.'

'I thought this place looked a bit like a museum.'

'Yes, there is some truth in that,' she laughed. 'In fact, we only keep it going because we supply the Royal Yacht which enables us to keep our Royal Warrant.'

She pointed to the Royal Coat of Arms with the lion and the unicorn rampant – just like the one on certain jars of marmalade and Gordon's gin.

'Let me show you round.'

I inspected the wine-tasting room and looked respectfully at various ancient and distinguished bottles of port. Then we came to a wall lined with books.

'These are the naval lists,' she explained. 'We used to supply the whole fleet but we sold our interest to Saccone and Speed.'

'I know the Royals like a drop, but surely they're no substitute for the whole fleet.'

'We still supply the shore bases.'

'Ah.' I turned. 'What's the significance of that life belt?'

'That's from HMS *Audacious*. It was given to us in lieu of debt.'

'You mean – '

'Yes, if a ship sinks, the debt's written off.'

'Christ Almighty! There must have been some hair-tearing in the boardroom after the Battle of Jutland. No wonder you sold out to Saccone and Speed. I suppose you've got a warehouse full of life belts somewhere.'

The room was now glowing amber in the weak spring sunlight. A seagull drifted past the window. I could just see the tops of the masts swaying gently. I sighed. I felt quite heroic.

'You don't seem to have many customers,' I said somewhat inanely to break the silence.

'You're the first today.'

'But I haven't bought anything yet.'

Our eyes met. Hers were bright and clear. Mine were as red as Liberace's dinner jacket. I took a step towards her. Her gaze, though quizzical, remained steady. I succumbed.

'Right! I'll have six bottles of claret. Sorry I can't take a dozen but it's a question of space. It's clout I'm after – not taste. I'll be on the high seas for three weeks before I can refuel.'

She didn't flinch when I proffered the plastic and the deal was soon concluded.

'You can buy spirits in the shop just past Taffy's Tattoo Parlour,' she called after me. Portsmouth was becoming more and more exotic, and the natives were friendly after all. It was nice to find such a haven of civilisation so far west of London.

My elation was cut short as I recoiled in horror from a wild-eyed apparition. It was my own reflection in a shop window. I still had toilet paper stuffed in my ears. Oh well – the number of customers she met in a day, she'd probably be pleased to see anyone, even if he was wearing a balaclava and pointing a sawn-off shotgun.

When I got back to the ship I met Reijo, the cook, standing outside the galley. He was smoking as usual. He looked so bad he made me feel good.

'What's for lunch?'

'Don't know. I no cook today. Feel ill.' He tapped his head, grimaced and spat over the side. 'Too much English pubs. I fall asleep on deck. Bastards from *Trade Wind* find me. Hang me up in rigging. I no cook today.'

I stuck my head in the galley. Gordon, the Australian pastry cook, was knocking up lunch.

'What are you cooking, Gordon?'

'Potato and carrot soup. Lashings of Worcester sauce. It'll be very tasty.'

He hadn't been exaggerating about the Worcester sauce. The recipe goes something like this. Take one gallon of it, add potatoes and carrots to taste, and boil for one hour.

After lunch everyone suddenly remembered that they had urgent appointments ashore and wandered off muttering about the need to make long-distance phone calls or collect vital supplies from the ship's chandlers. Half an hour later we all met in the Kentucky Fried Chicken near the town centre.

We spent the afternoon loading up the ship with provisions. Vans and lorries arrived on the quayside at regular intervals. We formed a chain down the gangplank and across the pontoon to the ship's side. I was last in the chain, which meant that I had to heave the cartons up above my head and over the ship's rail to Derrick, a barrel-chested steeplejack who took them from me as if they were full of air. Most of the cartons had their contents printed on them. There passed through my hands, in steady succession, tins of ham, olives, fruit salad, sardines, marmalade, plum jam, powdered milk, cornflakes, sacks of spuds and so on. After two hours we'd put on enough food to keep the QE2 going. The *Amorina* was visibly settling in the water.

Then came the medical supplies: bales of bandages, transparent bags of syringes, packets of sinister-sounding drugs and even a brand-new stretcher. They must have been expecting mayhem. Finally, and this is when I cheered up, came alcohol. They'd obviously learnt from their mistake on the first leg from London to Portsmouth. I counted over 200 cartons of drink, each containing an average of twelve bottles of spirits, liqueurs or fortified wines. It's a pity Harveys didn't get the contract to supply the *Amorina*. Perhaps they did.

My optimism turned out to be ill-founded. On the first leg the bar prices had been high – one pound for a half-pint can of beer. Most of us had expected that once we had waved farewell to Land's End duty-free prices would come into operation. This was not to be. The prices remained the same except for an occasional happy hour to celebrate a special event such as when we reached the halfway stage to Tenerife or when we first sighted Porto Santo, a small island just north of Madeira.

Already each ship was assuming a distinct personality according to its size, nationality, captain, crew and trainee crew.

The *Amorina*, being Swedish, was a peculiar amalgam of puritanism and excess. Petra, who acted as barmaid between six and eight, smiled when you ordered your first drink, looked blank when you ordered a second and pursed her lips when you begged for a third. She usually finished the evening with her lips wrapped around the back of her teeth. I hoped she'd swallow herself.

I managed to avoid her ire for a greater part of the time through Welsh cunning. I'd stride confidently to the bar and order a beer. Then I'd turn, wave to a group in the furthest corner, unfocus my eyes, mouth something unintelligible, hold up a few fingers and then order two more. She was quite impressed by my generosity.

The *Bounty*, moored ahead, was a dry ship. It had no keel so in order to prevent it from skating or bouncing off the waves, they had to take aboard ballast in the form of ingots of pig iron. They must have been crazy. Later I understood the rationale behind the *Amorina*'s contradictory attitude. Load up with as much booze as you can carry instead of ballast, charge extortionate prices and sell off what will probably be a substantial residue when you get back to Sweden. I determined to thwart their plans.

Then there was the *Trade Wind*, a Dutch ship, with a predominantly Australian crew. It had a black hull and was obviously going to be the black sheep of the fleet. It was moored alongside us, so the crew had to use our deck as a thoroughfare if they wished to go ashore. They looked a rough bunch, refugees from the set of *Treasure Island*. Adriaan, one of the few Dutch crew members, looked like the archetypal pirate. He had everything bar the parrot. The Australians, Yakker, Frank, Ashley and others, looked as if they had stepped out of a Castlemaine advert. I was impressed.

The *Trade Wind*'s policy towards alcohol was a compromise. It was only available for one hour before the evening meal. This was probably just as well, otherwise they would have had to charter a tanker full of Foster's to follow in their wake. I resolved to visit them later.

I had just heaved up the 150th box of booze when there was a break in the proceedings. I wiped my brow and lit a cigarette. Derrick grinned down at me. There seemed to be some problem on the quayside. A plastic bag was being passed down the line. It was full of corks with holes in them.

'What are these — Irish corks?' asked Derrick.

'They're optic corks,' I said, marvelling at Swedish attention to detail.

'What do you do with them? Stick 'em in your eye?'

More cartons started to arrive. A tall, thin stringy fellow with a big nose and a demented look in his eye arrived beside me. At first I thought he had come to help on the basis that he'd take one box and I'd take the next — share the burden. But no, he wanted to do it all. He hurled himself into the task with frightening enthusiasm. He used up as much energy loading one box as I did loading three. What was wrong with him? Had he escaped from somewhere? When he tried to force a box that was too big between the rails, I seized my opportunity and, grabbing the next one, heaved it over the rail. This upset him. He threw himself into the task with such frenzy that I knew I was redundant. Perhaps this last lot were his own personal supply. He seemed so obsessive about them. I went up on deck and watched anxiously for a while. I'd dropped a box of Martini myself, but the way he was juggling with them was going to give me nightmares.

At five o'clock I climbed over the rail and dropped on to the steel deck of the *Trade Wind*. There was nobody in sight. I stuck my head into what looked like a kiosk in front of the galley. Four faces looked up at me as if I'd come to deliver a summons. I'm not good at names but this lot had been pointed out to me so often that I needed no introduction. Yakker, Adriaan, Ashley and Fred.

'Can I have a look below?' I'd got it right this time.

'No!' said Adriaan, looking at me from under hooded eyes.

'Are you the Captain?' I asked, knowing full well that he wasn't. There was an explosion of derisive laughter.

'Don't take any notice of him,' said Yakker. 'Do yer want a coffee? Find somewhere to park yer arse.' Adriaan swept a pile of important-looking charts and nautical manuals on to the floor. It was a scene of some squalor. The wall racks were jammed full with a mixture of official documents, postcards, photos, magazines and long-redundant cigarette packets. Fred brought me a sweet, black coffee, kicking aside a sextant on the way. I didn't dare ask for milk.

'So how far are yer going . . .?'

'Marcus,' I said. This set them snorting and scratching.

'So how far are yer going, Mark?' asked Yakker, suppressing the last syllable of my name. It was obviously too redolent of the declining years of the Roman Empire and dubious sexual practices.

'I'm going the whole way.'

They mulled this over for a while. 'Have yer robbed a train or something?'

I explained my mission. They didn't change their behaviour or start telling me their life stories. It was a relief. Some people had begun with the exact second, minute and hour of their birth and ended with the colour of their car. Explaining that I intended to change ships for some of the legs, I asked them to tell me about the *Trade Wind*.

'We call her the submarine,' said Yakker, who seemed to be the self-appointed spokesman.

'Why is that?' I asked, my suspicions aroused.

'She can turn over ninety-five degrees and still right herself.'

'But that means the bloody mast would be under the water,' I said, my voice rising several octaves. They were delighted by this outburst of genuine horror.

32

'That's why we call her the submarine,' said Yakker.

A lot of people get drowned. Some of them can't swim but most of them can. In fact, excellent swimmers fall into the high-risk category because, either through arrogance or over-confidence, they get themselves into difficult situations. I'm not a bad swimmer. I've spent a lot of time wallowing about in the South China Sea and the Malacca Straits. I've nearly been drowned twice and I'm not including the time I fell into a canal in Bangkok with a surfeit of wood alcohol inside me. The last time was off an island called Rawa near the east coast of Malaysia. I only just made it. I spent half an hour on the beach coughing up prawns and particles of dead coral.

I had the terrible feeling that when the conditions were right – forty-foot waves and a force ten gale – they would decide to test the ninety-five-degrees 'stability factor'. I didn't want to be around when they did. I crossed the *Trade Wind* off my list.

They started talking about 'sailing' as opposed to scooting along powered by a Perkins diesel. Only pooftas (sic) used engines. Engines were the last resort. It was clear to me that this bunch weren't capable of recognising the last resort. It wasn't on their map.

'So you're Dutch,' I said to Adriaan, trying to change the subject.

'Dutch? *Dutch!* I'm not bloody Dutch. I'm Frisian.'

'Frisian?'

'Ya! Frisian. From Friesland. Not bloody Dutch.'

'Isn't Friesland part of Holland?' I asked recklessly. Adriaan's eyes came out from under their hoods and bulged alarmingly.

'I'll be off then,' I said.

'See you later in the pub. The Invincible,' shouted Yakker. 'Turn left out of the gate. You can't miss it.'

'Anything special about the Invincible?'

'Yeah – it's where we drink.'

As I left I was overcome by a feeling of fatalism. I knew that if

I went drinking with them I'd end up on the *Trade Wind* for at least one stage of this crazy journey.

I spent nearly twenty minutes in my cabin scribbling notes. I began to feel restless. It was just after six so I went up on deck in search of the action.

Reijo was still feeling ill. Derrick and Gordon had already gone ashore. The tall, stringy fellow was cavorting about up in the rigging, alone. I made a note to check up on him.

I went to the bar and ordered a Carlsberg. Petra smiled. The place was empty apart from a small group in the corner. I was under orders to be friendly, so I wandered over.

They were a jolly crowd. They were lashing back the bitter lemon. They hadn't yet started the 'dib-dib-dib, dob-dob-dob' stuff. They prefaced nearly every remark with, 'I must admit . . .' They seemed to have a hell of a lot on their consciences. I listened.

'Anyone want a packet of crisps?'

'Yes. I must admit I do like crisps.'

'This is the life.'

'You can say that again.'

'Peanuts anyone?'

'I must admit I do like peanuts.' Gobble. Crunch.

'You drinking beer, Marcus?' said one of them. I wasn't sure whether this was a question or an astute observation. I looked down at my hands. My right was holding a tin of Carlsberg and was in the process of transferring the fluid therein to a glass held, somewhat shakily, in my left. I had to agree.

'Yup . . . I don't like drinking on an empty stomach.' They looked puzzled.

'I must admit I do like a beer now and then,' said another. Everyone turned and stared appreciatively at him. It took them some time to digest this confession.

'What a day. I feel exhausted.'

'I'll sleep like a log,' said three of them simultaneously. Chortles of merriment. And so it went on.

I began to feel depressed. Talking to them was like throwing pennies down a dry, bottomless well. I decided to move on. Invincible here I come, I thought. The crew of the *Trade Wind* would pass as intellectuals in this company. I guzzled down my drink and rose to leave.

'I'm going ashore to eat. I must admit I do feel hungry.'

Their eyes lit up. It was the first thing I'd said that they'd understood. I'd established some sort of bond with them at last.

'I must admit I feel hungry as well,' echoed the star of the group.

'I'm going to a Tibetan restaurant,' I said quickly.

I left to a chorus of, 'Don't do anything I wouldn't do.' No wonder I drink.

I left the Invincible at about eleven o'clock. I declined Yakker's invitation to carry on to a party. I needed to keep a clear head. Mark was driving down from London the following morning, ostensibly to deliver an electric typewriter and see me off. I was sure his real reason was to make certain that I was still aboard.

When I got back to the *Amorina* it was like the *Marie Celeste*. There was nobody on watch. The radio on the bridge popped and fizzed. The sink in the galley was full of unwashed plates. The bar was locked. Clever move. I went back to the galley and stole an apple.

I was pleased to find that I still had the cabin to myself. Kerstin, the Swedish girl in charge of allocating berths, had promised to do all she could to see that I remained alone. I spread a map of the world on the top bunk and began to study it.

Portsmouth to the Canary Islands looked fairly straightforward. Turn right out of the harbour and keep on going to Land's End. The next stage, which I didn't like the look of, entailed sailing across the gaping jaws of the Bay of Biscay. The most arrant landlubber knows that this area is in the grip of a permanent storm. Then came Cape Finisterre. This got the red lights flashing. I used to love listening to the gale warnings on the radio late at night. It made me feel safe and cosy to think of all those trawlermen out there in the howling storm, risking their lives just to keep us supplied with fishfingers. 'Humber, Dogger, Fisher ... Faro, Rockall ... Biscay ... Finisterre.' Finisterre was positively cyclonic from what I could remember.

The last, though longest, stage didn't look too bad. Carry on in a southwesterly direction down past the coast of Portugal and there were the Canary Islands, hanging off the southern coast of Morocco. Hanging? They looked as though they were falling into the huge blue void of the Atlantic. There was a hell of a lot of blue between the Canaries and South America.

Drinking in the Invincible all evening had restored my confidence but now it was ebbing away as fast as my body was metabolising the weak English beer. Beer distends the stomach but leaves a vacuum behind. The size of the vacuum depends on how much you've drunk. My stomach felt like the Postojna caves and was churning with a mixture of hunger and fright.

I went up to the galley again and raided the fridge. I made a sandwich out of ham, salami, cheese, tomato and pilchards. I was standing on the deck straining to get my jaws round it when I heard a commotion on the quayside. Shadowy figures lurched towards the *Amorina*, brandishing ropes. Yakker's voice rose above the din. The night before they had had an altercation with one of the natives who decided to camp out in a public telephone box. They had passed a rope round it and tied a knot of Gordian complexity. I remembered Reijo's fate. I dropped the sandwich into the sea and fled below.

There was a lot of cursing and crashing about above my head as they negotiated the *Amorina*'s deck and fell on to the *Trade Wind*. Eventually there was silence.

My stomach now sounded like an orchestra tuning up in the Albert Hall. I opened the wardrobe and extracted a bottle of Bell's whisky from one of my green yachting wellies. I'd known all along I'd find a use for them. I took a long pull. The gurgling subsided. I took off my hat and went to bed.

I woke early but still missed breakfast. I got no sympathy, but managed to extract half a cup of tepid coffee from the pump thermos. I took it up on deck, saw Portsmouth and immediately retreated to the other side of the ship. I leant against the cold metal wall of the galley and contemplated the chilly waters of the harbour. Muffled snores rose from the *Trade Wind*. They were at peace. I began to relax.

Suddenly a pair of feet interposed themselves between my eyeballs and the horizon. *Bare feet.* Feet that were horrible to look upon. Feet that resembled some rare species of reptilia that lurks in the primal slime of an Amazonian creek — yet recognisably human feet, battered, splayed and corunculated from an excess of jogging and other athletic pursuits.

I regarded them with a mixture of horror and distaste. Was I hallucinating? Was this the first sign of what my doctor had been gloomily prognosticating for some years now? I'd been told one first saw squirrels running up the wall. Feet would be a new one for the textbooks. Either way, they upset me. I was just about to test the veracity of their existence by prodding them with my cigarette, when they abruptly disappeared. The tall, stringy fellow appeared, sliding hand over hand down a rope. He looked as though he had spent the night in the rigging.

We stared at each other with mutual hostility and then he loped off. To be confined on a 120-foot ship with such a person or even a portion of his anatomy would severely test my powers of endurance. I expect to see feet when I'm lying in the gutter singing but not when I'm upright and sober. What if more people like him were on board or joined the ship at a later stage?

I remembered that on the original voyage, John Power, one of the convicts, had escaped at Tenerife by shinning down the anchor chain and stealing a dinghy. He had rowed to a small island but had been recaptured the next morning. He had made the mistake of falling asleep on the beach. I resolved to give it a try as far as Tenerife. If I had any more trouble with feet I could follow Power's example and get a cheap flight home.

After this harrowing episode I felt I could contemplate Portsmouth with equanimity so I moved across the deck to watch out for Mark. He was due at nine o'clock. At nine-thirty there was still no sign of him. The fleet was supposed to leave at eleven to anchor for the night off the Isle of Wight before actually setting sail the next day. Then there would be the final sendoff with the Red Arrows giving an aerobatic display and the Queen sailing past to inspect the fleet. I was fed up with all this shillyshallying. Why couldn't they get going? It was like hanging about in a dentist's waiting-room. Still, I shouldn't grumble. The original fleet was delayed four months by adverse winds, supply problems and bureaucratic inertia.

Then there was a welcome diversion. Walther introduced me to Sven, the new Captain. He was old but obviously hard and fit; and he actually did have the aquiline features that novelists are so fond of bestowing on such characters. His eyes were as grey as the Baltic in March. He was straight out of a Conrad novel.

We shook hands. I was improving – we connected first time. Then I knew what Holden Caulfield of *The Catcher in the Rye* fame meant when he said that some guy 'bust about forty of his fingers'. It wasn't just American hyperbole after all. I managed to light a cigarette with my left hand while Walther tried to explain in a mixture of Swedish and English why they had the misfortune of having me aboard. I didn't like the sound of this at all. The English bits were bad enough. What the hell was he saying in Swedish?

A few minutes later I spotted Mark's Saab edging along the quayside, its sleek lines marred by a peculiar contraption on the roof.

'What's with the ladder rack?' I asked anxiously, as we shook hands.

'Ladder rack? Oh that! It's a ski rack.'

I sighed with relief. I note little details like that and imbue them with a greater significance than they warrant. I didn't want to end up in the middle of the Atlantic without a literary agent if Mark suddenly found window-cleaning more remunerative.

By now I was suffering from a crisis of confidence.

'What am I going to write about? What if nothing happens?'

'Something will,' said Mark ominously. 'Anyway, you're bound to meet some interesting characters.'

Adriaan limped by. His eyes were double-glazed. Mark winced.

'I have already. It's not them I'm worried about. There's this horribly jolly crowd on the *Amorina*. You know – the type that loves playing Hunt the Slipper. They've already started singing "My Bonny lies over the Ocean". They'll drive me mad. They like everything – even macaroni cheese. I think they've escaped from the set of *Blue Peter*. They're all so friendly. What if there's no friction?'

'There will be with you on board,' said Mark reassuringly.

I felt irritated. I get fed up feeding him lines. I changed my approach.

'Walther said I might see a whale.'

'A pink one, the way you're going on. You'll end up in a park nursing a bottle of cider.' I ignored this and reverted to my whinging pom role.

'I'll go nuts in a confined space with that crowd. Sartre says that hell is other people. He demonstrates this brilliantly in his play *In Camera*.' I paused. Mark was looking worried. Perhaps now I'd get some sympathy.

'I hope you're not going to carry on like that in the book.'

'Why not?'

'It's too intellectual. Publishers don't like it.'

'You know I hate pleasant, well-integrated people. I was quite happy in London with a close circle of friends.'

I looked at him. He looked away and started studying his fingernails. He was obviously thinking about the times I'd disgraced myself in restaurants.

'You're trying to get rid of me,' I whined. 'Nine months. What are you doing to me?'

'More, if you decide to take a look around Australia.' Mark smiled to himself.

Now I knew how the original convicts felt.

'Hadn't you better spend half an hour with Rosamund? She's bringing the typewriter I promised you.'

'Excellent. You managed to get that Rank Xerox 575 Compact Electric with the 255-character correction memory. Only ten kilos. There it is now.' Rosamund appeared, struggling across the quayside.

'Will all trainee crew board ship. Will all trainee crew board ship.'

'What?' I said. 'It's only twenty to eleven.' But they needed twenty minutes to haul up the gangplank and throw off the ropes. Luckily, Rosamund and I had said our goodbyes in London. I hate public displays of emotion. I stepped towards her and relieved her of her burden. Then we embraced. I pushed back her hair and whispered in her ear. What I said is strictly private and is reserved for my accountant and Her Majesty's Inspector of Taxes.

On 13 May 1787 the First Fleet, much to the relief of the citizens of Portsmouth, had, after months of delay, slipped quietly away at dawn with its cargo of convicts. They were to found a nation. We, on this re-enactment of the seminal voyage, were to confound and divide a nation. The Australian government, a curious blend of tepid liberalism and unfocused socialism, had invested millions of dollars in the schemes to celebrate their forthcoming bi-centennial. They had already chartered a rival fleet of tall ships, many weighing up to 3,000 tons, to grace the blue coves of Sydney Harbour in January

1988. Their rôle was cosmetic – to give the media and public something to film and photograph. To instil some drama into what would be little more than a display of sail, they had arranged for a 'tall ships' race' from Sydney to Hobart, Tasmania.

On the other hand, the fleet now anchored at Mother Bank off the Isle of Wight on 13 May 1987, awaiting the signal to depart from the Queen on the Royal Navy frigate HMS *Sirius*, had an eight-and-a-half-month voyage ahead. We considered ourselves to be the 'real thing' and looked upon the tall ships as an expensive publicity stunt which bore little relation to the original event. We also envied the financial security which the tall ships enjoyed under the patronage of the Australian government.

The resources of the First Fleet Re-enactment Company were slim to the point of being anorexic. Funded by private enterprise, it was to lurch from one financial crisis to another. Investors were reluctant to put big money into such an ephemeral project. The fares paid by the trainee crew would not be enough to cover the expenses incurred by chartering the ships needed to make up the fleet. Profits, if any, were to be made by the sale of books, pamphlets, video tapes, souvenirs and the entrance fees paid by the public to view the fleet at each port of call. The bulk of these notional profits would not be reaped until the later stages of the voyage when the fleet reached Fremantle and Sydney. It was not an attractive investment proposition and yet just enough money had been raised to bring together the core of the fleet here in Portsmouth Harbour. In fact it very nearly failed to set sail.

Walther told me the owners of the *Amorina* had threatened to pull out of the venture the day before because they hadn't received the charter fee for the Portsmouth–Tenerife leg. The loss of the *Amorina* with its sixty berths would have scuttled the entire fleet. The owners of the other ships also threatened to pull out if the *Amorina* didn't sail.

Disaster was averted when a First Fleet Company executive delivered a carrier bag bulging with £5 and £10 notes to the quayside a few hours before we were due to leave for our anchorage at Mother Bank. Thus the *Amorina* was able to pay off an irate crowd of ship's chandlers and avoid impoundment.

The fleet was given a spectacular sendoff. Helicopters hovered overhead and the Red Arrows performed suicidal aerobatics and traced with red smoke huge arabesques in the chilly blue sky. Hundreds of small yachts, motor launches and cruisers swarmed round us. The Queen and the Duke of Edinburgh on HMS *Sirius* reviewed the fleet from a distance. Arguments raged about the colour of the Queen's shoes. I tried to resolve the issue with the aid of the *Amorina*'s binoculars but it was like looking through two bottles of smoke.

'They could come a bit closer,' Gordon grumbled. 'I can hardly see her. How do we know it's her? Could be a stand-in.'

Many of the Australians were disappointed. They had expected her to come aboard and shake hands with them.

'They'll be coming to Sydney to welcome our arrival. Perhaps you'll get a closer look then,' I said to console him.

'Ah well,' he said, 'I'll be seeing Ronnie Biggs in Rio.'

'Seeing Ronnie Biggs?'

'Yeah. I got his phone number off a mate in Australia. That's my other reason for coming on this trip. I want him to sign a T-shirt.'

'Can I come with you?'

'Sure. Something for you to put in the book. It'll be better than this.' Gordon stalked off in a huff.

On HMS *Sirius* signal flags were hauled up conveying the Queen's message: 'You may weigh anchor and heave away and I wish you a pleasant journey to your destination.'

We were off, or so we thought. The flagship, the *Søren Larsen*, acknowledged with her own flags, but an accident in the engine-room prevented her from hauling up anchor. Ten ships hoisted sail and set off slowly through the mêlée of small boats. As we approached open sea the *Kaskelot*, *Royalist*, *Lord Nelson* and *Johanna Lucretia*, hired on a short-term charter to make up the eleven for our ceremonial departure, set a different course to return to their home ports. The *Trade Wind* and *Our Svanen* were called back by the Department of Transport for a safety check. Head winds from the southwest blew up and forced the remaining five ships to seek shelter in the northeast lee of the Isle of Wight. But despite this inauspicious start, the financial problems and the air of gloom that hung over the remnants of the fleet, it was to be a successful journey. On 26 January 1988 eleven ships sailed through the heads of Sydney Harbour to a tumultuous welcome. Seven of the ships and thirty-two people – twenty-four professional crew and eight trainees – had sailed the whole way. I was one of them.

4

Southwestward Ho!

We were about midway between Land's End and the Bay of Biscay when I first felt seasick. The *Amorina* was lurching along like a drunk with a surgical boot. She was butting through ten-foot waves that were sweeping across the bow at forty-five degrees. Not only was she seesawing from bow to stern but she was also rolling from side to side.

That morning lasted for ever. I felt as if a septic octopus were lying in my stomach with one rubbery tentacle thrust up my throat as far as my Adam's apple. It lay there amongst last night's carrots and this morning's porridge and cinnamon. Being sick would have been a blessed relief. To feel the carrots sluicing past the molars would have been a pleasure more exquisite than any devised by the most dedicated hedonist. But the octopus refused to budge.

Nothing mattered any more. If they'd announced that the ship was sinking or that Ken Livingstone had been elected Prime Minister, I wouldn't have cared. I stood at the rail staring bleakly at the lumpy surface of the sea.

Somebody slapped me on the back. I turned slowly. It was Gordon. If it had been anyone else I would have thrown him overboard.

'Stick yer fingers down yer throat. Have a good chunder. You'll feel better then,' he advised. 'See yer later.' He walked off quickly when he saw the look in my eyes.

I gripped the rail with one hand and tried it. Nothing doing. I

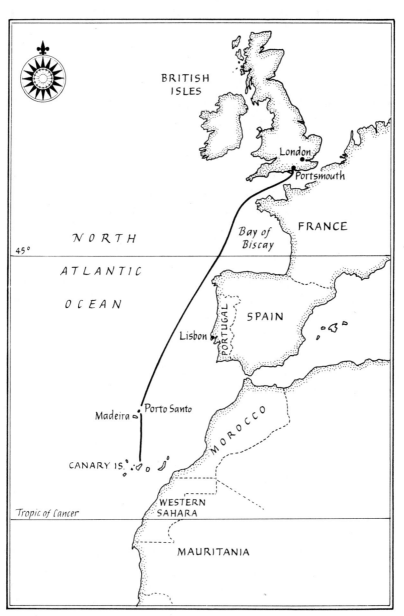

LONDON TO TENERIFE

pushed my fingers deeper in an effort to grab the tip of that tantalising tentacle. Still nothing.

By now I was desperate so I tried the ultimate emetic. I tried visualising being locked in my cabin with Barry Manilow, Wedgwood Benn and Billy Graham. My body was wracked by a terrible spasm as the octopus retaliated by bracing itself even more powerfully against my stomach wall and anchored itself by thrusting another tentacle deep into my intestines. My eyes were watering.

Nigel wandered by. His face was as green as a rancid olive. I felt slightly better. Seeing other people suffering is a good tonic, especially someone like Nigel. He was a handsome young man in an obvious sort of way and knew it – knew that he was handsome and knew that it was obvious. He just didn't know that it was in an obvious sort of way.

His main conversational gambit was to say 'YEAH' very loudly and then repeat it *sotto voce*. It certainly seemed to work with the girls and by the time we got to Tenerife, he'd got through a few. I don't know how many but I reckon they had a collective IQ of forty.

This is not sour grapes. I had my kicks in the swinging sixties and I'm quite reconciled to growing old, bald and boring, as long as the claret keeps flowing. I'm not one of those silly old buggers you sometimes see in discos, still wearing blue jeans and doing the twist to Duran Duran while the DJ bounces the light show off my sweating dome.

Bérenice appeared at the rail. She patted my arm gently.

'Try thinking of the worst thing that's ever happened to you. That's a good cure.'

'This *is* the worst thing that's ever happened to me.'

'Don't be silly. Think of the most painful experience you've ever had. Really concentrate. Relive it in your mind. And when you stop thinking about it, your seasickness will go – poof – just like that.' She snapped her fingers and walked off humming, the wires of her Sony Walkman tangled up in her pigtails.

I decided to try it. I thought of the time I had been stung by a Portuguese man-of-war in the Straits of Malacca – like being whipped with red hot wire. No good. I thought of being struck by lightning in the Malaysian jungle which had set my nerves jangling like a Peruvian harp. Still no good.

'You're not concentrating.' It was Bérenice again. 'I can see you blinking. You must really concentrate. You must think of every detail. Close your eyes. Concentrate.'

I closed my eyes and thought of the most horrible thing that had ever happened to me . . .

Some years ago I had been sitting in a pub in Fort William. I had just swilled back a pint of sour beer with icebergs in it when my fillings started to vibrate in time to some Pict strumming the electric banjo. Within seconds I had the most appalling toothache. I went back to the Bed and Breakfast and asked the good woman in charge of that granite mausoleum if there was a dentist in the area. But she had a remedy. She produced a bottle of pills. Unfortunately she wasn't going to part with them until she'd had her say. It went something like this (and I'll translate as I go along):

'Ma wee bairn (six foot lout) ha' just bust a leggie (multiple fractures of the femur, self-inflicted) from falling dune sa steps (off the doorstep of the pub) after a wee dram (ten pints of Tennant's Super Lager with whisky chasers). The doc, Mac-Gregor, he lives dune the road by the Chinese takeaway opposite the kirk, ye know the place.'

I nodded frantically and pointed at the pills.

'The doc,' she continued, keeping a firm grip on the pills, 'ha given ma wee Donald sa pellets ta keep awa the pain.'

She was just about to hand over the pills when a crash from the back room distracted her. It was followed by a dreadful caterwauling. She pressed the bottle close to her scraggy bosom.

'Ah, that's ma wee chick. He can sing like a bird.' He sounded like a capercaillie tangled up in a gorse bush.

'From Loch Rannoch, to Loch Grummet, to Loch Aber I will
    go,
Ah saki by the Crummochs to the sea.'

(Bang. Crash. Tinkle.)

'Tis the fair cookins are pullin aver me
Ah saki by the Trossaks to the sea.'

(Bang. Crash. Tinkle.)

'Aaaah. Do ye wan a bite o ma han china?'

There was a final crash that sounded like a wardrobe falling
over. Then silence.

'Och, you see. He'll be going to sleep already tonicht and
they're not even closed yet.'

'The pills,' I gibbered as my filling vibrated like a silicon chip
in a stock-exchange computer. 'Give me the pills, the pills, the
pills.'

'Have you tried seasick pills, Marcus?' It was Derrick.

'Pills?'

'Yeah! Seasick pills. Go and ask the doctor. He'll give you
some. There he is.' Derrick pointed in the direction of the bows.

'Where?'

'There.'

'Where?'

'There. Are you going blind as well?'

All I could see was the long stringy fellow sitting on the
bowsprit in a haze of spray.

'You mean he's the doctor?' I asked in horror.

'Yeah. He's very good. A qualified surgeon. He'll put you
right. I'll get him for you.'

I didn't argue. The way I felt I was prepared to consult the
devil himself.

'This is Pete, the doctor.' We didn't shake hands. Pete looked down his nose at me. There was foam on it.

'You're an interesting colour,' he said, failing to hide his satisfaction. I nearly told him to go and pull his rope.

'Why didn't you ask me for a Scop disc?'

'A what?'

'A Scopolamine disc.' He produced a yellow plastic disc about the size of a pound coin and stuck it behind my ear. 'Scop discs are impregnated with a drug that you absorb transdermally. I won't tax your mind with the finer details but they are effective for three days or more. You should have put one on six hours before we sailed. They used them in the America's Cup Race. They really do work.'

'What the hell am I going to do for the next few hours?'

'I'll give you some pills as well. Here. Take two, three times a day. Be careful. They'll make you feel sleepy. And don't drink alcohol with them. *Bon voyage.*'

'Thanks,' I mumbled and staggered off to my cabin. I took four pills. Doctors always err on the side of safety. I once took half a bottle of aspirin for a headache. Didn't touch it. Nasty bout of internal bleeding though.

I slept like a hog in a dung heap for the whole afternoon. When I woke up, the octopus had gone. I didn't feel even a hint of nausea. The sense of relief was so great that I felt unusually elated. It was six o'clock. Marvellous. Even my internal body clock was functioning normally. I decided to celebrate.

I went straight to the bar and ordered a lager. Petra smiled. As always, it made me feel uneasy.

I popped back two more seasick pills, just to be on the safe side, and surveyed the scene. The bar was almost deserted. Vilhem, a seventy-six-year-old retired judge, sat in the corner. He was puffing on his Sherlock Holmes pipe and sipping a large brandy. Oddly enough he was the least sanctimonious of the Swedes on board. He was the only one who didn't tell me off for throwing beer cans into the sea. When he wasn't on watch, Vilhem was always to be found in the bar, cocooned in acrid blue coils of smoke.

The lager went down well – a bit too well. Petra expected you to take half an hour to shift one.

'Another drink, Vilhem?' I shouted.

'Ya. A *large* brandy.' His English was a bit too precise for my liking.

'A large brandy for Vilhem. I'll have another lager. Blue can this time, please. They're the strong ones, aren't they?'

I braced myself. Petra smiled. What had happened to the regulation blank stare? Perhaps she'd got lockjaw. Then I understood. If I was drinking in such respectable company, she had to grin and bear it. I resolved to test her powers of endurance.

I joined Vilhem. He was a likeable Anglophile, and thus far I had not disillusioned him. We chatted away about politics, the Second World War, Sweden's neutrality and Churchill. Churchill was Vilhem's hero.

'Ya, Churchill. A great man. Not like zese vimps ve haf today. He gave me a cigar vonce. A ver goot cigar. Now I vish I had not smoked it. I should haf put it in a museum case. You vant a trink. It's my shouting, as you English are happy to say.'

Petra smiled again but her eyes were bleak. There were beads of sweat along her upper lip.

And so it went on. I bought Vilhem another drink and then he felt obliged to reciprocate. Petra usually went at eight. After that we were on trust to sign for our drinks in the book. She was obviously determined to see us out tonight.

At nine o'clock Vilhem announced that he was off to bed. I went to the bar and ordered another. Petra's smile was fixed. She was doing a good impression of Humphrey Bogart. Her teeth were so dry that her lip wouldn't slide back down. She pushed a can towards me without opening it.

'Aren't you on watch from four till eight?'

1 *Amorina* successfully negotiating Tower Bridge

2 *Amorina* refitting at Portsmouth

3 Walther in a tangle up the rigging

4 The fleet arriving at Cape Verde

5   *Amorina* loitering under quarter sail

6   A view of the *Bounty* from the porthole of *Amorina*

7 *Anna Kristina* tilting in a light swell

8 The flagship, *Søren Larsen*, ploughing ahead

9 Captain Sven Strömberg and the author waiting to ring the dinner bell

10   *Anna Kristina* showing off under full sail

11   The author serving the Captain in the bar of the *Amorina*

12 Suzanne and Lindo at the 'halfway' party

13 Young Bill awake

14 Ronnie Biggs holding up his share of the Great Train Robbery

15 Ronnie and the author at the end of a long evening

I looked round the bar. It was empty. Petra was smiling horribly at me. I thought of looking under the seats but decided against it. Petra already thought I was eccentric.

'Aren't you on watch from four till eight?' Dear God, there it was again. I looked frantically around the bar. Nothing. I put down my lager. This was quite sinister. Nearly as bad as the feet.

'Aren't you . . .' It was Petra. What a relief.

'You're a ventriloquist.'

'VAT?' she grated between clenched teeth and rigid lips.

'You can speak without moving your . . . I'll see you in the morning. I'll take the drink down with me.'

Once back in my cabin I felt inspired. I like to smoke and drink when I write so I strapped a plastic bag over the smoke sensor and got out a bottle of whisky. I'm not sure what happened after that. I don't remember going to bed. I woke up after a black hiatus which, I suppose, was unconsciousness rather than sleep.

Somebody was pounding on the door and screaming my name. The light was still on. I leant out of the bunk and twisted the key. The door was flung open and there stood Walther. He was very agitated.

'Are you all right, Marcus?'

'Yeah. What's up?'

Walther's eyes took in the scene. There was paper strewn everywhere and a whisky bottle rolled back and forth across the floor. Thank Christ I'd thrown the fag ends out of the porthole. He stared at me intently. I looked at my watch. It was five-thirty.

'Why didn't someone call me earlier?'

'Zey did. Ve haf been calling you for one and a haf hours. Longer! Jill, she call you at fifteen to four.'

'Oh dear.'

'Ve haf been hammerink on ze door till our fists are sore. I was nearly getting ze fireaxe. Vy you lock your door? Doors are not to be locked. You might be ill and zen ve cannot heal you. No more locking ze door. Ya!' He waved his finger sternly at me.

A glockenspiel started up behind one eye. I felt sorry. Genuinely sorry. Sorry for myself and sorrier for upsetting Walther. I told him so.

'No, no. You mustn't be sorry. You mustn't vorry. Ve are glad you are still here.'

'What?'

'Ve thought maybe you fall overboard. Ve thought maybe ze door was jammed. Ve search ze ship. Ve vas wery vorried.'

'What?' Why?

'I think maybe you hang yourself. You hate ze sails so much. Artists, wery sensitive people.'

'Artists?'

'Ya. Painters, poets, carvers, writers. Zey all trink much in Sweden and zen zey kill zemselves.'

He patted me on the shoulder and looked at me with admiration.

Then I understood. I'd been wondering all along why he hadn't read me the riot act and got out the plank. Normally they went berserk if somebody was ten minutes late on watch.

Of course. Walther had this habit of categorising people. His world was inhabited by stereotypes. Artists drank a lot. It was to be expected. He was delighted that I had confirmed his notion of how artists behave.

He was staring at the paper on the floor. One sheet had a footprint on it. The rest were covered with an indecipherable scrawl. All very Bohemian. Another work of genius lost to the world. I hoped he didn't expect me to start carrying on like Dylan Thomas.

I started to get up and smashed my head on the bunk above. I sank back. Walther got excited again.

'You stay. No need to get up. Ve manage vithout you.' He

peered at me through his tiny glasses. Each lens was about the size of a tenpenny bit. They were pulled tight across his eyes. They were ideal for gale-force winds and flying spray but they made him look even more serious than he already was.

I groaned. Walther beamed at me.

'You stay,' he repeated. 'But no more locking ze door. And no more vorrying about sails.'

I lay there for a few minutes listening to atonal music played by a steel band. I couldn't go on behaving like this, not even to impress Walther. What had happened to all my good resolutions? My notebook was beginning to read like the diary of an alcoholic not a travelogue celebrating the birth of a nation.

I got up and went on deck. I looked terrible but, apart from the resident orchestra in my head, I didn't feel too bad. At least I didn't need a Sony Walkman. I went to the stern, and gripping the rail, gazed morosely into the swirling grey void that prefaced the dawn.

This was no gorgeous tropical blood-letting such as I was to see off the coast of Brazil. A consumptive pallor leaked through the slit between the sea and the sky. A fan of light shed an eerie luminescence over the turbid waste of the Bay of Biscay. There was a magical instant when the myriad motion of the sea was jolted to a halt. It was like looking at the negative of a black-and-white film. Each wave was sculpted by light and edged with tarnished silver. But only for a moment. The fan closed. The scudding clouds coalesced. The sky became a granite dome that compressed the horizon into a vein of Parian whiteness.

Then the sea broke back into life. The waves advanced in rank after relentless rank, fifteen feet high from trough to crest. And although they marched forward with a monotonous regularity, each was a miniature mountain, unique in the details of its topography. Each had knife-edged ridges that rose, disintegrated and reformed. Each had hanging valleys that suddenly closed in on themselves to become smooth, sweeping slopes – slopes that heaved and transformed themselves into tottering cliffs which collapsed and tumbled in ruin on to the screes below.

I was just about to turn away when something alien caught my eye. At first I thought it was merely a fleck of foam. But this grey smudge had a separate life. It was a bird, hardly larger than a robin. I couldn't identify it. My knowledge of migrants is limited to such obvious visitors to our bleak islands as swifts and swallows. Whatever it was, it was brave and tenacious.

It fought against the wind to reach the rigging. It would advance twenty feet, only to be blown back ten. I watched and willed this handful of delicate bone, blood, flesh and feather to gain the haven of the ship. It hovered over the crests and then swooped, zig-zagging down the troughs. Once I thought it was gone but then it reappeared, wing feathers splayed and bent, as it staggered across a deepening valley.

It was, perhaps, ten feet from the sanctuary of the ship when the sails whipped and crackled in a freak gust of wind. I saw its eyes – black, intent, expressionless – a second before it punctured a rising glassine cliff which crumbled into foam under the hull of the *Amorina*.

Walther arrived. He was panicking again. He probably thought I was suffering from a bout of artistic angst – getting ready to hurl myself into the bosom of the brine like Hart Crane. There's very little opportunity for cries for help on a ship. One really has to be sure. There are no basement windows to jump out of.

'Vat are you doing?'

'It's OK, Walther. Getting some fresh air. Got a light?' He had started to go but then turned.

'OK. You poison yourself. You pollute ze sea vith your beer cans and cigarette butts. Ze sea is pure, beautiful. And all you vant to do is smoke.'

'The sea is the sea is the sea,' I told him wearily. 'It's water and waves and . . . vales. It's indifferent. No, that's wrong. It's not even capable of indifference. That's a human failing. It's just there – out there. It's H_2O with salt in it. The sun sucks it up and purifies it. Then it falls on the land. Rain. Fresh water. Trees, flowers, grass. I know I'm simplifying, Walther, but . . .'

'Ze land is vere there are vars and brothels and greed and nuclear power stations.'

'Do you mean whores and brothels or wars and brothels?'

'Vat's ze difference? Evil is on ze land.'

'You have to have a brain to be evil.'

'Ya! It was a serpent in a tree on ze land zat started all ze trouble.'

'Serpents don't just grow in trees, Walther.'

'Oh Marcus, you are a cynic. A trinker. A grumbler.'

'You grumble about the land. I grumble about the sea. It's dangerous and unpredictable. It can be beautiful. It can be horrible. And tedious. Certainly tedious.'

'Tedious?'

'Boring.'

'*Boring?* Ze sea is ze source of life.'

'Jesus Christ, Walther, we also need air, fresh water, food . . .'

'Fish are goot food.'

'We also need art. How many fish do you know that have composed a symphony, written a poem, designed a cathedral? The sea is just a mindless mass governed by the wind and the moon.'

'You are a mindless mass. You cannot understand ze mysteries of ze sea.'

'Know the one about the mermaid and the killer vale?'

'Just another English sick joke, I do not doubt. Vait till you see a vale. Vait till you see ze phosphorifying light on ze vaves at night. You vait. Zen you vill change your mind. Vait till you see a storm.'

'What the hell do you call this?' I spluttered as the wind deposited the crest of a wave on my head.

'Zis? A storm? You land crab. Zis is just a draught under ze door. You vait. Oh ho ho. You vait.' Walther strutted off, chortling. 'Time for breakfast,' he called over his shoulder. 'Our vatch is finished. You come for breakfast now.'

Breakfast was a help-yourself meal. The porridge wasn't too bad if you didn't ladle the cinnamon powder on like the Swedes. I wasn't going to make that mistake again. The food was laid out on the tops of the two chest freezers between the galley hatch and the mess tables. Some people skipped breakfast, usually those who had been on the midnight-to-four watch. Nevertheless there was a queue this morning. What was the hold-up?

It was Sven again. There was only one butter dish out. Watching Sven butter a piece of toast gave me brain damage. He turned a simple process into a complex ritual that had everyone grinding the porcelain off their back molars. It went something like this:

1   Take a piece of toast in the left hand and a knife in the right hand.
2   Carefully scrape thin shavings of butter off the semi-frozen block.
3   Apply butter evenly in a two-inch strip down one side of toast.
4   Rotate toast ninety degrees and repeat sequences two and three.
5   Rotate toast ninety degrees and repeat sequences two and three.
6   Rotate toast ninety degrees and repeat sequences two and three.
7   Apply butter to butterless square in centre of toast.
8   Repeat sequences two to seven inclusive, but this time with pink caviare.
9   Do two more pieces of toast as before.
10 Wish everyone good morning as you make your way to the mess.

And don't think the pink caviare bore any resemblance to the black stuff that comes in tins marked 'Fortnum and Mason'. This stuff looked like blood-soaked tile grout. It was so salty it shrivelled your gums and made you suck your teeth until you were doing a good impression of a trumpet fish. Thankfully there was marmalade, real English marmalade, thick-cut marmalade, not that orange slop that the French dish out.

Sven was still at it. Scratch. Scratch. Scratch. I was about fifth in the queue. Everyone was staring stolidly ahead like mesmerised hamsters. Suddenly I had an idea. The queue always formed on the left-hand side of the breakfast buffet. You helped yourself, working your way around to the right-hand side, and then carried on to the mess tables the other side of the stairwell which divided the room. Why not have two queues? That would speed things up.

I double-backed round the companionway stairwell. It was so easy. Plenty of elbow room. I hacked a substantial wedge off the butter block. Sven smiled amiably. I piled up the toast and marmalade and headed for the mess.

It was then that I came face to face with the rabid horde who had followed my example. I tried to edge by but it was difficult. The ship was lurching and rolling even more than before. Sven had completed his arcane ritual and was prodding me in the back with his plate. I made a determined attempt to shove my way through to the mess. The *Amorina* listed sharply to starboard. I scrabbled at the wall with one hand while trying to keep my plate horizontal with the other. The man I was trying to squeeze past leant backwards over the buffet. I noticed that he had one hairy arm deep in the porridge.

The *Amorina* righted herself and then listed sharply to port. Probably a squall. I over-compensated and stepped backwards involuntarily into Sven. I turned to apologise. The amiable smile had gone.

'You haf a toast of mine on your back. Be so good as to revolve yourself.'

He peeled it off. I returned to the fray encouraged by the close proximity of Sven's aquiline nose. I wove my way through the queue in a series of elegant pirouettes as my other companion withdrew from the clammy embrace of the porridge tureen. He stumbled forward and wrapped his arm, from which hung a ragged curtain of glutinous oats, around Sven's waist.

As I settled down with my toast I could hear an uproar coming from the serving area. Walther's voice rose above the din.

'Who is ze von starting a new queue? Now you can see vy ve haf zese simple rules.'

'Marcus!' chanted the chorus line.

'Yeah. He fused the toaster yesterday,' somebody called out. 'Tried to get the toast out with a screwdriver while it was still on.'

'Missed his watch last night,' piped up another. 'Dead drunk on the floor of his cabin with the typewriter on top of him.'

I was tempted to linger and take notes. Some of this was news to me. But then Sven entered. He had changed his blazer. He sat down three tables away, facing me. His mouth was like a scimitar and his eyes were as grey as a Sunday in Aberdeen.

I decided to take my toast out on the deck and once again I broke one of those simple rules so important to the smooth running of life at sea. I started to push open – and it took some strength – the door on the windward side of the mess. I got it open about six inches. There seemed to be quite a gale going on outside. I transferred the plate of toast to my left hand and, grasping the handle with my right, applied my shoulder. Suddenly my toast mastered the art of levitation and took off for the ceiling. Before I could set off in pursuit, the fickle wind, instead of resisting, now decided to assist my egress to the deck. It gusted and flung open the door with considerable violence. I found myself quick-stepping in an arc concentric to that described by the edge of the door. I crashed into the rail at waist height. The bottom half of me came to an abrupt halt. The rest of me – brains and broad shoulders give me a high centre of gravity – continued onwards and outwards over the Bay of Biscay.

Fortunately a stanchion rose from this section of the rail. I managed to grab it and thus averted a potentially fatal immersion. And yet, as I hung there, cursing with fright, a portion of my brain was sufficiently detached from the business of self-preservation to note with some pleasure my toastless plate skimming like a discus over the waves. Interesting how one thing leads to another. A wave exploded against the hull. A sheet of water, like a murky pane of green glass, hung before my eyes. Then it collapsed over me and insinuated several pints of itself down my neck and up my sleeves.

I turned my back on the sea and, keeping one hand firmly on the stanchion, dabbed at my eyes with a paper handkerchief. As the stinging subsided, I found myself watching what appeared to be a scene from a French farce. The people in the mess were performing a drunken, high-stepping pavane. Somebody had opened the door on the leeside. The wind was howling through. Paper napkins swooped and soared around their heads like seagulls. Soon they were lost in a blizzard of cornflakes.

I wasn't on watch again until noon so I went to the bar. It was empty and smelt like an English pub at opening time. I felt a pang of nostalgia for the easy-going life I had left behind. But at the same time it made me take stock of my situation. I realised that I had been treating the ship as a floating pub. I was carrying on as if I were still in Hampstead. I was making no concession to the fact that I was now at sea – really at sea. Now, at last, the harsh light of reality began to penetrate my smokescreen of flippant cynicism.

It was 17 May. I had only been at sea four or five days and already I had nearly fallen overboard. There were still roughly eight months to go. Since we were replicating the voyage of the original fleet, we weren't due in Sydney Harbour until 26

January 1988. We had just entered the Bay of Biscay. Ahead lay two crossings of the Atlantic Ocean and the southern latitudes of the Indian Ocean. It was obvious that I would have to change my ways.

Apart from the dangers and demands of the sea itself, the nature of the watch system severely disrupted the normal pattern of daily life. The trainee crew were expected to join the professional crew on watch twice every twenty-four hours. I was on what was known as the 'four-till-eight' watch. The ship's company had been divided into four teams and each team took a particular watch shift for a week at a time. Each team was known as 'the watch'. The table below shows the different watch periods in twenty-four hours and their sequence as it would affect me during the month:

Week 1	4 a.m. to 8 a.m.	4 p.m. to 8 p.m.
Week 2	8 p.m. to midnight	8 a.m. to noon
Week 3	Noon to 4 p.m.	Midnight to 4 a.m.
Week 4	8 a.m. to 4 p.m. (The Day Watch).	

Each watch had various duties to perform under the supervision of one of the professional crew. They were:

1   To steer the ship, or 'man the helm' in sailing parlance. Each watch member took a half-hour turn at the wheel.

2   To act as companion and backup to the helmsman in case he was taken ill or drunk and to attend the radio and take messages.

3   To be on 'look out' from the boat deck. This was the upper deck which formed the roof of the bridge, galley,

mess and bar. The importance of the task stemmed from the fact that the helmsman's vision was limited to about ninety degrees; 180 degrees if he constantly turned his head from side to side. Ships don't have wing mirrors. In any case, the helmsman would be concentrating on the compass and wind direction meter. The boat deck afforded 360 degrees vision. It was always possible that a supertanker could race up astern at twenty knots or burst out of a fog bank.

As sailors never tire of stating, there are two types of accident at sea – the avoidable and the unavoidable. If the *Amorina* got caught in a hurricane or mixed up in a waterspout, there wasn't much we could do about it except cancel the milk. But it helped to have some warning, as I was soon to discover.

If we weren't conscientiously performing one of these three essential duties, then we were supposed to seek out Dan, the bosun, and volunteer our assistance on one of the many maintenance jobs. This became a game of hide-and-seek. We hid and Dan sought. The *Amorina* was sufficiently capacious to contain all sorts of nooks and crannies in which to ensconce oneself briefly, away from Dan's reproachful gaze.

Dan brought the word 'ubiquitous' to life. No sooner had I settled in the bar to enjoy a cigarette out of the wind than I would spot him coming along the portside deck. Exit me through the bar door, starboard. Five minutes later I would be puffing away in the engine-room when Dan would enter, ostensibly to borrow a shifting spanner. Exit me through the door to the crew's quarters. I used up more energy evading Dan than I would have expended chipping paint off a lump of iron to which it was attached with a tenacity that made you wonder why you were chipping it off in the first place.

All in all we were expected to steer, put up and take down sails, wash dishes, clean and touch up paintwork, sweep and mop floors, clean the 'heads', as the toilets were called, whip ropes, splice ropes, take apart pulleys and reassemble them, grease shackles and attend knot-tying lessons and much more besides.

And yet, despite the seemingly endless process of cleaning and maintenance, I was left with a lot of free time. There I was sitting in the bar at ten o'clock in the morning. I wasn't on watch again until four in the afternoon. Nothing was required of me unless there was an 'all hands on deck' call and these were rare. Some people on the 'four-till-eight' watch went back to bed after breakfast. I found that I didn't need that much sleep. Years of late nights and debauchery had proved good training for the disorientating effects of the watch system.

Last night's débâcle had been partly due to the soporific effect of a surfeit of seasickness pills. I hadn't been late on watch before and I resolved not to be late again. Still, I realised that I would have to curb my alcohol intake for my own sake, and the sake of my companions. I certainly wasn't going to sign the pledge or start acting like a muscular Christian, but I would have to compromise. Moderation was the obvious solution. I would ration myself to two or three lagers a night and go to bed at ten o'clock. I would touch neither whisky nor wine until we reached Tenerife. There, obligations had to be met. I had promised to celebrate landfall with Reijo as soon as we got ashore.

Then I started to rationalise. Why should I feel guilty? Why should I change my ways at the age of forty-one? It takes all types, as the overworked saying goes, to make the world. And the *Amorina* was a floating microcosm. Why should I try to become something I never could be? I would only be putting on an act. And, anyway, was my behaviour so out of keeping considering my circumstances? With or without alcohol I would be a handicap to the ship. If they really wanted to replicate the events of 1787, then my behaviour could be viewed as being positively authentic.

I remembered from my research that alcohol had caused

trouble all through the original voyage, and even before the fleet had left. One of the first problems that confronted the Commander-in-Chief, Arthur Phillip, when he arrived in Portsmouth, was a liquor feud. The marines, with the support of their officer, Robert Ross, refused to guard the convicts unless they were guaranteed an allowance of 'spiritous liquor' not only en route but also for three years after their arrival in Australia. It was an allowance which they considered 'indispensibly requisite for the preservations of our lives, which change of climate and the extreme fatigue we shall be necessarily exposed to, may probably endanger'. I knew how they felt.

And it wasn't just through drinking that I was living up to the spirit of this crazy re-creation of the founding of a nation. Somebody, I forget who, had branded me 'the reluctant sailor' because of my acerbic remarks about everything from the absence of lemon slices in my gin and tonic to the notional delights of hauling on a rope at four-thirty in the morning in a forty-knot wind. I don't think he realised the significance and historical relevance of his observation. The more I thought about it, the more I appreciated the aptness of his words. I was a reluctant sailor. And so too had been nearly all those who had set sail 200 years ago for an unknown continent on the other side of the world.

The convicts had certainly been reluctant – some to the extent that they were overcome by a fatal apathy that sapped their will to live. Their guards, the marines, had been reluctant to the point of being mutinous. And even the sailors themselves caused trouble (not without reason, for many were owed months of back pay) by refusing to unmoor ships and going on strike. Five sailors from the *Fishburn* deserted and eight more had to be sacked. Thus the First Fleet had not set sail fired by the spirit of endeavour and adventure.

On the contrary, after months of frustrating delays, those on board the fleet as it sailed away from England on 13 May 1787 were consumed with apathy, trepidation, sullen resignation, and a determination to blot out their sorrows with copious draughts of alcohol. From such an inauspicious start grew the nation of Australia which, as Gordon never failed to impress upon me, whether in London or Rio, Cape Town or Salvador, Tenerife or Cape Verde, was the greatest place on earth to live. Well – I would find out for myself in January 1988.

Nor was the reluctance to sail halfway round the world confined to the convicts and the lower ranks. Ralph Clarke, a Second Lieutenant of the Marines, kept a journal in which he expressed his most intimate thoughts and private feelings. As they passed Plymouth where he had hoped the fleet would put in and give him a last chance to see his wife, he wrote: 'Oh my God all my hopes are over of seeing my beloved wife and son. Oh cruel wind why will you not change and grant my fond heart the longing wish?'

Coincidentally we, on the *Amorina*, did make an unscheduled stop at Plymouth to put ashore one of the engineers. He had developed kidney stones and was in considerable pain. It gave me an opportunity to scribble a short letter to my wife. Peter, the doctor, posted it when he went ashore with the patient. It seemed an incident hardly worth recording at the time. But now in retrospect I see it as the first of many unplanned parallels between the two voyages, some tragic, that occurred in the following eight months.

Thinking of these things made me feel happier. I felt that by being myself I was balancing the initial ecstasy of the sailing enthusiasts, which was not at all in keeping with the mood of our reluctant forebears.

I wasn't unhappy. On the other hand, I wasn't thrilled to bits at the prospect of being involved with ropes for the next eight months. As the *Amorina* bobbed up and down like a champagne cork in the Trevi fountain, I began to have a clearer idea of what I had let myself in for.

The other problem I had to think through was how to write this book, this travelogue, this account of the re-enactment.

Jonathan King, whose brainchild the whole escapade was, had already written an account of the original journey.

What approach should I adopt? I toyed briefly with the idea of a diary but it seemed to me too rigid and unimaginative an approach. There would be days and days at sea when nothing out of the ordinary would happen. One officer on the First Fleet had dismissed the leg from Portsmouth to Tenerife in a single word – 'uneventful' – despite the fact that there was a convict uprising, deaths, births, accidents and a number of floggings. I admired his insouciance. Most diaries are a heterogeneous mass of tedious and inconsequential detail.

By now there were several people in the bar – some reading, some staring vacantly into the middle distance and some writing up their diaries. I got up and went behind the counter. I managed to locate a can of lager buried beneath the jumble of Coke and bitter lemon tins in the cold box. I returned to my seat by a serpentine route made necessary by the way the floor rose, fell and tilted. This enabled me, on the frequent stops to steady myself by grabbing the backs of chairs, to get a squint at the literary pits into which the diarist can fall.

> *16 May* Got up at 11.30. Had rice salad for lunch. Steered the ship for half an hour. The Captain said I was very good. The sea was too rough for deck work. Dan sent me to the mess to unpick ropes for Baggywrinkles.

Baggywrinkles! What the hell were Baggywrinkles? They sounded revolting. No doubt I would soon find out.

I zigged across to another diarist and peeped over his shoulder. 'My cornflakes got blown away at breakfast.' This sounded more promising. But no. 'Had to have porridge instead. Found some hairs in it. Disgusting.'

That did it. My doubts were fully confirmed. Diaries were of no interest to anyone except perhaps the writer's great-grandmother, who relied on him to hump her on and off the commode. At least there was no competition on board. I zagged my way back to my seat where I continued my internal debate.

I came to the conclusion that I would have to be totally honest about myself and those around me. There was no use pretending that I was keen on sailing – I wasn't. And never would be. Or so I thought.

I tried to imagine a sailing buff writing the book; eulogising on the canvas, wiping the spray off his brow as he hauled away at a halyard, singing sea-shanties in the bar and comparing rope burns with his fellow hemp addicts. How many times could he describe putting up and taking down a square sail before the reader started picking his nose and looking out of the window?

My reverie was interrupted by the ship's bore.

'I never see you writing, Marcus.'

'Don't need to. I've had a transmitter implanted in my hippocampus. Latest thing from Japan. All I have to do is sit here thinking and it all appears on a telescreen in my agent's office.'

'I don't understand. What's a hippocampus?' He paused. 'I'm writing a book too. Would you like to see what I've done so far?' Before I could decline he shoved a huge leather-bound tome on my lap.

'Aren't you worried I might plagiarise?'

'What?'

'Steal your best lines.'

'Oh no. I'm getting off at Tenerife. Mine will be out before yours. I thought I'd write a detailed account of this leg. *Three Weeks at Sea* I'm calling it.'

I opened it and read:

> *15 May* First real day at sea. Our position at noon was longitude three degrees five minutes west and latitude fifty degrees seventeen minutes north.

Hmmn. Very evocative. Great sense of place.

'I thought we were longitude three degrees *four* minutes west. You've got the latitude right.'

'My God, you're observant. Perhaps I'd better check with the ship's log. But if you say so . . .'

'Pretty sure I'm right.' He was clearly impressed.

'I was wondering about you,' he continued. 'Couldn't think how you could write a book if you didn't take notes. You spend so much time . . .'

'Yes?'

'Well I suppose all writers . . .' He looked embarrassed.

'Yes?'

'Drink.'

'You don't,' I said.

'Do you think it helps?'

'Helps what?'

'Helps you write.'

'No. But it helps me get through the bits in between writing.'

'But I never see you writing.'

'That's why I'm drinking. Actually I write late at night when there are no distractions.'

'When do you sleep?'

His remorseless logic was exhausting. I lay back and closed my eyes. He didn't take the hint.

'Would you look at this bit about putting up a square sail? I'd like your opinion.' He turned back a page or two. I read on.

> The *Amorina* has five square sails which are rectangular in shape. The top one is called the *royal*, the next one down the *top gallant*, the next one down the *fore upper topsail*, the next one down the *fore lower topsail* and the bottom one is called the *forecourse*. Putting up a square sail is a very complicated process.

There followed a description of the various lines and their functions which was mind-numbing in its exactitude. I quite admired his stamina.

My can of lager fell and rolled away across the floor. I hadn't opened it, so I waited. The *Amorina* obligingly tilted the other way. The can rolled back to me. I retrieved it with a nonchalant flourish. I had surprised myself. I was adapting to life at sea faster than I'd imagined. I tucked it into the gap between the cushions and returned to the saga of setting a square sail.

'Would you mind if I borrowed this later?' I asked, handing it back to him. I wasn't just being polite. I meant it. It had given me an idea.

'I'm going out on deck to have a look at the sea. Need some fresh air.' I left my lager behind – unopened. I had a lot on my mind.

I went out on the leeside and stood there gripping the rail. One does a lot of rail-gripping at sea so I won't mention it again. One has to contend with the perpetual motion of the ship even in relatively calm conditions. We must have been well into the Bay of Biscay. The *Amorina* was rocking and rolling with increased violence. I estimated the height of the waves, from trough to crest, to be twenty feet. What the hell was it going to be like in the South Atlantic? The *Amorina* would be doing somersaults.

Between rocking and rolling, she returned to a twenty-degree list to port as a strong wind from the northwest drove us southeastwards. The angle of the list depended not only on the wind strength but also on how much sail was up. Walther, in a fit of enthusiasm, once managed to get the old tub careering along with sparks flying from the hull at eight and a half knots, listing thirty degrees.

Finding one's sea legs involved a lot more than just being able to adjust one's gait to the angle of the deck and the rhythm of the waves. A freak wave could catch you on the hop. I'm using the word figuratively and literally because people did a lot of hopping, as well as skipping, running on the spot, fox-trotting, side-stepping, about-turning and goose-stepping, both backwards and forwards, as they made their way along the deck. And these are but a few of the more mundane options, or combinations thereof, available to the experienced sailor.

The really spectacular choreography was demonstrated by those who hadn't found their sea legs. When they were out in force on the deck, it was like watching one of the more eccentrically esoteric of modern ballets in which the music alternated between a lugubrious lento and a frenetic allegro. What looked like a group of stilt-walkers stumbling up a sand dune could suddenly be transformed into whirling dervishes dancing on broken glass. Those whose joints had lost their elasticity shot along the deck on legs that resembled a pair of pneumatic drills welded together. Those who had problems with their motor nerves looked like drunks on roller-skates trying to go up the down escalator. And those who were merely landlubbers but otherwise sound in mind and body wobbled along like humming tops running out of spin. Such histrionics were often induced by a careless helmsman wandering twenty or thirty degrees off course. Then the waves would strike the ship at a different angle and start the show.

And there was more to it than accommodating one's feet to the heaving of the deck. One had to be perpetually alert. I'd be halfway up the companionway when somebody would tread on my head as it inclined from its normal sixty-degree slope to the perpendicular.

As their name implies, companionways are quite intimate places. People tend to get thrown together. Many a romance at sea must have started in the companionway. I got quite excited about the possible origin of the word. It seemed so logical. Weeks later I consulted a dictionary. I was disappointed to find the derivation is banal. It either comes from the Dutch word *kompanje* or the old French word *compagne*, meaning a storeroom.

I encountered many other hazards while finding my sea legs. It's not pleasant suddenly to find yourself imbibing lager through the nostrils or that your cigarette smoke tastes of someone else's earwax. Inanimate objects came to life. Doors slammed on fingers. Toilet seats and lids snapped at one's accoutrements. Mirrors dodged around. Wash basins tipped soapy water and shorn stubble over your Y-fronts. Trays tobogganed across tables. Fridges vomited yesterday's leftovers. Walls took offence at being leant on and hurled you away. Toilet rolls unwound themselves. Bunks decanted their sleep-starved occupants. Recalcitrant drawers relented and inverted in the short drop to the floor. Nothing was safe.

Even the most innocent objects were imbued with malicious cunning and psychopathic tendencies. The metal door of my shower-room cabinet, which usually had to be prised open with a screwdriver, swung silently open over my head when I was cleaning my teeth. I was still picking the scabs off my scalp in Brazil. And my wardrobe, which had refused to accept another garment, suddenly found the space to accommodate a pair of long johns and jeans, a thermal vest, two pullovers and a wax jacket – with me inside them.

As for ropes, never again will I doubt the authenticity of the Indian Rope Trick. Ropes! I'll leave them for now. They'd fill a chapter on their own. Months later, on the *Anna Kristina*, a homicidal rope nearly killed Gordon.

Vilhem strutted by as if he were kicking pigeons. He wished me a curt good morning. When he reached the foredeck he crashed to attention, executed a ninety-degree turn and passed in front of the bridge. There he read the thermometer before continuing his constitutional. The deck was deserted. I turned to 'the ever-changing face of the sea'. But there's a limit to how long one can watch the constant metamorphosis of the waves. Corn undulating in the wind is beautiful. Wood smoke drifting through autumnal foliage is beautiful. But how long can you stare at these things before the bolt falls out of your neck and you start wondering if you can beat the lunchtime rush to the pub?

It took four days to cross the Bay of Biscay. On the second night I woke to find that the toilet had come adrift. The bolts holding the pedestal to the floor had come loose. The toilet, held only by the waste pipe, was swinging back and forth like a horizontal pendulum. I didn't lose my temper. I got some cardboard boxes, crumpled them and wedged it tight.

When I got to the mess Walther was there alone, pouring coffee.

'My, my. Ve are being very goot. You are ze first von up. It is still only fifteen to four.'

'I've taken to sleeping fully clothed. Saves time. I can never find the legholes when the bloody ship is rolling about like this.' I told him about the toilet.

'So now you haf taken to sabotaging the ship instead of yourself. Vat are ve going to do with you? I am thinking ve vill haf to build a cell. No, no. I only joke. Tell ze engineers. Zey will fix it.'

I did. They didn't. I couldn't blame them. They had problems. The steel plates, four foot by four square, which made up the engine room floor over the propeller shaft, kept coming loose. Chasing them was a dangerous task as they cartwheeled and clanged around the bowels of the ship. They were heavy enough to cut a man in half. Or a woman.

On the last day in the Bay of Biscay the toilet succeeded in detaching itself completely. It didn't have as much room to manoeuvre as the steel plates in the engine-room but it did have allies — a slippery floor and clammy tiled walls.

I tried to grab it. The ship listed to port. The toilet eluded my grasp and retreated. I felt my feet skidding. I braced myself against the walls with both hands, but even so, inch by inch, I slid down towards the vile fluid that oozed up from the hole in the floor. I was leaning back at an angle of seventy degrees when the toilet counter-attacked. It bounded towards me. In defence I stuck out my right foot (I'm right-footed). The toilet swallowed it. The situation was perilous. I was now leaning back at an angle of sixty degrees with a toilet stuck on my foot.

The ship lurched to port again. The toilet retreated. I didn't go with it but one of my green wellies did. I was just about to collapse into the mire below when my hand got a grip on the light switch. With a supreme effort I catapulted myself into the cabin.

Brains, not brawn, were going to solve this. I thought about it while the toilet careered around attacking the walls. I went for help. Lars and Sigge, the electrician, came to my rescue. Sigge leant in and deftly extracted my wellie. Lars stuck a rope into the pan and grabbed the end as it appeared out of the waste pipe. They lugged it away.

By noon, conditions had improved. The wind had eased. The ship no longer rocked and rolled so unpredictably. But I still had a problem. A brown soup six inches deep slopped back and forth in my shower room. Lars used his brains. He gave me a plastic bucket and told me to bail it out of the porthole.

I plugged the hole with the base of the toilet brush holder. Then I spent the afternoon bailing, attired only in underpants and wellies. Occasionally a wave appeared at the porthole and left behind a few gallons of Portuguese territorial waters. I didn't mind. It helped to dilute the foul brew. When I'd finished I poured half a gallon of green disinfectant over myself, showered and went up for afternoon tea.

Margaret, one of the few trainees going the whole way, had instituted the genteel English ritual of afternoon tea. It was strictly by invitation only. One was expected to be punctual, and conduct oneself with decorum. I was ten minutes late.

'Ah, there you are,' she said, looking pointedly at her watch. Gordon and Petra were looking bemused. Margaret passed me a cup. I reached for the biscuits. Margaret's stare froze my hand midway.

'A biscuit, Marcus?' she asked, holding out the tin.

'Thank you.'

Margaret moved the tin out of reach. There was a strained silence.

'Ahem,' I said.

'Pardon,' said Margaret.

'The weather . . .' I said.

'I hear you're going the whole way as well,' she said to Gordon.

'That's right. The *whole* way. I got on in London.'

'What made you decide to come on this trip?' I hastily interposed. I knew that Gordon felt strongly about what constituted 'the whole way'. Margaret had joined the fleet in Portsmouth. As far as Gordon was concerned, this didn't count.

'Well, I've always wanted to go to sea, but my husband was so protective. It's in my blood. I come from a sea-faring family. My grandfather was the captain of a sailing ship – the *John of Grimsby*. And my father, Captain Andrew Thomson, served his apprenticeship under sail but then changed to steam. My grand-father was furious. He said steam would never last.'

Gordon's teacup set off down the table.

Margaret skilfully arrested its progress a few inches from the edge.

'More tea, Gordon?' she asked, holding up his cup.

'Yes please. And I'll have another biscuit.' Margaret raised her eyebrows.

'Yes. I've always been attracted to the sea. I have a house in Barton-on-sea in Hampshire. It's in a beautiful position. I can see the Needles.'

'When are we going to get the rest of it?' Gordon asked.

'Pardon?'

'The rest of the food,' he persisted. Margaret looked puzzled. I explained that 'tea' in Australia was an early evening meal, the equivalent of supper.

'Well,' Margaret continued, 'I've spent so much time looking at the sea that when I heard Jonathan King talking about the voyage on the radio I just knew it was what I had to do.'

She paused. Traditional oaths could be heard from the deck.

'I've never heard such language before. I suppose I've led a rather secluded life.'

Derrick entered in spray-drenched oilskins. We looked at him quizzically.

'Some idiot let a lifebelt fall into the sea.'

'Quick. Throw a man overboard,' I said.

'*Marcus*. How could you say such a thing?' Margaret was genuinely shocked. She returned swiftly to her story. 'Anyway, I booked a place through *Twicker's World*. Then I found that my passport had lapsed. I – whatever is that dreadful smell?'

Gordon and Petra were staring hard at me.

'I think I'll go out on deck for a cigarette,' I said hurriedly.

'Some people are so rude. He didn't even say thank you,' Margaret said as I left.

Day by day the weather improved as we sailed southwards down the coast of Portugal. This meant deck work and my first encounter with Dan the ubiquitous bosun.

I was on the boat deck trying to coil a rope. It was a stubborn one with a kink in it. Every time I attempted to untwist the kink, it would reappear six inches away. I soon lost my temper. I dropped the rope and put the boot in.

'That's no way to treat a rope,' said a quiet voice behind me. I turned to tell whoever it was to go dance in cod shit. I didn't. Dan was tall, thin and wiry. He had a presence that commanded respect.

'That rope looks like a snake's honeymoon,' he observed.

'That rope's a bugger,' I said.

Dan took the rope. He twisted his wrists. The rope relaxed. Then he fed it through his hands and poured it on the deck to form a perfect coil. The rope lay there as still and smug as an ammonite. When Dan had gone I gave it another kick.

My next encounter with him taught me a lot. It was a fresh, clear morning. I was on lookout. I was lying in a huge coil of mooring rope, smoking a cigarette and contemplating the blue 'inverted bowl we call the sky, whereunder crawling coop't we live and die'.

A shadow fell across me.

'Are you on lookout?' asked Dan.

'Yup.'

'You're not going to spot anything looking at the sky.'

'I'm not going to spot anything looking at the sea. Anyway I had a look around about ten minutes ago. Three hundred and sixty degrees of nothing.'

'Get up.' He said it quietly, almost sadly.

I struggled to my feet, dropping the cigarette into the coil. Dan extracted it with distaste and flicked it into the sea.

'Hey! I hadn't finished it – Jesus Christ! Where did that come from?'

Less than half a mile away a colossal container ship was steaming northwards.

'That came from the horizon.'

'But there wasn't a sign of it ten minutes ago.'

'It's doing about twenty knots. The *Amorina* may have been in the trough of the swell when you looked. How carefully *did* you look? You might have spotted a smudge on the horizon. They saw it in the wheelhouse fifteen minutes ago. What if it had been coming from astern?'

'But they've got eyes as well. And radar.'

'There are other people in the world like you. Do you think they spend the whole time on the bridge glued to the radar? They're probably smoking and playing cards. One of those bastards arrived in port with a yacht wrapped round its bows and they didn't even know it.'

Dan had the knack of being crushing without being offensive.

'Being on watch is an important and responsible duty. There's a lot to look out for apart from other ships.'

'Such as?'

'A squall, for example. Look over there.' Dan pointed to the west. The sea stretched away in a series of monotonous undulations. Grey clouds were building up on the horizon.

'Well?'

'There's nothing to report at the moment. But let's say you saw a patch of sea out there where the waves had white crests. And let's say that this patch of sea was moving towards us. That would be a sign of an approaching squall. It could hit us abeam in minutes. It would be helpful if the helmsman were warned. And there are other things to look out for. Somebody spotted a fishing net afloat yesterday.'

'So what? Ramming one of those isn't going to sink the ship.'

'No. But it could indicate that there were trawlers in the vicinity. Report everything you see. It could provide valuable information. Even debris.'

'Debris?'

'Yes. There could be somebody clinging to it. Lots of small yachts sail down to Gibraltar and Tenerife. Sometimes they get into trouble. How would you feel if you were hanging on to a plank and a ship sailed by because some goon was in a trance?'

I got the point. I resolved to mend my ways.

The next day on lookout I performed my duties conscientiously. I scanned the horizon, studied the surface of the sea and strained my eyes looking for debris with men clinging to it.

The weather was unsettled and blustery. Cones of sunlight, like inverted searchlights, poured gold on the waters. Squadrons of clouds passed above us and raced ahead southwards. Darker clouds, low on the horizon, kept pace with us as they shed their burden.

Then I saw something to starboard and slightly astern. Two water spouts, elemental monsters from out of the grey wilderness of the Atlantic, were stalking the ship. Their swirling skirts tapered away into surrealistically elongated waists so that they resembled gaunt Dalinian cooling towers. Giants with their heads wrapped in the clouds, they groped and reeled along the horizon on a parallel course.

'Water spouts!' I shouted. A group of zombies sat on the deck sewing a sail, their faces frozen in imbecilic rapture.

'Water spouts!' I shouted to those on the deck below. They were staring blindly at the sea, following their own internal dreams.

There was a stampede as everyone charged below to fetch their cameras. Dan strode up to me.

'I saw them first,' I said proudly.

'Why didn't you tell them in the wheelhouse?'

'I . . . er . . . Oh dear.'

'All you had to do was shout down this,' said Dan tapping the mouthpiece of the speaking tube. I'd been using it as an ashtray. Somebody must have been walking around with an earful of ash.

'Those things are bad news. They could turn us over. We'd be lucky to get away with just the masts ripped off. They're unpredictable. They could veer towards us any minute.' Dan and I watched them for a few moments. Then they peeled away and disappeared. Dan looked at me, sighed and shook his head. He started to walk away.

'Hey, Dan,' I called. He turned and I pointed to the west.

Another water spout was struggling into existence. Hundreds of feet tall, like a blind worm it probed the sky. Then it tottered and collapsed. Dan walked away.

An exhausted dove had taken up residence in the shelter afforded by the anchor winch on the prow. I'd been feeding it for a week. I placed small piles of crumbled biscuits, bread and porridge flakes near by. It emerged occasionally to sample these offerings. Dan disapproved. A few days short of Porto Santo where we were to make a brief unscheduled stop Dan cracked.

'Clear this up,' he ordered, kicking at the porridge flakes.

'Why?'

'It's in the way. Somebody could trip over it.'

'Like who? Tom Thumb!'

'They could slip on the pigeon shit.'

'It's dove shit.'

'I don't care if it's angel shit. Clear it up. Like now.'

I walked away muttering mutinous but muted curses. Dan cleared it up.

We sailed on down the coast of Morocco under cobalt skies. To the north a Himalayan range of cumuli sank slowly beneath the horizon.

We heard over the ship's radio that the *Trade Wind* wasn't far behind. This news caused some excitement. The other ships, because we had put into Plymouth, were a day's sail ahead of us. Walther offered a free can of lager to the person who spotted her first. A crowd gathered on the stern. Wenzel, who had fled the economic reforms imposed on Czechoslovakia by Russia and now ran a thriving garage, spent two days up the mast scanning the horizon. He gave a new lease of life to the redundant expression 'up the pole' but he won the prize.

On the morning of 26 May we sighted the island of Porto Santo in the Madeira archipelago. Discovered by the Portuguese in the fourteenth century, it had been used as a staging post by Christopher Columbus.

At first sight it appeared to be a barren wasteland of volcanic rock. Vertiginous cliffs, riven with iron-red gulleys, plunged straight into the sea. Behind rose an ochre mountain, the lower slopes faintly striated with abandoned vineyards.

We rounded a bleak promontory and burst into a bygone age. Five ships, sails furled, lay at anchor in a serene blue bay. Their masts in the slanting morning sunlight cast tremulous shadows on the sparkling water. The few white houses lining the shore did not dispel the illusion. Inland dun-coloured, sun-slaked fields rose to the pine-clad slopes of a perfectly shaped extinct volcano.

Walther took our passports to the customs house and by the afternoon we were ashore. We had little time to explore. We were leaving that evening. There wasn't much to see. Gordon and I rambled aimlessly around the narrow cobbled streets, admired the bougainvillaea and wondered what to do.

It was a quiet place; too quiet for my liking. It had atmosphere – the atmosphere of an endless Sunday afternoon enshrined in still sunlight. The white walls were like blank pages confronting a mind locked in stasis. The windows were sealed with wooded shutters. The inhabitants slept. Siesta. An ancient silence lapped at the sills broken only by sparrows chirping in the eaves and the ticking of hot metal from the few parked cars. No wonder Columbus had decided to discover America.

Perhaps I'm being unfair to Porto Santo. What can one learn about a place in a few hours? Was it a haven of tranquillity or just dead? Were there gems of architecture hidden up some unexplored side street? I missed Columbus's house. Could I have spent a month or a fortnight here and let the slow rhythm of life extinguish the restless flame? I doubted it. It struck me as a place for exiles. But if you want a holiday far from the madding crowd, free from the distraction of anything out of the ordinary and if you have something to expiate, then Porto Santo is your place. You could always climb the volcano and hope it erupts.

We retraced our steps to a small square near the landing stage. There the main restaurant was full of 'first fleeters'. It sounded like an aviary of kookaburras. I didn't want that either.

We roused a taxi driver from his torpor. After much gesticulating (it's difficult to mime a fish) and after much shouting of 'restaurant *pescadoría*, *piscina*, maritime' and finally, in desperation, 'fish', he stopped scratching his ear, nodded and set off.

He drove us about two miles through fields where the main crop seemed to be rocks and dropped us at a modern house set back about 200 yards from the road. It was brick built and rectangular in shape. Two rows of windows pierced the front elevation. It had a sloping roof. (The architect had obviously lost his nerve at the last minute.) An aperture at ground level permitted ingress and egress but, above it, no sign denoted that victuals and drink could be obtained within. There were no other buildings in sight. The taxi had gone.

'What the hell is this place?' I raved. 'It's just a house. The bloody fool.'

Gordon lit a cigarette and shrugged. We picked our way through the builders' debris. As we neared I was somewhat mollified to see light refracting on bottles at head height. We entered. It was a large functional room devoid of décor except for that afforded by cigarette ads and an eclectic array of bottles behind a small bar. It was furnished with plastic mock onyx tables and metal chairs. Four men sat round one of them contemplating a carafe of wine. They ignored us. I didn't expect them to leap to their feet and pump our hands but such rapt immobility I have not seen since I was a ward orderly at the brain surgery unit at St Francis's Hospital.

The dining area was easy to identify. Half the tables were draped in dazzling white linen. The management had realised that only a blind man could eat off what resembled a disc of fossilised vomit. I swerved away from the first group of tables. Above them, point downwards, hung stainless-steel blades the size of sabres. I chose one free of Damoclesean suspense.

The waiter spotted us straight away. He presented us with a vast menu and had the sense to inform us that everything was off except swordfish and mixed barbecued meat. We ordered the former, two beers and a bottle of red wine. I prefer red to white. I can drink it with anything, even ice-cream.

I cast nervous glances at the sabres. Gordon puffed away placidly, staring straight ahead. As usual he seemed oblivious to the surroundings. The waiter brought our drinks without going through an intermediary. He seemed a pleasant young man. He didn't have a hare lip, obsidian eyes, a nervous twitch or platform boots. Who were the sabres for? Staff or customers?

I studied the four somnambulists at the other end of the room.

Maybe they were made of wax. Suddenly one of them leant forward and slapped the man opposite on his bald pate. The bald man didn't flinch. A few seconds later he decanted some wine and imbibed. He lowered his glass slowly to the table and relapsed into immobility. *Slap.* He had retaliated. He struck his aggressor on the cheek. Now I expected mayhem. The sabres hung motionless. What the hell had we got ourselves into? I looked at Gordon.

'Flies,' he said. 'I've seen 'em doing that in the outback.' He leant over and brushed one off my shirt.

The place was filling up. A fat man took the table next to us. He caught the waiter's eye and pointed at the sabre. The waiter unhooked it and took it to the kitchen. When he returned a few minutes later, it was sheathed to the hilt in sputtering gobbets of beef, pork and mutton. He hung the impaled, oozing flesh over the table. It looked like a flayed, mutilated limb. The last few inches of the blade were slimed with grease and gore. A tear of blood gathered at the point and fell to the salver below. The fat man reached up. As he drew the first morsel down the blade it squeaked on the steel. I'm not a vegetarian but this carnivorous ritual nearly converted me.

We rose to leave. Tenerife was a taxi ride and two days' sailing away.

5
Under the Volcano

My first sight of Tenerife was a purple bruise through a pink band of gauze on the horizon. I watched the rising sun banish the haze and engrave the contours of Mount Teide into the deepening blue. The pale nipple of the volcanic cone, at an altitude of over 12,000 feet, hovered above a heavy ermine mantle of cloud draped across the broad shoulders of the island's colossal bulk.

As the fleet approached the harbour the ships fell in line astern, the *Amorina* bringing up the rear. By the time we had rounded the breakwater and ground to a halt, shredding rubber tyres against the concrete quayside, the brass band had shouldered their instruments and were marching away.

Gordon and I contemplated the sweltering stacks of containers. A vaguely familiar figure knelt on the quayside snapping photographs. We grinned obligingly. He approached. It was Malcolm, a freelance photographer whom we'd met at St Katharine's Dock.

'I've decided to join the fleet,' he announced. 'Flew in a few days ago. I'm staying in a small hotel on a fruit farm up in the hills. Very quiet, good food, swimming pool, lovely gardens. There's a few rooms left. Want me to book you in?'

'Sounds like a good idea,' I said.

'Don't mind if I do,' Gordon affirmed.

Malcolm told us the owner, George Nelson, would be happy to pick us up at noon the next day. This suited me. I had two things to settle before heading for the hills.

'Ready then?' Reijo said. 'I know some good bars.' I sighed. Having a good time is hard work. It takes dedication and stamina.

'We'll look at the other ships tomorrow,' I said to Gordon. 'It shouldn't take long to make a decision.'

'Come on,' Reijo said. Adriaan and some other ruffians from the *Trade Wind* beckoned. I sighed again. I accepted my fate but I knew if I went with them I'd be needing a week on a health farm. Perhaps a fruit farm would do.

Gordon and I walked along the quayside on a tour of inspection. We had decided to change ships. We went on board the *Tucker Thompson*, where they were preparing lunch. A muscular, bronzed young man was arranging a salad on a large stainless-steel salver. He started to construct a frill of orange quarters around a mosaic of sliced peppers and cucumbers. He looked up, said hello and returned to his orange quarters. Everyone else said hello and then resumed slicing, dicing, shredding, peeling and eviscerating mounds of vegetables. Their 'hellos' sounded like 'goodbyes'. There was no sign of meat. The only sign I could see said No Smoking Below. We left.

We stepped on board the *Anna Kristina* and went below. It was a scene of some squalor. Electric cables snaked across the floor. Tools lay everywhere. The sink was full of unwashed crockery. Clothes and rancid blankets hung from bunks recessed in the walls. A kettle steamed on an ancient cast-iron stove. Breakfast debris littered the solid pine table bolted to the floor. Beer bottles glinted in a huge wooden bin built into one corner.

'Just brewing up. Want a cup of tea, mate?' asked a spritely old fellow with white hair and a stubbly white beard. He had a strong Liverpool accent. His face was a shocking pink. So were his eyes. He looked rough. Cut six inches off him and he could have starred in *Snow White and the Seven Dwarfs*.

'I'm Old Bill. That's Young Bill,' he said, pointing to an

amiable-looking youth hacking away at a salami the size of a torpedo. He looked up.

'Aaargh. Mum – mum – mum – mumph,' he said. And he wasn't talking with his mouth full.

'He's glad to meet you,' translated Old Bill. 'His old man sent him on this trip to straighten him out.'

Young Bill giggled. An electric saw whined above. Golden grains of sawdust trickled down from the open hatch. Some landed in my tea. The *Anna Kristina* was the only ship in the fleet with a hatch. We were standing in what had once been the hold. Originally built as a cargo ship, she had spent her working years carrying salted cod up and down the Norwegian coast.

'Mum – mum. I gor pimwissed lar nigh.'

'He's telling you he got pissed last night,' said Old Bill, patting him on the shoulder. 'We call him the ship's log. Can't get the bugger up of a morning. It's like trying to push-start a bulldozer. Still, he's got a heart of gold. And a wallet to match.'

Young Bill grinned and giggled some more. He waved the salami at Old Bill. He had to use two hands. The salami was also a shocking pink. I rubbed my eyes.

'Jesus!' I said. 'That can't be Italian.'

'It's Danish,' said Old Bill. 'The Danes call it the road accident. They just push the whole cow through the mincer – horns, hooves and shitting tube. Then they dunk it in a vat of preservative. It's not biodegradable. The only way to get rid of it is to shoot it into orbit or eat it.'

Young Bill was piling slices up on a piece of bread.

'Yum yum,' he said.

'Hey. I understood that,' said Gordon.

A piece of wood fell through the hatch. We looked up. A face haloed by sunlight streaming through golden hair looked down.

'It's OK. We're still alive,' said Old Bill. 'That's Henrik, the First Mate. He's Danish too.'

Henrik disappeared. A plank threw a long shadow across the floor. The saw whined. The scent of pine drifted down.

'Want a drop of this in your tea?' asked Old Bill, producing a bottle with a lurid label.

'What's that?'

'Spanish brandy. Takes the paint off the back door.'

'No thanks. Still feeling a bit rough from last night.'

People bustled to and fro but we didn't feel we were in the way. Old Bill introduced us to John, the Captain. He was about twenty-five. He had a flattened nose. I couldn't tell whether it was congenital or the result of an over-indulgence in fisticuffs. He was Danish. Cut two inches off him and he could have co-starred with Old Bill.

'So you're thinking of joining us?'

'Yeah. If you've got a cabin. I'm not sleeping in one of those bone racks,' I said, pointing to the bunks cut into the hull. He opened what I thought was the door to a broom cupboard. Inside were two shelves. 'Compact', as an estate agent would have put it. If a farmer had kept chickens there, he would have had the RSPCA around in no time at all.

'Best cabin in the ship,' said Old Bill. 'Apart from John's.'

'Do you want to swap?' I asked.

'Not unless you want to run the ship.'

Gordon and I looked at each other. We shrugged. We had made a decision.

'Heard the good news?' asked Old Bill.

We looked blank.

'We're not going direct to Rio. We're breaking the journey at Cape Verde and Bahía.'

'Bahía? Never heard of it,' said Gordon.

'Bahía de Todos os Santos. Bay of all the Saints. Better known as Salvador these days. I'll take you round the hot spots,' he said, turning to Young Bill.

'Mum – mum – mum.'

'It's OK. Thank me later. I'm really pleased about Cape

Verde. It's right off the tourist trail. Another one for my collection. I've been to over two hundred countries. Want to do 'em all before I hand in my dinner pail.'

Young Bill got to his feet. He was wearing sandals, floral shorts and a Hawaiian shirt.

'Christ!' exclaimed Old Bill. 'The way you're dressed says: "Here I am. Please rob me." I'll come with you, sunbeam. I'll look after your wallet.'

'We'd better go too,' I said. 'Malcolm has booked us into a hotel. It's a fruit farm up in the hills. The owner's coming to pick us up at twelve. See you in a week.'

The terrace was roofed with vines intertwined with scarlet cataracts of bougainvillaea. Passion-fruit flowers glowed like exotic lanterns in the darker recesses. Some 2,000 feet below lay the sea – an aching expanse of blue stretching away into the heat haze. Behind rose arid, carious ridges of volcanic rock. The slopes were strewn with boulders and clothed in cacti and knee-high scrub. Over it all hung a pall of shimmering heat.

A dust devil meandered along a line of abandoned terraced fields. The aviary fell silent. A zephyr hissed through the foliage and expired with a sigh of infinite regret in the vastness of the gulf below. Fragile blossoms trembled and were still. The canaries resumed their inane twittering. The parrot in the kitchen guarding the telephone shrieked like a flame.

'Well, what do you think of it?' asked Malcolm, expecting congratulations.

'I told you I wanted a place where I couldn't see that,' I said cruelly, pointing at the sea.

'It's a long way away,' Gordon said.

'You don't have to look at it.' Malcolm was aggrieved.

'Sorry, Malcolm. This is a lovely place.'

Malcolm, somewhat mollified, went to his room. He was already installed in the main building. When we had finished our drinks George showed Gordon and me to ours. They were in the annexe the other side of a Hockneyesque swimming pool where serpents of light writhed and sparkled.

Later, when the afternoon heat had eased, George took me on a guided tour of his little Eden, where the fruits of the earth from the tropics to the temperate zones multiplied and prospered. There was a lesson to be learnt here somewhere.

Cabbages and cauliflowers slumbered in the shade of banana and mango trees. Sunflowers towered above geraniums. A thorny Jesus plant spilt bright beads of blood over a pumpkin, while oranges and lemons chimed colourfully among reticent limes and avocados. Apricot, nectarine, grapefruit, mandarin and peach trees stood among carefully watered patches of lettuces and feathery carrot tops. A traveller's palm strove to unfold its fan beside a dateless date palm. And there were plants I hadn't come across before.

'This is a kaki. It's a form of tomato. And this,' George said proudly, pausing for effect, 'is a parmelon. It's unique to Tenerife. We had a lady here from Kew Gardens. She'd never heard of it. Took some seeds back with her.'

We pushed through a screen of hibiscus and vine and came out by the swimming pool. Malcolm and Gordon were chatting to some other guests.

'Pork chops the size of tennis racquets,' said a man with a Newcastle accent. 'It's only two kilometres up the mountain. You can't miss it. It's the only restaurant in the village.'

'Right! Let's go,' said Malcolm.

'I thought we were going to walk down to one of the local bars,' I said.

'It's OK,' said Malcolm. 'I've rented a car. Picked it up this afternoon.'

It was soon apparent that this was going to be the most dangerous part of my nine-month voyage to Australia. Malcolm looked everywhere but out of the windscreen. He couldn't speak without looking you in the face – perhaps to ensure you were still awake. His main conversational gambit was to repeat what you'd just said. He did, however, throw in a few original remarks – original in the sense that he'd thought of them on his own.

'Look at all the cactuses.' We dutifully looked. Malcolm looked at us to make sure we were looking.

'Cacti,' I said pedantically and immediately regretted it.

'Where?' asked Malcolm, swivelling his head 180 degrees.

'Forget it,' I said hurriedly as we mounted the unmade verge, crushing some adventurous preadolescent cacti. Stones drummed under the mudguards as we hit the opposite verge.

'Looking forward to this meal,' he said, addressing himself to Gordon. This necessitated an almost complete about-turn.

'If we get there,' I said.

'What?' Malcolm asked, contorting himself in an effort to meet my eyes as I lay slumped in the seat with my feet on the dashboard.

'Nothing,' I said before I suffered severe compression of the spinal column. We'd hit a pothole the size of a bomb crater on the left-hand side of the road.

'They drive on the right over here,' I croaked.

'We drive on the left in Australia,' Gordon said.

'They drive on the left in Australia,' Malcolm said to me, almost inverting his head. I sat up quickly.

'Who do you think you are? Robert Mitchum!'

'What do you mean?'

'Keep your fucking eyes on the road,' I snarled, my instinct for survival overcoming social niceties.

'There's no need to be like that.'

'Just fucking drive.'

Malcolm relapsed into silence, for about twenty seconds. I was sucking on my cigarette so hard that the tip was like a thermal lance.

'What a view!' He waved his arms expansively as we traversed a culvert at the head of a gulch about 400 feet deep. The rusting debris of previous expeditions lay in the dried-up watercourse.

'That looks like a BMW,' Gordon said.

I turned before Malcolm could respond.

'Shut up,' I hissed. 'Don't talk to him.' Gordon looked confused but kept silent for the next five minutes.

'Here we are.' Malcolm stopped in the centre of the road.

'Aren't we going to park?'

'I want you to guide me in.' He pointed to some wasteground the size of a cricket pitch.

It was a small village. About twenty mean, white-washed houses straggled along the road.

'I wonder what they do here for kicks?' Gordon remarked.

The bright red badge of a Coca-Cola sign proclaimed the restaurant. We pushed through a bead curtain. As my eyes adjusted to the twilight I made out a formica-topped bar. Old-fashioned tin advertisements decorated the walls. A group of swarthy natives with prognathous jaws sat playing cards. They looked up briefly, their faces expressionless. A jukebox, one of those fifties jobs with a wide chromium snarl, rumbled in a dark corner. It was pure Hemingway.

Malcolm looked agitated. Gordon stood, hands in pockets, whistling. He's the only person I know who can whistle with a cigarette in the centre of his mouth.

A tall, thin man who could have been Salvador Dali's brother materialised behind the bar. He stared at us, his face im-mobile.

Malcolm started a grotesque mime. He leant forward and scooped his hands from his waist to his mouth. Silence. The locals put down their cards and stared hard at us. The barman raised one eyebrow.

'*Comida*,' I said.

The barman tilted his head towards the arch. We entered a larger, lighter room. We sat at a bare table near the window. Dali's brother padded in. He laid out cutlery, ashtrays, glasses and mineral water.

'*Vino?*' he asked.

'*Tinto*,' I replied. '*Dos litros. Vino de casa?*'

He inclined his head.

'Menu?' Malcolm described a square in the air with two fingers.

Our host held up the palm of his hand. Then he left. I went to the window. Twenty feet below a few dejected hens scratched in the dust at the edge of a cactus-choked fissure.

The wine arrived. It was almost black. It tasted strongly of tannin. We diluted it with mineral water.

The first course arrived. A large oval bowl was placed in the centre of the table. We looked at the amorphous contents suspiciously.

'Sea slugs?' I hazarded.

'Offal!' Gordon said.

'How do you know? You haven't tasted it yet,' Malcolm said as he speared at a tube. He chewed it for a while. Eventually he gulped and swallowed. His eyes watered.

I poked around with a fork and found what looked like a urinary tract. I put it back. We couldn't eat it and, since we didn't wish to offend the chef who was hurling pots around in the kitchen, I tipped it out of the window.

When our host collected the empty dish, I thought I saw a shadow of surprise pass across his eyes.

The main course consisted of gigantic smoked pork steaks in a lake of amber grease and enough baked potatoes to cobble Trafalgar Square.

'This is more like it,' Malcolm said.

I picked morosely at the pork and gave up. I ordered another litre of *tinto*. I used it to bludgeon my protesting stomach into submission.

We declined coffee. The bill was very cheap. I went to the window as we rose to leave. The chickens still scratched at the dust. The offal had landed on the cacti. Tubes, greasy ribbons and other less easily identifiable portions of a pig's innards hung from their thorns. Horrified, I turned. Our host was waiting patiently. He had scraped the leftovers on to one plate. I knew what he was waiting to do. I hurried away.

I awoke to a golden dawn. Sunlight streamed through the half-drawn curtains printing the shadow of a vine on the wall. I was encapsulated in the cool luxury of a bed as still as a sarcophagus. Almost perfection. I stretched out my arm but the sheet beside me was smooth and cold; the pillow plump and firm – a linen lacuna. I lit a cigarette. Gordon appeared in the window.

'Coming for breakfast? They stop serving in half an hour.'

'Ah, my rod and staff. Over turbulent waters thou hast accompanied me.'

'What yer on about, yer silly bugger?'

After an Empire-building breakfast we took our coffee on the terrace to enjoy the best cigarette of the day. Gordon began to make noises like a punctured accordion.

'What's up with you?'

'Can't get it up,' he wheezed. 'Can't take a breath deep enough to get behind it.'

I looked away. The air was sharp with fragrance exhaled from the garden below. The sun laboured up the curve of the sky. The shadows visibly shrank. The aviary seethed with sound.

'Bloody budgiewhoooofs,' Gordon exploded. He launched into a violent coughing fit. His chair vibrated across the tiles. Eventually he expectorated with a '*thoom*' of such a resonant timbre that it would have been the envy of the most ac-complished double-bass player.

'That's better,' he said in his normal voice.

'Canaries!'

'What?'

'They're canaries not budgies.'

'I don't care if they're penguins. They woke me up at five this morning.'

Malcolm stumbled up the steps.

'Morning all! Ready to go then?'

'Where?'

'To see the oldest tree in the world. Look!' He pointed to a photo in his guidebook. It had a trunk riven with vertical seams and foliage like a Brillo pad.

'I'm not risking my life to see that. Anyway, I want to stay here and get on with the writing.'

Malcolm's driving apart, I had already decided to defer sightseeing expeditions until we reached those more exotic ports of call, the Cape Verde islands and Bahía de Todos os Santos. I had nothing against Tenerife except that it was already well known to hordes of British tourists who came mainly to fester in the sun. All the travel agencies I'd visited in London stocked glossy brochures extolling the natatorial delights of the beaches and the punctuality, permanence and tanning properties of the sun. And so I spent an idyllic week at La Finquita, 'the little farm'; a tranquil oasis notwithstanding the canaries; a miniature Eden fructifying on a barren hillside.

I got into a routine. I wrote in the morning and at noon walked down the hill to a bar-restaurant on the main road for a two-hour lunchbreak. It was clean, functional and efficiently run. There was none of the pretentious clutter that you find in so many English restaurants to distract you from indifferent food. Each table was equipped with an ashtray, a jar of toothpicks and a stainless-steel paper napkin dispenser. As I lowered myself into a chair, one of the two waiters wiped the formica-topped table, presented me with the menu and asked what I wanted to drink. He then got me a beer while I perused the menu. When I laid it flat on the table he perceived that I'd come to a decision and made himself available to take my order. His powers of observation and deduction were remarkable. When my beer glass was empty *he* caught *my* eye and adjusted his physiognomy to denote polite enquiry. A single nod accomplished instant replenishment and a change of ashtrays.

And he did all this while attending to the demands of at least ten other tables. I was amazed, genuinely amazed, but then I hadn't been to a European country for eight years. (England is not in Europe and has not been civilised since the Romans left.)

And though a constant stream of customers kept Ramón and Federico busy, they did not once look harassed or flustered. They waited at tables, served drinks and snacks at the bar, sold ice-cream and cigarettes and all the while they chatted, whistled, hummed and gave vent to occasional bursts of song.

The secret of this happy state of affairs is quite simple – they did not confuse service with servitude. They realised that people on the move, however short their journey, would prefer to leave the stove and kitchen utensils at home.

At lunch a few days later I was established as a regular.

'You are the writer,' Ramón said, handing me the menu. I found his use of the definite article very elevating. I wasn't just a writer, but *the* writer. The cleaning lady up at La Finquita was obviously spreading the news.

'Have you visited the volcano yet?' he asked, pointing through the ceiling. The cone of Mount Teide was lurking up there somewhere behind a series of ridges.

I admitted that I had not. Out of politeness I pretended that it was on my agenda.

'I also have not been there ever,' he said. 'It *es* just a big hole high in the sky. Better you stay down here. Write about here instead. Volcanoes are not good places. Here is better.'

He went off to get me a beer. I pondered over his advice. He was right. I'd learn more about the people and the way of life in Tenerife in this humble roadside bar than by stumbling about in a sulphurous crater.

I thought of the few days I'd spent in Rome. They linger in my memory as a blur of frenetic sightseeing: the Vatican, St Peter's, the Colosseum, the Forum, the Spanish Steps and the Trevi Fountain – all isolated marvels connected only by traffic-choked streets sour with exhaust fumes. And the result? I failed to gain that illusive yet vital ingredient which all travellers should, but often fail to, experience – a sense of place. The lesson: if you've only got a few days in a place, stay put. Confine your exploratory urges to a small area and walk. Visit the local bars and restaurants. Linger in them. The people are as interesting as the monuments

I stayed under the volcano. It no longer loomed.

I studied the clientele. At the bar, lorry drivers in greasy overalls rubbed shoulders with businessmen in immaculate lightweight suits. Delivery men, their jackets blazoned with their firms' logo, stayed on for a beer. The place seemed to be in constant need of supplies; they had a high turnover. A policeman sat on a bar stool drinking beer, the butt of his heavy revolver touching the thigh of the man next to him. Village elders in sombre clothing conversed with young men in designer T-shirts. A group of workmen dined at tables next to a family in their finery, though Grandma still wore the traditional black uniform. The wine flowed. Even the children were given a little wine diluted with water.

What a contrast to England. People here, as in France and Italy, expected and got good food and service. They drank as much as they wanted, unhurried by 'time's winged chariot'. The policeman's chariot was in the carpark and it stayed there for over an hour. And they drank without worrying whether the sherry trifle would put them over the limit.

6

The Anna Kristina

As soon as the *Anna Kristina* sailed out of the security of the harbour breakwater I knew I was in for a tough time. She bucked and jolted through the short waves with a violence I had not experienced on the *Amorina* even in the Bay of Biscay. I felt vulnerable on the wide platform of her open deck. Apart from the kiosk of the radio room, there was no central superstructure to provide a leeside haven from the wind and spray and there were no grab handles. On that open deck one could stumble twenty feet, building up momentum, before crashing hip height into the pin rail.

Within half an hour I was feeling seasick. I had forgotten to put on a Scop disc. I sat on the hatch cover listless with nausea and consumed with self-pity. I was vaguely aware of chaotic and frantic activity around me. The shouts which always accompanied the setting of sails seemed remote and disembodied. I was so demoralised I couldn't summon enough interest to watch Tenerife recede in our wake. Two people vomited over the side simultaneously. I envied them.

Someone shook my shoulder. I looked up. It was Henrik.

'Coming below to help me cook dinner?'

'What do you mean, cook dinner?'

'We take it in turn to cook. There's no cook on this ship,' he explained. 'But if you're feeling sick I'll get somebody else. Stay up here in the fresh air. Concentrate on the horizon.'

I remembered my Uncle Godfrey's advice about making

friends with the ship's cook. Dear God. I'd have to make friends with everyone on this ship.

Henrik reappeared and stuck a Scop disc behind my ear. He was the medical officer as well as being First Mate and chippy.

'You should have put one on six hours before we sailed,' he admonished.

'What about some pills?' I asked.

'I don't believe in pills.'

'Well sod you, mate.'

'What?'

'Nothing.'

I sank deeper into the slough of despond. Then somebody shook my shoulder again. Christ Almighty! Why couldn't they leave me alone? It was John.

'We need some muscle on the main sail sheet,' he announced. 'At least you've got that even if you can't tell one end of a rope from another.'

The main sail sheet was a thick rope that ran between two huge blocks. One hung from the end of the boom and the other was attached to a metal ring on the deck. The free end of the rope ran from the deck block, passed through a bull's-eye and was secured to a short mounting post.

John and I heaved on the sheet to reduce the angle of the main sail. Each heave brought the boom a few inches closer to amidships. Tricia sat on the deck taking up the slack by pulling the sheet around the mounting post.

'A couple more heaves and it'll be right,' John grunted. Then it happened. The helmsman allowed the ship to run across the wind and, at the same time, Tricia failed to take up the slack. The boom started to swing with tremendous force out to starboard. John hurled himself at the mounting post. He managed to belay the sheet but not before I'd been jerked off balance. My hand smashed into the block and exploded into a crimson star of pain. I lay on the deck in a foetal position cursing between clenched teeth. Eventually the pain subsided to a dull throb. Henrik took a look at my hand.

'It's badly bruised,' he said, manipulating my knuckles. This set me cursing again. 'But you'll live. Lucky you didn't lose a few fingers.'

'Why didn't you let go?' John asked. 'Didn't they teach you anything on the *Amorina*?'

'No they bloody didn't. Hardly got a chance to get near a rope. Every time I touched one some interfering busybody would interpose himself. Or herself for that matter. Have you ever had a seventy-year-old hag with a crewcut and eyes like cracked Wedgwood plates climb up your back to lay hands on a rope? Christ! Put you off ropes for life. And there was this Peter Doc fellow. It wasn't safe to look at a rope when he was around. There must have been something in the water.'

'You're not feeling sick any more,' Henrik observed. 'So you can help me cook.' We went below.

Stuffed peppers were on the menu for the evening meal. It was a straightforward procedure. Cut the peppers in half lengthways, line with thin slices of cheese and fill with a mixture of mince, onions and tomato purée. But nothing is straightforward on a ship, especially a ship like the *Anna Kristina*.

When I'd visited her at the quayside in Tenerife I'd gained a somewhat amorphous impression of a slaphappy yet convivial domestic jumble; an impression that, now we were at sea, was rapidly assuming a harsher and more sharply defined Spartan reality.

The floor of the mess was now slippery with oily dishwater decanted from the impractically shallow sink. This was where sixteen people were to eat, sleep, cook, wash up and try to relax in rough weather. There were six bunks recessed into the walls and three cabins opening off. I refer to them as cabins but, in reality, they were bunks partitioned off with thin planks. My cabin had a floor space of two feet by two, the rest being taken up by two stepped shelves.

Now that the hatch was battened down it was gloomy and depressing. A pallid, watery light filtered down through glass cones embedded in the ceiling. The small, flat electric lights exhuded a weak, amber glow. A large antique oil lamp hanging from gimbals over the table was decorative rather than functional, though it was used as a night light.

While Henrik tinkered around trying to secure a saucepan on the stove with string and wire coat hangers, I attempted to chop onions one-handed. I was hanging on to the tap with the other. An onion rolled away. I let go of the tap and grabbed it. Then I found myself skating backwards. After a series of minor mishaps of a similar nature, the mince and the onions were finally brought together; but we couldn't find the tomato purée.

We searched the cupboards which, I noted, were stocked largely with accessories of cooking – packets of curry powder, bottles of sauce and jars of spices – rather than with the more substantial victuals generally considered necessary to sustain life. We searched the coffin-like storage crates with padded lids that doubled up as seats. As we went through them I began to feel uneasy. All I could find were packets of sunflower seeds and bags of corn of the variety favoured by chickens. But where was the food – the real food?

'There's storage space under J. D.'s bunk,' Henrik said. J. D. was in his bunk. He was a marasmic, hatchet-faced, lantern-jawed youth. He was feeling seasick and, as it turned out, continued to feel sick for most of the voyage. He was a great sailing enthusiast but for some perverse reason refused to wear a Scop disc. His face was the colour of cold porridge.

He would not or could not move. We rolled him against the wall and folded the thin foam-rubber mattress over him. We prised up a plank and found the tomato purée among assorted tins of tuna, fruit salad, corned beef and asparagus tips. This seemed a paltry amount of food for sixteen people but I consoled myself with the thought that they'd restock at Cape Verde only ten days' sailing away.

By evening we were in deeper water. The short waves had given way to the long undulations of a swell that rolled up from behind. The *Anna Kristina* rose and fell and surged forward with a more pleasant and more predictable motion.

Later that evening I went up on deck to smoke in the warm night air under a sky strewn with stars like finely crushed ice. Gordon got excited when he spotted the Southern Cross, hanging atilt, low on the black rim of the horizon.

'We're getting somewhere at last,' he said with nostalgia.

Young Bill, Old Bill and Salo were sitting near us playing bluff poker with dice and drinking Spanish brandy. Young Bill waved the bottle at us.

'Want some of this?' Gordon declined. I accepted.

'My old man didn't send me on this trip to straighten me out. It's more of a last fling, actually.'

'Last fling!' Old Bill snorted. 'I said that thirty years ago and I've been flinging ever since.'

'Onions,' Gordon said. 'Don't put so many bloody onions in the food. They repeat on me.' He belched. I was just about to comment on the stars when Old Bill answered Gordon with a crepitating trumpet blast from the nether regions.

And so I spent a pleasant evening drinking brandy and red wine. The air was velvety, the night wind cool, the stars cold and the company warm but undemanding. I was beginning to enjoy myself.

I knew that we were sailing southwest, edging out into the Atlantic. Tenerife was only about sixty miles off the coast of Morocco. The Cape Verde archipelago was just over 300 miles off the coast of Senegal. From there we would take the plunge across the vast blue expanse of the Atlantic to Brazil. It was an interesting prospect on a ship like the *Anna Kristina*.

'Another country,' said Old Bill dreamily. 'I've worked it out. Cape Verde will be my two hundred and third country.'

'Crap,' Salo said. 'There aren't two hundred countries in the world.'

'Oh ignorant youth,' said Old Bill, giving him an amiable cuff. 'England, Wales, Scotland, Ireland, the Isle of Man.'

'The Isle of Man,' I exclaimed. 'That's part of the United Kingdom.'

'They issue their own stamps,' Old Bill replied. 'That's how I count 'em.'

I went below to sleep. Gordon elected to sleep on the deck. It would save him getting up every two hours for a cigarette.

The next day I began to get a clearer idea of what I'd let myself in for. Breakfast was laid out on a shelf running the length of the table – salami, a selection of cheese which included a foul-smelling Danish goat's cheese, and assorted cereals. And this was to be the formula for the rest of the trip. The salami and cheese were also to feature with monotonous regularity at lunch as a backup to whatever the 'chef' of the day had heated up.

Henrik was chewing on a piece of rye bread laden with garlic cloves. I sampled a psychedelic disc of salami and spat it out.

'There's porridge on the stove,' Henrik said.

I sampled the porridge and spat it out.

'Some idiot's put sunflower seeds in it,' I said in disgust. Henrik looked at me balefully. The kettle started to steam so I made myself a cup of instant coffee. I spat that out in the sink.

'The kettle with the green tape on the handle is for salt water,' Henrik informed me. 'For washing-up.'

Then I noticed a metal teapot. I reached for it.

'Herb tea,' Henrik said smugly. I grabbed a bottle of beer and went on deck to perform my duties as a member of the morning watch.

I took a turn at the open helm. It was firmer and more responsive than the *Amorina*'s power-assisted wheel. The *Anna Kristina* was only eighty tons compared with the *Amorina*'s 500.

I found it quite exhilarating spinning the wheel while sitting astride the steel cowling that housed the steering mechanism, a

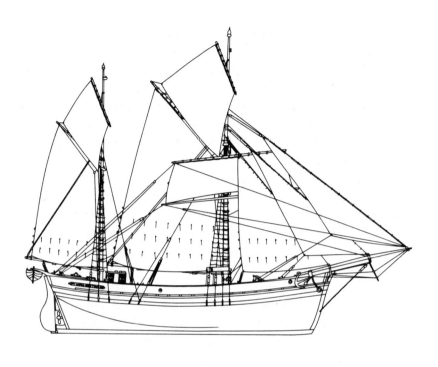

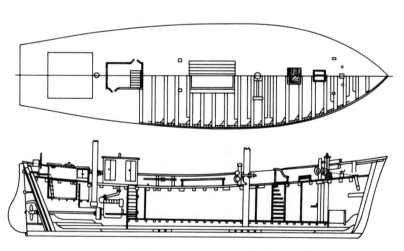

THE *ANNA KRISTINA*

system of cast-iron cogwheels. In front of me stretched seventy feet of deck tapering to the bowsprit which scratched and probed at the retreating horizon. One foot behind was the stern rail and the sea heaving up in a twenty-foot swell. And as each wave loomed over the stern it seemed that the ship would be enveloped, but each time she rose gracefully up the liquid slope, gaining a brief extra momentum before sinking back into the following trough.

After half an hour I relinquished the helm to Gordon. He had been standing by eyeing the wheel enviously. He was a good helmsman. His movements were precise and economic. He nursed the ship along. He did not indulge in the wheel-spinning histrionics that I had to perform to keep the ship on course. Nor did he go 'whee-he-he' as the ship skidded and surfed along the bulging brow of a wave.

John was detailing the tasks of the day. 'You can help Mons scrape the deck,' he said as I tried to make myself invisible. Gordon grinned and clung to the wheel possessively.

Mons (pronounced Muntz) was a young Norwegian. His hair was the colour of bleached straw and there was a slightly deranged look in his wandering blue eyes. He wore a permanent half smile as if he were enjoying some endless private joke.

John took us to the bow and pointed at a pile of grey rocks. They were rough and porous.

'Pumice stone,' he said. 'From the volcano.'

Mons smiled vaguely and stared out to sea.

John dropped to his knees and scrubbed away vigorously. This part of the deck was badly stained by oil seepage from the anchor winch.

'That's how you do it,' John said, dropping the stone. 'You've got till Rio to finish the job.'

Mons and I sat on the deck. After what seemed an age of intensive scraping the result was a few faint scratches. I cursed.

'Patience,' Mons said. We carried on for about half an hour in a desultory fashion.

'Bugger this,' I said and threw the stone overboard. Mons looked amazed.

'Look,' I said, 'it's obvious that it'd take us ten years to scrape the deck clean this way. The job could be done in two hours with an industrial sander.' I picked up another chunk of pumice and lobbed it over the rail. Mons threw his over.

John approached, puffing phlegmatically on his pipe. We waited for the outburst. Mons smiled at the sky. I started to speak. John held up his hand. He looked down at the scratches.

'I knew it was a stupid idea,' he said, 'but Hans has this passion for authenticity. He read somewhere that this was how it was done in the old days. He spent some time on the slopes of Mount Teide personally selecting these.' John prodded the pile of rocks with his toe. 'I had to humour him. Chuck 'em in the sea.'

Hans – Hans van de Vooren – was the owner. He had, over a few beers, told me the history of the *Anna Kristina* – a history which I think is worth relating at this point since she was the oldest and most authentic vessel of the fleet.

Built in 1889 in Norway, the *Anna Kristina* was one of nearly 2,000 Hardanger *jakts* (sloops) that traded up and down the coast. They were known to be excellent sailing ships, small, sturdy and fast, reaching a top speed of fourteen knots.

The *Anna Kristina* achieved early but brief fame a year after she was launched in a regatta from Trondheim to the Lofoten archipelago. Her Captain, Johannes Skarsvag, took a calculated risk and sailed her, fully laden, up the coast outside the protective chain of islands. There, the winds were stronger but the sea much rougher. His gamble paid off. His sturdy ship won. Unfortunately she wasn't a registered entrant so the *Anna Kristina* received much public acclaim but no official recognition. After that she plied the Norwegian coast until 1977, fulfilling her less exciting role as a cargo ship, carrying dried and salted cod but making occasional trips to Riga in Russia to transport timber.

Her recent history is more interesting. It is inseparable from Hans's enthusiasm and determination.

In the early seventies he and his family enjoyed a comfortable and secure life in Holland. He worked as a consultant for a construction company, spending his spare time and money restoring old ships. His aim was to bring history alive rather than create inert museum pieces.

In the summer of 1973 he was in Bodo on the west coast of Norway. On impulse he bought a dilapidated sixty-eight-foot *jakt*, the *Anna Rosa*. She was in such bad condition she nearly sank while being towed to the shipyard.

He returned to Holland and gave up his job to devote himself full-time to the restoration. He sold his house to finance the project. Then he drove back to Norway in a VW camper with his wife Hetti and son Salo, then a baby.

The boatyard replaced the keel but Hans and his wife, sometimes with the aid of friends, did all the remaining structural work, masts and rigging. He managed to get a charter from a film company to use the ship in a film of Knut Hamsun's short story 'Benoni and Rosa'. The ship had to be ready by the spring of 1974.

They worked twelve hours a day, seven days a week in temperatures as low as minus twenty-five degrees centigrade. By spring the ship was ready. But Hans was running out of money. The shipyard wouldn't release the *Anna Rosa* until full payment was received. The film company wouldn't pay Hans until the ship was at sea. Deadlock. Imminent bankruptcy. Then the Dutch Consul intervened on their behalf. He persuaded a bank to provide the necessary money. The film was made. Hans was afloat.

After this most people would have bought a toupé and crawled back to the office. Instead Hans bought another wreck – the *Anna Kristina*. This created even more problems for him and is probably the cause of his present hunted look.

It took him ten years to restore her. He spent £100,000 on an iron shoe to straighten the keel. Another £150,000 went on the main engine, generator, water maker, navigational equipment, weather fax and general restoration. Because he was a Dutch citizen he received minimal aid from the Norwegian government despite the fact that he was restoring a piece of their history.

To gain credibility and the necessary papers from the authorities, the *Anna Kristina* was sent on various journeys – first to northern Norway, then to Europe and finally to Spitzbergen (Svalbard) on latitude 80° north – a process of gradual dispensation, as Hans put it.

And so here we were rolling down to Rio on a ship that was yet to make an Atlantic crossing.

I had decided to join the *Anna Kristina* because of the friendly atmosphere of Scandinavian informality. Other factors such as comfort and convenience I had, perhaps unwisely, not considered.

She was a complete contrast to the *Amorina*. The grace and purity of her lines were unsullied by any additional superstructure. She was lissom and manoeuvrable. She was pretty, perhaps even beautiful; certainly colourful with her rust-red sails and green and yellow hull.

Hans had restored her to her original state as far as modern safety regulations would allow. I think these had been stretched a bit. Externally she was authentic in almost every detail. If you didn't look too closely you wouldn't notice the small radar pod high on the mizzen mast. Below, Hans had contrived, too successfully for my liking, to keep the intrusion of modern facilities to a minimum.

Now that we'd disposed of the volcanic rocks there wasn't much to do. Because of her totally wooden construction there was no need for the frenetic, endless round of rust-proofing that took place on the *Amorina*. No Wagnerian dwarfs with seven-pound hammers pounded on a 500-ton echo-chamber.

Mons and I basked in the sun. Abby and Katrina lay bare-breasted on the deck. In this environment they were curiously sexless. We stepped over them as if they were logs. Jill, the fleet dentist, who had left all her equipment on the *Amorina*, would not expose her breasts despite, or perhaps because of, many oblique promptings. Old Bill, Young Bill and Salo sat, cross-legged, playing bluff poker. It would take them three weeks to tire of this mind-numbing game.

'Oh wunnerful, wunnerful, do-da-dee,' Mons moaned. I realised he was talking to himself. I presumed this outburst was the product of some erotic reverie.

'Oh wunnerful, wunnerful, do-da-dee,' he moaned again.

'What the hell are you on about?' I asked.

'The sea is wunnerful, wunnerful,' he replied.

I sat up and looked at it. It was blue. So was the sky. The swell rolled along propelled by some inner dynamic beyond my comprehension. Not another Walther, I thought.

'Why?' I asked.

'Because there are no cars, no streets, no people hurrying to work at boring jobs in factories.'

'You prick,' I replied. 'If it wasn't for me you'd still be scraping the deck with a lump of volcanic rock. A most stimulating occupation.'

'What's prick?' he asked.

'Forget about that. Just answer my point.'

Mons, as I was to discover, was the master of evasion.

'At sea there are no worries. Life is pure and simple,' he said.

He had a point here. I thought about it for a moment. It was true that no brown envelopes with transparent address panels landed on the doormat with depressing regularity. On the other hand I never opened these outrageous demands for money backed up by the might of a top-heavy state machinery. Rosamund did; and she worked to pay them while I guzzled pints and played pool with our richer and more leisured brethren – Telecom workers.

'Anyway, why are *you* here if you don't like the sea?' he asked quite reasonably.

'To write a book.' I explained my mission in more detail. He was not impressed.

'I'm also getting a free trip,' he said. 'And I don't have to write a book.'

'What does Hans pay you?' I asked.

'Nothing. It's a privilege to be here.'

'Go on,' I prompted.

'When I first saw the *Anna Kristina* I knew I had to sail with her. I telephoned Hans. He agreed to take me on if I helped him get her ready. There was much to be done. I worked on her for two months before she left Norway. Lived most of the time on spaghetti.'

I made a noise expressing a mixture of disgust at his diet and admiration of his stoicism.

'That's nothing,' he continued. 'I once lived for six weeks on a sack of white rice and tabasco.'

Now I began to understand the casual attitude towards food on the ship. Mons, Henrik and Katrina, John's live-in girlfriend, were vegetarians. Since there was no resident cook the purchase of supplies was haphazard and dictated by the whim and eccentric tastes of Henrik and Katrina. Mons didn't really care what he ate as long as it hadn't been running around on four legs. The rest of the ship's company were blessed with that euphemism for a complete lack of culinary discrimination – healthy appetites. My jaded appetite craved more titillating fare than lasagne or macaroni in gorgonzola sauce, damp rice and doughy bread shot with sunflower seeds. My desire for roast beef and two veg, or a hamburger, was regarded as symptomatic of British imperialism and Western decadence respectively. I was a lone voice crying in a watery wilderness.

Well, not quite a lone voice. I had an ally in Gordon, but he was not given to overt grumbling or rabid diatribes, fuelled by alcohol, against the system. Gordon just smiled and stated that he was going to 'bugger off back to the *Amorina*' at Cape Verde.

We had been warned by various people in Tenerife that the *Anna Kristina* was a 'hippy ship'. The information was always imparted in a low voice behind a cupped hand. Requests for elucidation were countered with 'you'll find out'. I hadn't taken any notice of these sinister warnings. To me the hippy, with the exception of Alan Ginsberg, was an extinct species. All the hippies I had known now wore Burton suits, had their hair permed in unisex salons and were labouring to pay off their mortgages within, they hoped, a decade of their decease.

There were no hippies on the ship. True, there was a certain irregularity of dress. Mons's tar-encrusted jeans lent credence to the tired old joke that 'they could stand up on their own'. And he really did have to bang them on the deck before he could get into them.

True, we looked a dirty crowd but this was superficial – the look, not the dirt. Although we were limited to one fresh-water shower a week, the sea was now sufficiently warm to take regular salt-water showers on the deck with the aid of a bucket. Nobody stank though the atmosphere below was somewhat foetid from the bilge water that oozed up through the floorboards.

It was not a hippy ship. There was no desire for instant gratification with the least effort and minimal financial outlay. And there was no self-conscious adoption of the more superficial but obvious characteristics of exotic cultures to fill the vacuum created by an inability to appreciate and comprehend the complexities of one's own cultural heritage. Nobody was 'laid back' or 'into' things, or went round chanting 'Hari Rama'. Nobody smoked pot or dropped acid in an effort to reach Nirvana. Johan, the engineer, occasionally strummed his guitar in an ineffectual way but these painful episodes became more and more infrequent as he realised his limitations. Later – a long time later – some misanthrope gave Mons a bugle, and some other very clever person threw it overboard.

But the crew, especially Mons, Henrik and Johan, did feel passionately about what they perceived as the gross injustices perpetrated by the West, especially America, against the Third World countries. Naturally they were also anti the nuclear bomb, industrialisation, sliced bread, paper money, plastic packaging, three-bedroom houses with integral garages, Coca-Cola and NATO. These opinions were to involve us in many heated but hilarious arguments on the Atlantic crossing. I think it was my penchant for polemic that made me stay on the *Anna Kristina* instead of decamping with Gordon back to the relative comfort of the *Amorina* as soon as we reached Cape Verde.

Mons and I were to become great friends. It was probably the mutual attraction of opposites; he a cross between an amiable, educated Caliban and Rousseau's Noble Savage and I, a world-weary cynical hedonist, though, at the time, I felt more like the Flying Dutchman.

Mons's habit of moaning 'wunnerful, wunnerful', while staring with eyes as serene and blue as the surrounding vacancy, irritated and provoked me. Perhaps I envied his self-sufficiency, his almost oriental fatalistic acceptance of empty days spent on an empty sea. I needed more concrete and varied stimuli than the constant susurrus of restless waves and the aching blue void. I needed art galleries, the six o'clock news, the *Observer Review*, Radio Three, the *Guardian* crossword puzzle, page three of the *Sun*, dog fights outside supermarkets, pool tables, pints of draught Guinness, the midnight movie, second-hand book-shops, Chinese restaurants, steak pizzaola, walks on Hampstead Heath, drives through the green Arcady of Sussex, the gratuitous violence and eroticism of films masquerading as art, take-away curries, roast beef and mustard, and the cold astringency of massive gin and tonics, with a slice of lime, not lemon.

I found I could do without Breakfast Television, *Eastenders*,

Oxford Street, Islington, Margaret Thatcher, Princess Di, Greek restaurants, Arthur Scargill, the Underground, demo-marches, the Gas Board, football fans, crusading inverts, dog shit, the last four months of the English winter, Brickwoods pubs, three-bedroom homes with integral garages and the Post Office Tower.

I tried to persuade Gordon to change his mind about returning to the *Amorina* at Cape Verde.

'They're bound to re-stock there,' I said. 'The food will improve.'

'The cooks will be the same,' he replied.

'Think how proud you'll feel at crossing the Atlantic on such a little ship.' He looked interested. I could see he was tempted.

'Only eighty tons,' I added.

'Only eighty tons,' he squawked. 'Thanks for telling me. If I'd known that in the first place I wouldn't have set foot on her.'

'You're doing a Bulkington on me,' I said reproachfully.

'Who? Never heard of him.'

'Bulkington,' I explained, 'is a character in *Moby Dick*. Melville brings him in at the beginning, sets him up as a shipmate, describes him in detail and then forgets about him until chapter twenty-three. I need you to provide continuity.'

'Yer got yerself. But I'll think about it.'

He was flattered. I felt optimistic. I was sure I could win him round but then two things happened in quick succession to convince him that his decision to leave was a wise one.

Most of us had taken to sleeping on the deck as the nights grew hotter and hotter. In my case it wasn't the heat but the noise that drove me up to sleep beneath the stars. Below there was more activity at night than in the day. The midnight-to-four watch made the bread. I was fed up with listening to them pounding the dough, especially as the end product was about as dentable as a breeze block. At two Henrik pumped the primus stove to make popcorn. At three-thirty they made coffee for the oncoming watch. The four a.m. watch washed up, cleaned the heads and mopped the floor. From five to seven the generator roared to boost the batteries and run the oven to bake the bread.

That night Gordon and I laid our sleeping bags down between the foremast and the anchor winch where there was less chance of being trodden on. At about three in the morning the top spar of the upper square sail snapped in half. I must have been dozing for I heard a sharp crack like the report of a field gun followed by a rushing, slithering sound. A tangle of ropes landed on us. The jagged end of half a spar jerked to a halt a few feet above Gordon's face.

'It could happen on any ship,' I said to him the next morning.

'But it happened on this ship. Anyhow I prefer the *Amorina*. More space. More privacy. This is a young man's ship.'

We were standing near the bow just behind the forecourse. This was a huge rectangular sail set so low that the bottom edge was at head height. It had often cuffed me. Gordon had his back to it. The wind was fitful, alternately gusting and dying away. Gordon stepped back a pace. The wind died. The forecourse flapped and hung slack. The port clew line sagged downwards and inwards across the deck. It dropped a languid loop over Gordon's head and slid down to his waist. Unconcerned he tried to brush it aside. The wind gusted. The forecourse bulged. The clew line snapped tight as 300 square feet of canvas harnessed the wind. It catapulted him across the deck like a whipped top and smashed him against the pin rail.

He was lucky. He could have been flipped overboard. He could have broken a femur. As it was he sustained massive bruising from hip to knee. I knew then he'd return to the *Amorina* at Cape Verde. I was tempted to go with him, but only tempted. Despite the discomfort, the cramped conditions, the lack of privacy, the appalling food, the bilge water oozing across the floor and the noise at night, it was a happy ship. I knew I would stay on her until Rio.

7

The Blue House

On the morning of 16 June we sighted the Cape Verde archipelago. As the haze cleared the stark profile of the island of Saint Vincente hardened into shape. It was a barren and treeless desert; but there was a bleak grandeur about the iron-red central mountain rising up 2,500 feet out of the ocean. The most interesting feature was an immense sandfield that started in the centre of the mountain's sagging spinal cord and poured in a widening yellow swathe down to the lower slopes. This sand had been blasted by the wind off the beaches on the other side of the island.

We rounded a headland, passing between the shore and a long stack of rock topped with an abandoned fort. The sea here was angry. It boiled and seethed as the swell forced itself through the narrow channel. And there was Porto Grande, looking far from grand.

Some 200 years ago the First Fleet had tried to put into Porto Grande in adverse winds. Commodore Arthur Phillip had called off the attempt when a Portuguese ship in difficulty was sighted off the harbour mouth.

The foreshore was lined with quaint old Portuguese colonial buildings in pastel shades of yellow, green and blue. There was nothing about them to excite the student of architecture. The sun flashed on the tanks of a small oil terminal. An ancient prison with narrow windows blended into the contour of the low hill behind. (The government had built a nice new one

112

inland depriving the inmates of a sea view.) No high-rise buildings proclaimed themselves.

And then I spotted it. High on a mountainside about two miles inland stood a blue house in startling isolation; a dark blue house in a waste of shattered rock. It intrigued me. Who and why would somebody build such a house in so desolate a spot? The Cape Verde islands are remote enough anyway; remote in the sense that they have nothing to attract the tourist. So why cut yourself off from the limited facilities offered by the town? The house itself seemed encapsulated in a remoteness of its own creation. Thus it was doubly remote. It could only have been built in despair.

We reduced sail as we passed the end of a modern concrete breakwater where three cargo ships were berthed, and dropped anchor 200 yards from shore in a small bay. Less than 100 yards away was the mutilated finger of an older, concrete landing stage. It looked as if it had been bombed. Whole sections were missing. It was disintegrating under the sea's constant attrition and from a disease within. It was slowly bursting open from the pressure of the corroding reinforcing rods that scarred it with livid weals and protruded in tangled veins oozing rust. Two boys sat on the end fishing. To the right of us was the burnt-out superstructure of a wreck. I could hear the melancholy gurgling of the sea in its innards. Two dogs chased each other up and down the greyish-yellow sand edging the road along the shore. A small crowd of perhaps thirty people had gathered opposite us. There were no brass bands, though somebody did wave. An air of desuetude hung over the place.

'What a dump,' Gordon said. I quite liked the look of it.

'Used to be a busy coaling station in the good old days.' I remembered the prophecy of Margaret's grandfather that steam would never last. Gordon was not mollified by this piece of information. The crowd on the shore began to drift away.

Eventually we were allowed ashore on condition we acquired

three passport photos each from a specified photographer who was obviously a close relative of the chief of immigration. It was a pointless exercise since there were no officials on the shore to vet us and we were on trust to hand them in.

'Somebody told me this place was communist,' Gordon said as we wandered aimlessly around the streets.

There was no evidence of the hammer and sickle. There were no red stars or posters of firm-jawed girls in boiler suits waving spanners. On the contrary there were a number of tawdry ads for powdered milk, toothpaste, tinned sardines and bicycles. And the spirit of free enterprise was alive in those who had enough energy to rouse themselves from the torpid apathy inflicting most of those not gainfully employed. A lot of people sat in doorways watching the shadows measure the sun's course across the sky. The town – and it wasn't big enough for a blind man to get lost in – was seething with guides. We'd already shaken off the attention of three young men who each knew the best bar, brothel and nightclub. These distinctions, we discovered later, were fine to the point of invisibility. But an old man with jug ears and a pencil-line moustache persisted. He danced circles around us, plucking at our sleeves.

'This *es* the cinema,' he said, pointing at the cinema. 'This *es* a shop,' he said, a few paces later, peering through the window to apprise the nature of the commodities therein.

'I think we can do without the services of this twit,' I said to Gordon, working myself up to be unnecessarily rude. Gordon headed me off. He took him by the hand and shook it vigorously.

'It's been nice knowing you,' he said. 'Very nice knowing you.' We strode away leaving him forlorn.

'This shop,' he bleated faintly, 'he sell sewing machines.'

It was hot; and the restless wind that blew throughout our stay was not refreshing. It was warm and oily and laden with fine particles of sand. The sparse foliage of the few carefully nurtured trees cast a tepid sun-speckled shade. Most of the streets were mean, but not dirty or littered; there was nothing to throw away. Goats with supercilious eyes expected, and were given, right of way. There was very little traffic. Many of the women were beautiful. They walked with a superb, haughty posture, sinuous yet upright. You have to walk like that if you're carrying the shopping on your head.

I sensed that Gordon was bored. We were passing a bar. Young Bill and Old Bill waved from the cool, tantalising depths.

'Fancy a beer, Gordon?' I suggested.

'Don't mind if I do,' he replied. Gordon was the most accommodating of travelling companions.

It was a strange bar. By the door was a long glass cabinet displaying an eclectic array of offerings laid out in neat piles with a parade-ground precision: Kit-Kat, denture glue, chewing gum, aspirins, Tampax, Mars Bars, soap, razor blades, Andrews Liver Salts; all the riches of the West. Above the bar a small blackboard proclaimed, 'Have Homemade Nescafé Here'.

The proprietress, Mitzy, was an aged negress with wise eyes. I ordered three beers and a homemade Nescafé. Gordon had been seduced by the blackboard's exhortation. She started to make Gordon's coffee. She measured out the exact amount of water with a cup. She poured it into a tiny kettle over a tiny flame. Then she waited for the kettle to boil.

'The beer,' I prompted, thinking she had forgotten.

'All drinks come same time,' she said with an air of finality. I could have drunk two beers by the time the coffee was ready. My throat was a torrid zone. Perhaps this place was communist after all. Eventually, and with great ceremony, three tins of Carlsberg were lined up on the counter behind three tall glasses. By now I was mesmerised. Mitzy opened one tin and proceeded to distribute the amber nectar equally among the three glasses. She wasn't going to give me a chance to snatch one and run for it. She then opened the second tin and distributed its contents, as before, among the three glasses, pausing frequently to allow the foam to settle. By the time she'd shaken the last drop from

115

the third tin I knew the name of her deceased husband and the names of half her tribe.

I joined the others, nursing my lager as if it were the Holy Grail.

'Somebody better order the next round now,' I said, after a long pull.

The place was immaculate. It was obviously a respectable establishment. Mitzy's granddaughter fussed around with a dustpan and brush and a damp cloth. Behind me loomed a Victorian cabinet laden with toiletries. It was like drinking in a chemist's. Young Bill got the next round. Gordon tactfully refrained from ordering Nescafé and made do with Coca-Cola.

'We've been here all afternoon,' Old Bill said. 'It's an interesting place. Watch.'

I watched. She did good trade. She was flexible. One customer bought a single razor blade which was wrapped with due ceremony in brown paper. Her granddaughter did this with great pride and concentration, her pink tongue protruding through pearly gates. People bought aspirin singly or in pairs after much consultory confabulation. Schoolchildren in well-laundered and neatly patched uniforms bought single fingers of Kit-Kat cut from the block. A Chinese sailor came in and, after much haggling, sold Mitzy a carton of Winston cigarettes and three tubes of Colgate toothpaste. These were locked in the cabinet behind us. This transaction was conducted quite openly without the usual sideways shuffle and surreptitious backhander. Mitzy was in the import business.

A tall negro with three ceremonial scars on each cheek waited patiently for his Nescafé after watching in anguish as Mitzy shook a few granules off the heaped teaspoon back into the tin. Young ladies in airy flower-patterned frocks that awoke in me vague atavistic yearnings purchased sachets of shampoo, half bars of soap and what Old Bill referred to as 'white cigars'. If they did blush it did not show beneath their ebony skin.

Another young lady who looked like the popular conception

of the village schoolmistress came in and, after a brief chat with Mitzy, sat on Old Bill's lap.

'Fucky, fucky,' she asked, caressing his bald patch. Young Bill looked alarmed and suddenly became enraptured by the contents of the cabinet behind us. Old Bill bounced her on his lap for a while but remained politely non-committal. She transferred herself to Gordon's lap.

'Fucky, fucky,' she said, caressing his silver locks. Young Bill was now trying to read the small print on a bottle of Optrex. Gordon smiled as if he were starring in a toothpaste commercial.

'Fucky, fucky,' she said, depositing herself on my lap and pulling my beard. I lit a defensive cigarette and set up a smoke screen. She gave up.

'OK,' she said to no one in particular. 'OK, you buy me ice-cream instead.' Young Bill complied with uncommon alacrity. Honour was saved.

The tall negro finished his Nescafé and came over.

'You need taxi,' he said. 'I am the man. All others are bandits. I take you wherever.'

I suggested the Blue House.

'Not now,' he said. 'Soon comes the night. I take you another time.'

One of the most disreputable-looking ruffians I've ever seen came in. He was filthy. His ragged clothes shone with grime. He stank. He was crazy in the true sense of the word. He obviously hadn't been sober for years. Long matted dreadlocks hung about his shoulders. His eyes were rotten purple grapes in scarlet nets. His pupils were black pits from which hope and despair had long been banished. He stood by our table moaning and gibbering.

'I think he wants a drink,' Old Bill said.

Mitzy shooed him out. He lingered on the pavement in the lengthening shadows. Loud music blared from the bar next door. The air pulsed and thrummed like a metal sheet flexing. He danced. He punched at the air. He kicked higher than his head. He limboed. He did the splits. He leapt. He span; and he did all this with great expression and style in perfect time to the electric, primal beat. (He made Travolta look as though he danced with one foot in a bucket.) Then he lay in the road and screamed for five minutes. And this was the quiet end of town.

We left to find a restaurant. We followed Old Bill. We wended our way through narrow side streets towards the dock. On our journey we picked up the guides we'd shaken off earlier. They followed us silently. We stopped outside a restaurant called Pica-Pau. The guides lurked in the shadows. A faded peeling sign suggested that prawns and lobsters might be had therein. I pushed aside the bead curtain. There were six tables covered in dirty green and white gingham. At the end of the room was a short mahogany counter. The man behind beckoned. I let the curtain fall back into place. I looked through the adjacent door less than two feet away. It was a small, 'standing only' bar. The other half of the mahogany counter graced the opposite wall. The same man beckoned.

'Come on,' Old Bill said. 'Make up your bloody mind.'

We entered the restaurant. We sat at a table against the wooden partition that divided the premises. The proprietor, a short, stocky man with olive skin, could hardly contain his excitement. He spoke good English. He explained that he'd worked on English ships as a cook and spent a few years in Liverpool. He recommended lobster. It was the most expensive dish on the menu. I did some arithmetic. A lobster would cost just under a pound.

'It comes with all the trimmings,' he said, noting my fingerwork.

'I'll have two,' I said. It was his turn to look surprised.

We sat back and drank white wine. I began to feel mellow and at peace with the world. The discourse was amiable and unmemorable. Our host patrolled his dual premises from behind the counter. I was vaguely aware of a shouting contest in the bar next door. It raged for a minute or two then died away in a diminuendo of disgruntled muttering. I noticed that the old man with the pencil-line moustache and jug ears was sitting at a nearby table. He winked and leered at us. I ignored him. The shouting contest started again; the old man winked and leered. The noise died down. My companions seemed unaware of the periodic altercations interspersed with intervals of silence and the leering old man. I studied the label on the wine bottle. It seemed a genuine import from Portugal. The print was regular.

After a while I began to notice a pattern. Whenever our host was in view there was silence. Whenever he disappeared there was an uproar. It was an interesting phenomenon.

Suddenly, the din reached epic proportions; it sounded like a Nuremberg rally. Even Young Bill noticed. Silence. Our host had appeared. He looked flustered. He came over.

'There are many guides in there,' he said, pointing to the bar. 'They all say they brought you. Only one can have brought you. Which one?'

The *escudo* dropped.

'None of them,' Old Bill said.

'He did,' I said, pointing at the old man. I'd been feeling a bit guilty about him.

Our host brought him his commission – a large white rum. Then he went to the bar and blasted the opportunist rabble.

The meal was excellent. We nodded over coffee and brandy. The room was filling up with unguiding guides. A car screeched to a halt on the cobbles outside. Jonathan King pushed his head through the bead curtains.

'What's the food like?' he shouted.

'Very good,' Gordon shouted back.

'What?'

I elbowed Gordon viciously. 'Tell him it's terrible,' I hissed out of the corner of my mouth.

'It's terrible,' Gordon shouted.

The car shot off.

'Why did you make me do that?' Gordon asked.

'Keep it a secret,' I said. 'This is a small place. If the rest of that mob get to hear about it, we won't get in here again.'

Our host returned from an expedition to the bar. He hovered. Then he got to the point.

'Tell your friends,' he said. 'Tell your friends that this is a good place to eat. You enjoyed the food?'

We were volubly appreciative. We praised the lobster, but we didn't tell him we weren't going to spread the word. He beamed.

The room had filled up with guides. They regarded us reproachfully. I looked at them. My heart sank. Tomorrow the town would be seething with 'first fleeters'. These guides were just a platoon from Cape Verde's army of unemployed. I knew it was hopeless. Nascent territorial imperative dimmed.

We ordered more coffee and brandy. This was the only night we'd have Pica-Pau to ourselves. Better enjoy it. The guides edged closer. Their eyes brimmed with canine anguish. A vague feeling of guilt soured my brandy. Our host was clearing away the pink debris of our feast. Empty wine bottles stood in mute testimony of our relative wealth. To the guides we must have appeared millionaires. Like a Roman emperor dispensing a favour to the mob, I made the necessary languid yet eloquent open-handed gesture in their direction. Our host brought them rum. They did not, as I had feared, inflict themselves on us in an attempt to show gratitude. They talked among themselves in low murmurs. We let the rum flow. They accepted our largesse with a quiet dignity, tilting their glasses towards us in unspoken recognition that justice was being done. And so, united in spiritous brotherhood, we drank the night away.

At midnight we paid the bill. It was so reasonable we left a large tip. This confused our host. He insisted we take it back. Old Bill and Young Bill went off in search of further adventure shadowed by the guides. Gordon and I caught the last dinghy back to the ship. We lay on the deck on top of our sleeping bags beneath the stars and the gaunt silhouette of the foremast. I listened to the waves lapping against the hull and the dogs howling on the beach. Gordon coughed. His cigarette glowed. The stars were spinning.

I woke to the mewing of a sea eagle in the rigging. Lindo was wandering around the deck like a lost soul. He stopped and took out his slimline portable cassette tape recorder.

'Here I am in Cape Verde . . .' he said, and switched it off. He was indeed.

J. D. woke up. He addressed himself to Lindo.

'It's your turn to make breakfast. You put out the salami, the cheese, the bread, the cornflakes, the milk, the . . .'

'Take it easy, J. D.,' Lindo said, patting him on the shoulder. 'Take it easy or you'll never make it to Rio.'

Young Bill and Old Bill waved from the beach. They were alone. I waved back. Horrible oaths rolled across the water.

Gordon and I rowed the dinghy ashore.

Old Bill looked rough. Young Bill was asleep on his feet.

'Had a good night?' I asked facetiously.

'Tried to sleep on the beach,' Old Bill said. 'Fucking dogs kept pissing on me.'

I'd booked into a small hotel on the Avenue 12 de Setembro. It didn't seem to have a name. It was above a sports hall. The facilities consisted of two table-tennis tables and a few stackable metal chairs. The walls were lined with sepia photographs of long-dead football teams posing rigidly in what looked like the Ghaza Strip.

On the first-floor landing was the reception desk. This consisted of a wooden table and a watchman. He was a young man studying law. He gave me a key from one of twelve hanging from hooks on a wooden board. I was the only guest. At night another young man reading law took over.

It was a cheerful place. It echoed with the song and chatter of three negro maids who cleaned and re-cleaned the twelve rooms until they sparkled and shone. Attempts to converse with them were met with shrieks and giggles. Whenever I left the room they dashed in and cleaned it. They replaced the towels about five times a day and the sheets every morning. It was one of the best hotels I'd ever stayed in.

Gordon and I set off on a sightseeing expedition. We had no plan. We headed inland. The cobbled streets gave way to dusty dirt tracks. The houses became poorer and poorer. We came to a shanty town. We hesitated and entered. It was laid out like a gridiron. The streets of impacted red earth were too narrow for cars. The houses were made of tins hammered flat, poles, planks, plastic sheets, iron rods, in fact anything durable that the inhabitants could lay their hands on.

It was easy to see inside; all the doors were open. The interiors, like the streets, were scrupulously clean. There was a certain pathos in the pride with which a few humble ornaments were displayed. Gaudily painted plaster statuettes of the Virgin Mary and the saints predominated. But the atmosphere of the township was not one of despair or apathy, despite the obvious poverty. The people seemed to have a sense of purpose as if they were imbued with a hope more realisable than that offered by the plaster saints. Later we learned from Mons that they received limited aid, but a lot of advice, from a Swedish society promoting self-help.

Further inland was a bare, conical hill about 500 feet in height. I suggested that we climbed it.

'Don't mind if I do,' Gordon assented as usual.

At the edge of the town the path took us down a steep slope. We paused halfway down to allow a file of girls with plastic water pots on their heads to pass by. They wended their way up with grace and dignity. Their laughter tinkled like a Chinese wind bell.

A few minutes' walk brought us to the base of the hill. We started up through what we discovered was the town rubbish dump. The air was acrid with burning piles of refuse and angry with flies. It stank. There were tins – tins packed tight with

human excrement. We hurried on up through this other
Gehenna where spavined dogs slouched.

Halfway up the air was clear. The smoke from the refuse only
rose a few feet before the wind obliterated it. We stopped for a
cigarette.

'What a dump!' Gordon said, without a hint of a smile.

We carried on up along a ridge. One slope was an ankle-
twisting jumble of loose rocks; the other a sweep of bright
yellow sand ribbed by the wind.

From the top we could see the fleet. We could identify each
ship: *Anna Kristina, Amorina, Bounty, Trade Wind, Søren
Larsen, Tucker Thompson* and *Our Svanen* lay like models in
the serene blue expanse of the harbour bay.

From the town below rose the hubbub of daily life and above
that again the vain ululations of a pig being slaughtered.

'They take a long time to kill a pig here,' I said.

'They bleed 'em,' Gordon said. 'Hang 'em by their back legs
and bleed 'em.'

Behind us rose a mountain and halfway up its slopes the Blue
House beckoned. I studied the mountainside. I managed to
discern the faint zig-zagging line of a track.

'We must go up there before we leave,' I said.

'Don't mind if I do,' Gordon said. 'But we'll take a taxi.'

The next few days passed in a pleasant haze of self-
indulgence. There were no art galleries, museums, ruins,
monuments or other distractions to keep me out of the bars, or
to be more precise, the Pica-Pau. It was fairly quiet there in the
day, although Lindo had taken up residence. He had adopted
'jug ears' as a general factotum.

'He carries my camera,' Lindo explained. 'And he keeps away
the other guides.'

'Jug ears' had found himself a brief sinecure. Lindo poured a
lot of drink down him.

In the evening Pica-Pau, as I had anticipated, became
unbearably crowded. I took to dining there at four o'clock and

drinking after seven in the more disreputable establishments further inland where sailors feared to tread.

On the last day I roused myself. After a brief nap in the afternoon to sweat out the poisons of the morning's debaucheries, I located Gordon. We went round to Mitzy's. 'Scarface' was drinking Nescafé.

'Can you take us to the Blue House?' I asked.

He looked at his watch. He went out and looked at the sky.

'Too late, too late. Soon come the night,' he said sombrely.

We went to the square and roused a taxi driver from his extended siesta.

'Take us to the Blue House,' I cried.

He looked blank. We piled in. I directed him inland. It was easy. There was only one road across the island. When we were out of town and at a sufficient altitude I stopped him. I pointed up and across the burning waste to the Blue House. The driver shrugged and continued. A little further on we left the main road and bumped up a rough track bulldozed out of the mountainside. We made slow progress as the driver had to negotiate small rock falls and hairpin bends.

Close to, the Blue House lost some of the grandeur lent by distance. It had no architectural features worthy of comment. It was really a large villa in the Mediterranean style. It was locked, bolted and barred. The secret lay within. And though we could see the town and the bay way, way below, the sense of isolation was complete. The waste of rock and stunted bulbous cacti broke round it stopping short a few feet from the walls. I walked along the front terrace to some outbuildings. A few chickens scratched in a small yard. I called.

An old man emerged jangling a bunch of keys. He shook with excitement. He had a bad limp. He hobbled along, pausing every few steps to make sure we were still following. He took us round the back and unlocked the door. We entered a long kitchen that seemed to run the length of the house and passed through into what was the main living-room. It was a huge room, lit only by a faint light leaking through the slatted shutters. Our guide threw them back with much banging and clanging of steel drop bars. I looked out. The view was a void. The terrace cut off the near distance. Blue sky and blue sea merged into a blue absence. There was nothing to hang a thought on out there unless one was prepared to dwell on infinity. Perhaps the owner had.

In the room itself some fifties style garden loungers contrasted starkly with the solid presence of a huge Victorian sideboard. I pulled open a drawer. A cotton reel, some unmatched cutlery, a biro and a jumble of other commonplace objects evoked by their very banality a sense of past habitation; a sense that people had lived here; laughed, quarrelled, loved and wept. The drawer was haunted; not the house. When I closed it the emptiness flowed back.

Our guide took us upstairs. He opened each door with a flourish and we politely inspected each whitened sepulchre. Emptiness, silence and light. There were no shutters upstairs. Each window was a square of blue; birdless and cloudless. Except for the drawer the place seemed to have been cleansed of all human habitude, rid of all memories.

I tried questioning our muttering guide. I asked him about the owner. I repeated the word 'owner' over and over again but it was no good. I ransacked my limited repertoire of foreign words.

'*Patrón?*' I said, pronouncing it with a short 'a'.

'Ah! *Patrón morte*,' he informed us. '*Patrón morte, morte, morte.*'

Then he raised an imaginary bottle to his lips and drank deeply. He did it again and again, pausing to shake his head sadly between each copious draught. He led us back down the corridor and unlocked what I'd thought was a linen cupboard door to reveal a narrow staircase leading up to a vast attic well lit by gable windows.

The floor was a glittering sea of bottles; thousands of bottles

NOR ANY DROP TO DRINK

long leached dry of false hope and brief solace; bottles in which the hard light of reality now coruscated and crackled in myriad mocking refractions – a shimmering legacy of some dim tragedy.

'*Patrón morte, morte, morte,*' the old man chanted.

On the way out we took another look in the living-room. At one end was an alcove I hadn't noticed before. It was full of books, each identical and anonymous in brown wrapping paper. There were hundreds. I pulled some out at random. Beneath the brown paper they were pristine in their original dust covers. Most of the great authors of the twentieth century were represented. I looked at a Graham Greene. I shivered with excitement. For a moment I thought I'd discovered a small fortune of modern first editions, but they all turned out to be book club reprints.

The caretaker gestured to me to help myself. I took the Graham Greene as a souvenir and a book called *The Captain* as a present for John. We gave the caretaker a generous gratuity.

Outside we paused. The warm wind soughed through the eaves and bled through the cacti.

'I'd go nuts if I lived there,' Gordon said.

'I need a drink,' I said.

The taxi dropped us at the Pica-Pau. It was quiet. Walther and Kerstin were studying the menu. We joined them. We all ordered lobster.

'It will be goot to have you back,' Walther said to Gordon. Then he looked at me. 'I am hoping you will stay on the *Anna Kristina*. Ze *Amorina* has been so quiet vithout you. Ze crew are now happy.'

I looked mockingly crestfallen. I was too convincing.

'Oh, no, no, I only joke vith you.'

'I'll see it through to Rio on the *Anna Kristina*,' I said, 'then I'll be back.' It was Walther's turn to look crestfallen.

The place filled up with 'first fleeters'. Most of them were pleasant people bent on enjoying a good meal, but there was a hard core of 'screamers'. A screamer can be identified by a laugh like a badly calibrated, twin-barrelled, quick-firing ack-ack gun. This laugh can be triggered off by such statements as, 'I'm going for lunch', or, more humorously, 'I missed breakfast'. The other salient characteristic is their method of greeting people. However brief or distant the acquaintanceship, they hurl themselves on their victim with screams of delight accompanied by much hugging, kissing and backslapping. They avoid me as I avoid them. I have a cold exterior, and intend to keep it that way.

I left early, driven out by the raucous bonhomie of this strident minority. I decided to pay a last visit to Mitzy's.

I stood at the bar, drinking red wine, and chatted with Mitzy. I told her about the fleet and she told me the names of the other half of her tribe.

'Scarface' came in. This surprised me. I'd got the impression that he suffered from noctophobia. I was wrong. I learnt that his gloomy pronouncements of 'soon comes the night' were the result of his self-imposed regime of abstinence during daylight. He did not want to be caught in some arid waste when the sun slipped behind a parched ridge, especially in a house full of empty bottles.

He bought me a drink. I bought him a drink. I accepted my fate. It was going to be a long night. 'Scarface' waxed eloquent. He told me his life story. I don't remember it. He told me he had many children and that he commuted between a number of wives. It is impossible to reproduce his English. We communicated mainly in grunts and disjointed sequences of mono-syllabic words accompanied by arm-squeezing for emphasis. We got along. By midnight he wanted to open a vein, seal our brotherhood in blood. The room started to rock. I thought I was back at sea. 'Scarface' realised my condition. He was most attentive. He took me outside and pointed me in the general direction of the hotel.

I set off. I got lost. I couldn't even find Pica-Pau. Then I got second wind. I was sober. My mind was like a cold scimitar of light rotating in a crystal. I was ready for more. I found the market. Near by was a street of seedy bars. I walked up it. From each emanated a subdued murmur. One was silent. It had scalloped, louvred swing doors, presumably to facilitate the ingress of fresh air and the egress of drunks. It looked like a place where some serious drinking was done. I couldn't resist it. I entered.

The dirt and squalor were ameliorated by the amber glow of low-wattage bulbs. I ordered red wine and was served a generous slug of imported Portuguese plonk from a ten-litre flask encased in plastic simulating basketwork.

I took my drink to a corner table and viewed the scene. Most of the clientele were drinking the local homemade white rum. Nearly all were catatonic. A white man in the opposite corner waved at me. I pretended not to notice. He was obviously one of those lonely drunks who, given the slightest encouragement, would unload his sorrows with much repetition and circumlocution. I avoided his gaze. A few minutes later I took a quick squint in his direction. Too slow – eye contact was established. I smiled faintly. He was a tough-looking sort. There were bands of scar tissue above his eyebrows and what looked like razor scars seamed his chin.

He hauled himself to his feet with the aid of an invisible crane and made his way over with exaggeratedly precise movements. I groaned inwardly. I knew what was coming next.

He sat down opposite and ponderously proffered a huge, grime-engrained hand. It swallowed mine to halfway up my wrist.

'You are a sailor,' he informed me in a tone of voice that brooked no contradiction. If he'd told me I was a solicitor, I wouldn't have denied it. He helped himself to one of my last two cigarettes.

'Feel free,' I said, before I could stop myself, but he missed the mild reproof.

'Free,' he said with some feeling, and stared at me through watery blue eyes in which a luminous fish of intelligence still swam in some deeper, turbid current.

'I am not free. I am the engineer on a Korean ship, registered in Liberia, with a Swedish captain and crewed by chinks from Hong Kong.'

He paused. I lit his cigarette. This was beginning to sound interesting.

'I have no one to talk to or drink with. The chinks, they save, save, save. They don't even come ashore except to sell their cigarettes.'

I managed to look neutral. He was getting boring.

'The Captain is a one-time bastard. He likes this sand dune. He likes little boys. Little boys are cheap here.'

I looked suitably shocked. He was getting interesting again.

'Whores are also cheap,' he continued. 'I have had three in two days. How 'bout you?'

'I've been around,' I said ambiguously. He nodded sagely. We sat in silence while he digested this remark.

'What ship you from?'

'The *Anna Kristina*,' I replied.

'Ah, one of the sailing ships. She is from Norway. All Norwegians are bastards. All Swedes are bastards. All one-time bastards. You are English, I know. The English are only part-time bastards.'

I warmed to him. I took this as a compliment.

'I'm Finnish, from Finland. In my youth I fought the Russians. Then I fought the Russians again but for the Germans. They paid me to kill Russians. I have killed many Russians. I lost my toes in Russia. I have done many cruel things but the Russians are worse. After the war the British lock me up. They put me behind sharp wire just for killing Russians. The Russians wanted me back for killing Russians. The last man I killed was a German officer. The British officer knew this. He

129

adjusted my papers. "I will adjust your papers," he say to me. The Russians did not get me.'

I nodded sympathetically. There wasn't much I could say.

'I get you a drink,' he said. 'A real drink.' I knew it would be useless to protest. He returned with two glasses of the neuron-splitting local rum.

'How you find the *Anna Kristina* with all those Norwegian bastards?'

'It's all right,' I said. I'm not a great conversationalist. He wasn't satisfied with this. I became expansive. I told him about the food. I told him how I had trouble sleeping because Young Bill talked all night when he should have been in bed.

'You are a tolerant man,' he said. He spoke slowly, with great care, pausing between each word. 'You need a shifting spanner,' he continued, leaning forward and lowering his voice. 'You need a Stillson, as they are called in English. On my first ship I was given a cabin. There were two bunks. Both were empty. I put my bags on top bunk. When I come back they was moved to lower bunk. A big Swede lay in top bunk. He told me to get focked. I did not care. I took lower bunk. Many days later I find my things on top bunk. The porthole is leaking. The top bunk is wet. The big Swede, he told me to get focked. Now I did care. When he sleeps I go to the engine room. I fetch a big Stillson. Then I break both his legs. No more problems. You need a big Stillson.'

He turned and scanned the room. He looked disappointed.

'No Russians,' he said. 'Here is often a good place for Russians. Here Russian ships let the crew come ashore. They know they will come back. Here is little better than Russia. Last year I fix two Russians very badly. I am very skilful. First I drink with them and then – bang, bang.' He crashed his fist into the palm of his hand. This got me worried. Perhaps he'd been lying about the English only being part-time bastards.

I decided to return his hospitality. I went to the bar and bought two more rums – less than five pence each. The men at the bar were like a line of statues. They stared straight ahead and held on to the bar with their left hands. Occasionally, with the jerky movements of automata, they raised their glasses to their lips, sightlessly, without moving their heads. You're really in trouble when you don't look at your drink.

When I returned to the table the scourge of Russia was fast asleep, his head buried in his arms. I gulped down my rum and rose to leave. I felt no qualms. He could look after himself.

'Scarface' appeared in the door. He pointed an accusing finger at me.

'You are here,' he said.

I could not deny it.

'They tell me you are here,' he elaborated. It was a small town. News travels fast. I hadn't realised I was a celebrity.

'I take you to hotel. Now.'

'I was just going anyway,' I grumbled.

'And do not drink with this man,' he admonished, pointing at the sleeping Finn. 'He is a bad good man.' What eloquence there is in simple words.

His taxi was outside. He drove me to the hotel. There was no traffic. I didn't offer to pay. He pushed me through the gate. We shook hands. He kissed me on the neck. There was nothing sinister in it. That was their way.

I woke early. Herds of wild beasts galloped through my head. Every cell screamed for water. I was numb. I felt as though there were two of me. One of me was a half-blind, shambling wreck that obeyed without question the simple but precise directives of the other me. There was a significant time lapse between the order and the action obedient. I moved like Marcel Marceau. I made no sudden movements.

I drank a few glasses of water. I sat on the bed. I lit a cigarette. I stubbed it out. I had a shower; first hot then cold. I dressed slowly, pausing for a rest between each garment. I drank more water. My cells still wailed. I checked and double-checked and triple-checked that I had my credit cards. I don't usually do this.

I went out on the balcony. I was struck by the beauty and harmonious composition of the building opposite. It was a rectangle standing on one of its shorter ends. Doesn't matter which. And this rectangular façade was in itself composed of many squares and rectangles in the sublime array of divine geometry. It was asymmetrical. On the right-hand side was a tall slim rectangle of glass – the stairwell. The base was composed of a broader rectangle of a shop window adjacent to a square of double glass doors split by a faint dividing line. Above rose a pattern of windows and balconies. The whole edifice was neatly capped with the thin rectangle of a penthouse flat, itself divided into rectangles and squares. It reminded me of a Mondrian, but gave me more pleasure. It gave me as much pleasure to look upon as Salisbury Cathedral or Chartres. It gave me an insight into what is loosely classified as modern art. I began to understand Mondrian. I realised I had a lot to learn. I remembered the time when I'd thought Picasso should have been relegated to linoleum catalogues. I also remembered how this unenlightened opinion had been blessedly dispelled on leafing through an art book in a library in Singapore. The same thing had happened to me in other countries with Matisse, Modigliani and Chagall. Cézanne and Henry Moore still elude me.

I left in search of coffee. The watchman had disappeared but his bike stood against the wall. I guessed he was taking a nod in one of the eleven empty, immaculate rooms.

I wandered the streets burdened with typewriter and briefcase. My head pounded. I met the town idiot. Like me he was up too early. He carried a plastic carrier bag full of litter. This is not unusual. There are plenty like him in London. I managed to communicate with him.

'Coffee?' I said.

'Coffee!' he replied.

'Coffee' is understood from Titograd to Timbuktu.

He led me up a street and pounded on a door. A tired-looking man, fully dressed thankfully, came to open it.

'Coffee,' the idiot said, pointing at me. The tired man nodded and ushered me in. I offered the idiot a few coins. He declined. I hadn't got any litter about my person. He went off, skipping every third step.

The tired man and his family lived on the first floor above a shop. They lived in Dickensian squalor. I couldn't count the children. They wouldn't keep still. I sat on a single chair at a rickety table. His wife, a haggard young woman, gave me coffee in a glass rimmed with dirt and a tin of milk. They drank rum from a bottle in which there was a two-inch layer of sugar. I juggled briefly with a filthy baby, managing to hide my disgust. I don't like babies – even clean ones.

When I left I offered them a few notes. They declined. I pointed to the children. They accepted. I felt depressed. Here in Cape Verde I'd been baptised from the font of human kindness. I realised that the line between the generosity of the poor and the despair which generates a desire for blood vengeance was as fine and delicate as a thread of mercury.

I sat on the beach. The ships rocked gently in the bay. Mons was coming to collect me at seven. Behind me the town murmured into life.

8

Cape Verde to Brazil

'Sure you want to leave?' I asked Gordon as we stood on the deck waiting for the rubber dinghy to pick him and Lindo up.

'I sure am,' he said with conviction. 'This is a hell ship. I like the crew but . . .' The dinghy snarled alongside. Gordon clambered over the rail. I passed his bags down.

'See you in Bahía,' I called down to him.

'Come on Marcus, move yourself,' John shouted from the stern.

I cast off the line. The dinghy shot off. Lindo fell over on his back but managed to keep my typewriter on his stomach. I'd lent it to him because I knew I wouldn't be able to use it on the *Anna Kristina*. John walked over.

'I thought you were leaving us.'

'What made you think that?' I snapped. I still had a headache.

'Well, you grumbled so much. So many criticisms,' he said.

'I don't grumble. I point out defects that need correcting. If everyone were like you lot we'd still be throwing rocks at each other.'

'You're still here though,' John said.

There were ten minutes' frantic activity as we hauled up the jib sails and then the main sail. John span the wheel to starboard. The *Anna Kristina* shivered under the wind's caress. The bowsprit described a forty-five-degree arc. John span the wheel half to port. She steadied and then went with the wind. Her rust-red sails blossomed. We hauled up the mizzen sail and the top square sail. She surged forward. The bowsprit bored at

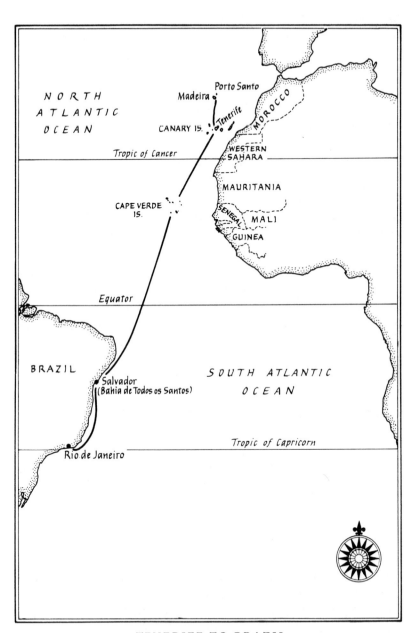

NORTH
ATLANTIC
OCEAN

Porto Santo
Madeira
Tenerife
CANARY IS.
MOROCCO

Tropic of Cancer

WESTERN
SAHARA

MAURITANIA

CAPE VERDE
IS.

SENEGAL
MALI

GUINEA

Equator

BRAZIL

Salvador
(Bahia de Todos os Santos)

SOUTH ATLANTIC
OCEAN

Tropic of Capricorn

Rio de Janeiro

TENERIFE TO BRAZIL

the blue concavity of the mocking horizon. We were off —
sailing into what seemed to me a blue infinity. It took us twenty-
one days to cross the blue void. They were the longest twenty-
one days of my life.

John was ecstatic. We were the only ship of the fleet to take
the wind from the start. The others had motored out of the bay
and then set sail.

Once out of the bay I had to admit — and I don't do much
admitting — that it was a splendid sight; seven ships now in full
sail setting off across the Atlantic for the coast of Brazil. The
Amorina, listing sickeningly, staggered through the short
waves. I began to pity those on board until I realised our motion
was worse. I was a sailor at last, albeit a reluctant one. The
Anna Kristina did not list as alarmingly but her motion was
more violent. The bowsprit described an invisible figure of eight
in the sky. The *Bounty* with her blunt prow bashed her way
through the waves with an even worse motion. In the distance
the *Trade Wind*'s lean black hull seemed to cleave the waves.
The *Søren Larsen*, her white hull sweeping through the blue and
her white sails straining, looked as impressive as she did in the
television series *The Onedin Line*.

Cape Verde fell behind. The Blue House still beckoned. I
watched it shrink to a blue dot and expire in the opacity of the
mountain's silhouette. I resolved to go back one day. I was sure
it held the germ of an interesting short story; the inchoate
melody of some unsung minor tragedy. As Cape Verde sank
slowly behind the horizon, the fleet began to disintegrate. The
Amorina and the *Bounty* fell behind. *Trade Wind* and *Søren
Larsen* forged ahead. The disembodied sails of *Tucker
Thompson* and *Our Svanen* ran a parallel course, port and
starboard, their hulls hidden by the curve of the world.

Later, *Our Svanen* made a dash for the coast of Brazil, motor-
sailing most of the way, to arrive five days ahead of us. She had
no trainee crew. The Board of Trade had refused her a licence to
carry paying passengers over some technicality about the safety

of the deckhouse. Since the demise of the *Marqués* off Bermuda in 1984 with the loss of nineteen lives their inspectors were nervous and perhaps over-zealous. Not until Mauritius was she able to take aboard a trainee crew.

The next day I lay on the deck basking in the sun. Mons lay near by.

'No nuclear bombs,' he said.

'What?'

'No nuclear bombs.'

'Are you all right?' I asked.

'You told John yesterday that if it wasn't for progress we'd still be throwing rocks at each other. Better to throw rocks than drop bombs.'

And so began the first of many arguments that were to rage and engross us through the long, blue, empty tropical days. It is a myth that life at sea is full of adventure. In the main it is a routine interrupted occasionally by bursts of activity. This first Atlantic crossing was to be largely, but not wholly, uneventful. Later, in the South Atlantic, things were to change.

On the *Anna Kristina* the watch system was more disruptive and demanding than on the *Amorina*. The hours were roughly the same but the watch teams were rotated every twenty-four hours instead of weekly. But even on watch there wasn't much to do except take a turn at the helm or pump out the bilges. The bilge pump was a squat iron carbuncle carefully sited to trip people up in the dark. To operate it one stuck a crowbar in the lever socket and cranked away. Pumping out the bilges was the high point of the day. People lingered near it eyeing it longingly. Actually, it was pumped out thrice daily, so there were really three high spots to the day. It only took about fifteen minutes but it was better than scratching away at the rail with a piece of sandpaper. Doing something boring is worse than doing nothing at all.

Lunch and dinner were the two other main events. 'Lunch'

and 'dinner' are perhaps the wrong nomenclature for dismal concoctions that would have disgusted even a British lorry driver. I tried to imagine what a restaurant critic would have to say about the *Anna Kristina*'s culinary arts. It would go something like this:

L'*ANNA KRISTINA* REVISITED
A Special Report by Prunella Leaf-Mould

Once again I was charmed by the simple rusticity of the long pine table and the brass-plated Taiwanese oil lamps glimmering on the wall. Above the table hung a genuine antique oil lamp on gimbals which, throughout the evening, periodically struck my escort between the eyes. George didn't mind. He's such a sport. I can take him anywhere. We sat on dinky little boxes; their canvas covers stained with evidence of many a jolly meal in the past. The *hors d'oeuvres* were already laid out on a raised shelf running down the centre of the table. I'm sure I recognised the salami from my last visit two years ago. It was a bit shorter, but there's plenty of time yet – it's date-stamped 'Consume before Dec. 2050'. The Danish goat's cheese was also an old friend. A green haze hovered over it. It had matured at last. Its aroma, like that of a Bombay storm drain, mingled pleasantly with the scent of the sodden foam rubber mattress stuffed in the beer bin and the pile of wellingtons in the corner.

L'*Anna Kristina* is noted for its set meals and regular clients often arrive early to watch the chef put the finishing touches to the *plat du jour*. We watched, fascinated, as he lifted from the oven a three-pasta pie. This sumptuous culinary creation was made up of layers of macaroni and spaghetti topped with lasagne verde. Blue-veined tentacles of gorgonzola oozed down its side. A touch of colour is so important, don't you think? Then our chef administered the *coup de grâce* to this *pièce de résistance*. With a flourish of genius he poured sunflower seeds over it. I gasped at his daring inventiveness. As he laid it on the table he actually spoke to us.

'It's amazing what you can do with pasta,' he said. The man opposite me told him what he could do with it. He was very rude. He had manic eyes. He never stopped muttering and swearing. Beside him was a horrible old man with red eyes. He kept dropping things on the floor so he could look up my skirt. I'll wear my purple culottes next time.

But, silly me, I forgot to tell you. One of the main attractions of the L'*Anna Kristina* is the cabaret. The artistes mingle with the customers. So *avant-garde*! The man with manic eyes poked and prodded at his portion and asked for a chainsaw. Finally he hacked off a piece and spat sunflower seeds all over me. The horrible old man gobbled it down. So did a handsome young man. Then they both banged the table with their spoons and shrieked for more. At this, the man with manic eyes flew into a terrible rage. He called them peasants and Philistines. He threatened to break their legs with a Stillson, whatever that is, but contented himself with belting the young man on the head with the salami. Then all three of them had a mock fight and spilt a lot of food on the floor. I thought this part of the act was quite unnecessary. The management had installed a very sophisticated piece of machinery in the basement which made the floor rise, tilt, and fall rhythmically. This novelty was the brainchild of the French philosopher J. P. Etunne as an aid to digestion. It was such fun trying to eat our meal while hanging on to the table with one hand, but I wouldn't do it every day.

'Manic eyes' stuck his fork upright in the layers of lasagne where it thrashed back and forth for a while before settling down to a monotonous hum. Then he went to the larder and snatched a tin of sardines. He opened them with difficulty, using a carving knife, all the while cursing the management's meanness in only providing one tin-opener with a loose cogwheel. Then the manager's mistress chased him round the room with a cleaver screaming, 'Eat the Cape Verde sausages first.'

Above was an open skylight just like a ship's hold. We could see the stars. So romantic. It was almost like dining *al fresco*.

'Manic eyes' returned. He took his plate and my bottle of wine without so much as a 'thank you' and went upstairs to dine on the terrace. A minute later we heard a loud splash. I thought he'd jumped in the canal. The horrible old man said it was just him throwing his dinner in the water. I'm going to write a letter to Camden Council. Apparently he does this every night.

The finale began with pink feet materialising before my eyes. They were followed by a pair of sexy masculine legs. A Scandinavian Adonis dropped to the table. He danced along it clad only in designer dirt-encrusted shorts. (George got quite excited and I had to smack him.) He helped himself to the side dish of rice *à l'eau* and jumped into a hole in the wall where he lay moaning, 'Wunnerful, wunnerful.'

The manager brought the evening to a close. He came over to the table and said, 'Whaah, that looks good,' at which everyone threw bread at him and the man with manic eyes shouted down through the skylight that he was a 'Danish hyena'. Quite extraordinary. George thought the evening had been stunning.

Many people may think this skit the product of a surrealistic or deranged imagination, but behaviour which would seem eccentric or even crazy on land was taken for granted at sea on the *Anna Kristina*.

Mons did habitually take a short cut down to dinner through the hatch and when his feet appeared on the table we chewed stolidly on without raising an eyebrow. Only once, when he trod in Old Bill's soup, was there a mild altercation. Henrik did make a three-pasta pie and state, 'It's amazing what you can do with pasta.' We did have mock fights using the salami as a truncheon; spill food, if it wasn't being spilt for us; and drop cutlery – but not look up skirts. None of the girls wore skirts, and most of them went around topless anyway. The only person who wore a skirt was the Captain. See what I mean?

John had bought himself a 'mini' sari in Porto Grande. He insisted on wearing this without underpants and since he spent quite a lot of time checking the rigging we were often treated to a view of his credentials. Jill blushed the first time she saw them but soon got used to the sight of male genitalia twenty feet above her head. The impulse to expose oneself seemed quite a common phenomenon among 'first fleeters', especially the Captains. Sven, with some justification, showed us what it took to make a Captain in the southern latitudes of the Indian Ocean – but that's another story.

Less amusingly, this desire to bare all led to the trainees and crew of the fleet being banned from the yacht club in Bahía because of an indiscretion committed in the swimming pool. As Samuel Johnson said, 'When men come to like a sea-life, they are not fit to live on land.'

And so the routine of eating, sleeping and keeping watch went on day after day, night after night. One day was much the same as another and I lost all sense of diurnal time; the watch system ruled. We kept watch from eight in the morning until noon, followed by midnight until four in the morning; from noon until six followed by four in the morning until eight; and from six in the evening until midnight followed by eight in the morning until noon. And then the cycle began again. Most of the time I did not know what day it was; nor cared. There were no weekends: Saturday and Sunday were no different from

Thursday or Friday. In many ways it was always a Monday with the atmosphere of a Sunday, the work being no more demanding than washing a car. On looking back it seemed like one long day in which I sometimes pottered around the deck with a tin of paint or lay in the sun arguing with Mons, while Old Bill in the background sang 'A sunbeam, a sunbeam, I'll be a sunbeam for you'.

In the mid-Atlantic I experienced for the first time a curious but not unpleasant feeling of unreality; a sort of hallucinatory detachment brought on by our remoteness and the empty impersonality of the ocean. There was no daily paper, no radio, no television to bring into focus the realities of life on land; whether banal or dramatic, trivial or tragic, ugly or beautiful. The ship was in the centre of an azure desolation under a cerulean void. The land was a chimera, not over there but down there somewhere far beyond that bright girdle, that filament of mercury circumscribing the vast blue vacancy of our prison. For twenty-one days we carried this blue vacancy with us until the serene white towers of Salvador rose slowly above the horizon.

On the eighth day out of Cape Verde we hit the doldrums. For two days we bobbed about 'as idle as a painted ship upon a painted ocean'. The sails were taken down and furled with the exception of the forecourse. It hung limp and lifeless though it did occasionally flap disconsolately when a lost zephyr wandered by. We drifted aimlessly on a current so weak it took a Coke tin half an hour to fall out of sight astern.

On the second day the *Tucker Thompson* motored over to within a hundred yards of us. We swam between ships. Russell the Captain swam over to see us – naked of course. He was provided with a towel. I swam over to the *Tucker Thompson*, modestly attired in elasticated black swimming trunks. I clambered aboard and managed to coax a beer out of them.

Later I was stooging around between ships with about four miles of water beneath me when the dolphins arrived. Normally they come close to the ship and ride the pressure wave in front of the bow. This time they held off, probably because there were about twenty of us thrashing about. I and a few others swam about 200 yards to where they'd last been sighted. I thought they'd gone. Then I looked down and saw their blurred shapes about six feet below me. When a Swedish trainee from the *Tucker Thompson* lent me his face mask I gained a perfect view of these our distant, prelapsarian ancestors. I looked down on them. They looked up at me. They hung vertically, their tails pointing to the ocean bed and their long, streamlined noses pointing up at me. I thought I could detect in their eyes a shrewd intelligence, but this may have been a romantic projection on my part – the result of listening to Mons and reading too many *National Geographics*. (Dolphins were to Mons what whales were to Walther – an obsession.) When I dived down towards them they let themselves sink into the deep purple murk of diffused light. When I returned to the surface they rose up towards me. And so it went on.

After a while I gave up. I couldn't get nearer than six feet. I swam back to the *Anna Kristina*. I still had the Swedish fellow's face mask. I was just about to swim back across with it when we caught a shark. We'd been dangling a line with a 300-pound breaking strain baited with salami. We'd forgotten it. Suddenly it snapped tight. It was hauled in with no great effort. We peered over the side. A six-foot shark languidly writhed in mild protest not a yard from the hull. Salo rushed to get the gaffe. We danced on the deck with delight – food, real food! Visions of shark steak swam before our eyes. Then, disaster. The shark's crude palate had finally assessed the nature of this pink morsel and transmitted the necessary distress signal to HQ. It lashed its jaws violently from side to side and sliced through the line. I was enraged; not so much at the shark's escape but at this dramatic demonstration of the salami's unsuitability for consumption by elasmobranches let alone naked apes.

'Bloody hell!' I raved. 'These bastards will eat anything. They've been found with number plates, radio-active satellites and rubber tyres in their stomachs – even re-treads. What more proof do you need, you Scandinavian swine?' This was a tirade remonstrative as opposed to the tirade abusive. I can never remember my tirades abusive. They usually take place late at night. I know when I've thrown one because people usually, but not always, pat me on the shoulder the next morning, compliment me on my vocabulary and suggest that I try Valium.

After this I certainly wasn't going to swim across to the *Tucker Thompson*. If you ever read this: thanks for the loan of the face mask, mate. It's still on the *Anna Kristina*.

We were running out of food. We were down to four frozen chickens, a bag of mince and a plastic tube of unsliced steak. Katrina had bought 'fresh' fish off a reeking slab in the wet market in Cape Verde. We'd eaten some of it and thrown the rest away when it started to dance with bacteria. She'd also bought some shrivelling peppers which had now shrivelled. We weren't going to starve. There was an abundance of sunflower seeds, husks, millet, porridge and rice – polished and unpolished. Nevertheless I was beginning to get nervous.

On the beginning of the third day of bobbing around in the doldrums I suggested to John we get moving – rouse the old Volvo Penta engine from its smug, oily sleep and point ourselves in the general direction of Brazil instead of describing lazy circles in the windless, aquamarine mirror. I was not alone; other omnivorous hominids backed me up.

'Let's get fucking going,' they chanted.

John sucked on his pipe, nodded, looked evasive and said he'd think about it. He said he'd give me a birthday present – that we'd get to Salvador Bahía on 11 July.

After a face-saving interval of a few hours we got going. The engine shuddered into life and we were off 'in search of the wind', as John put it. The next day we found it, just up the road. It was a slight wind but enough to fill the sails and make them strain. It gradually strengthened until we were hissing along through a gentle swell.

On the first of July we ran out of beer, wine, brandy and cigarettes simultaneously. The gods in the four adjacent niches of this particular section of the modern pantheon had obviously decided, impelled by Saturn, to strike as one. Only the god of cheap, return to warehouse, Tenerife sherry opted out. We had about forty bottles of it but no one could drink it – not even Old Bill. I certainly couldn't.

Perhaps a more rational explanation lay in panic buying. A few days before I'd dipped into the beer bin and found it necessary almost to invert myself to grope for a bottle. Others with shorter arms, legs and bodies had to draw upon their pot-holing skills to lay hands on a bottle. The wine and brandy disappeared rapidly. I bought the last three bottles of red wine and stashed them under my mattress with my last forty Winston.

The last ten days of the journey were virtually dry except for a crate of beer reserved to celebrate Young Bill's twentieth birthday. Some of us donated a bottle from our private and untouched hoards – Old Bill a bottle of brandy and I a bottle of red wine. I did not suffer from alcoholic deprivation. The sea remained a serene azure. Monsters did not arise from the deep. My cells did not crave or run wild.

But cigarettes were a problem. Forty wouldn't last me a day normally. I tried to ration myself to four a day. It was hopeless. Smoking was banned below deck. There was nowhere to hide. As soon as I lit one of these precious cigarettes Salo and Young Bill would hover. It's quite unnerving smoking a cigarette with two pairs of eyes boring into one. They became very friendly. They followed me everywhere, no difficult task on a small ship. I gave up and shared them. There was plenty of pipe tobacco left. John lent me a pipe. At last I had a full-time occupation.

On 3 July we crossed the line. This called for the usual

initiation rites. Old Bill and I had crossed the line before so we became the Masters of Ceremony. I was Neptune and Old Bill Neptunia, my wife. John made a trident and saw to our make-up. He was very imaginative. He made me a wig from unpicked rope and a cloak from a shredded green towel. He strapped a large metal kettle on my head and filled it with a foul mixture of cold tea, ketchup, Worcester sauce, mayonnaise, milk, curry powder and whatever else he could find in the larder. Old Bill was made up to look like a ravaged whore. We primed ourselves with a bottle of my wine and half a bottle of Bill's brandy and went up on deck to deal with our waiting victims.

It was a simple ceremony. Old Bill and I sat either side of the wooden rope tub filled with seawater. John brought the novitiates up one by one. Salo was first. He knelt before me.

'I Neptune, King of the Deep, Ruler of the Waves, blah, blah, blah . . . baptise you Salo the Salmon.' On the word 'salmon' I tilted my head forward and let some of the vile unction trickle over him. Then immersion. We grabbed him and threw him in the tub. Everyone submitted meekly until it was Young Bill's turn. 'Bill the Barnacle', an apt appellation since he spent most of life asleep, submitted to the vile unction but feared immersion. He struggled. We reeled across the deck and collapsed against the rail, which dealt me a severe blow to shoulder and neck. Old Bill came to my aid and Young Bill was immersed. The remainder of the ceremony passed without incident.

I hadn't felt much pain when we'd fallen against the rail but when I woke from an afternoon's nap to metabolise the Spanish brandy, I thought I'd broken my neck. Attempts to move my head a single degree in any direction brought on an exquisite pain that ran from my neck into my shoulder. It felt as if there was crushed glass between each of my upper vertebrae. Sudden movements brought agony and temporary paralysis. I couldn't have wielded a Stillson. I had to walk with the limited, deliberate movements of a robot. If I wanted to turn my head I had to turn my whole body. Henrik reckoned it was a pinched nerve. On the third day it went.

A few days off the coast of Brazil we had visitors. A pair of humpback whales approached. At first they kept their distance and then, overcome by curiosity, they came closer and closer until they were alongside. Walther would have expired with ecstasy. This was the closest sighting of whales on the whole voyage. The larger one came to within six feet of the hull and kept pace with us for ten minutes. It was about sixty feet long. Take away the bowsprit and it was nearly as long as the ship. We could have jumped across and skated on its back. It surged through the surface at regular intervals. We didn't see its head though we occasionally saw its huge flipper and its corrugated flank. It seemed free of the parasites that often scar a whale's body. It did not vent much water through its blowhole. Perhaps this was because it was surfacing every twenty seconds or so.

9

Bahía de Todos os Santos

On the dawn of 11 July we saw a vision. The rising sun threw a
wand of light across the sea and conjured up the white towers of
Salvador Bahía. They hung like an hallucination in the
quicksilver band of light that separated the tarnished waves
from a pastel blue vault of expiring stars. The land lay hidden
behind the curve of the world; and, like a city in the sky, they
floated in the shimmering rise of vapour. I was gratified to note
that everyone, including Mons, gazed at these manifestations of
Western decadence with an anguished anticipation mingled
with apprehension as if, like a mirage, they expected these
towers to fade away into the blue abyss.

'I wonder if there's a McDonald's there?' Young Bill said,
visibly salivating.

They remained at a tantalising distance as we sailed for an
hour on a course parallel to the invisible coast before turning in
towards Barra yacht club. Barra was a rich suburb of luxury
hotels and apartment blocks lining the orange beaches north of
the city. Here the white towers jostled each other to the very
edge of the red laterite cliffs veined with lush tropical
vegetation. Some of them seemed suspended in space until one
noticed that they were supported by tall concrete piles rising
from the crumbling red slopes scored with rain-eroded fissures.
Their precariousness was an illusion. They were built upon
rock.

It was the hovels of the poor that were in danger of being
swept away in a tropical downpour. Built of driftwood and tin

sheets, they clung to the slopes on narrow ledges hacked out of the soil or tottered over the gulf on buckling stilts. The lucky ones had anchored their shacks to the concrete piles and enjoyed the shelter of the monoliths above.

Pewter clouds condensed ominously over them. The towers flexed in the oily air and then disappeared behind a curtain of rain. A few warm, heavy drops exploded on the deck but the sun still shone on us. Within ten minutes the deluge was over. The white towers rose once again, brilliant and serene, cleansed and radiant. Threads of silver laced the steaming cliffs. A shack slid in slow motion down a drenched incline, shedding planks as it went, until it was no more than a scattered trail of debris. Human figures edged across the slope to salvage what they could of the strewn wreckage.

'They'll soon have it back together again,' Old Bill observed. 'Happens all the time.'

We took down the sails and motored into a small cove where we dropped anchor a hundred yards from the yacht club landing stage. They had offered us temporary membership and full use of their facilities.

Customs and immigration officers came on board to shuffle and pound papers. After two hours Mons rowed Old Bill, Young Bill, Gary and me ashore. It was an impressive club: Olympic-size swimming pool; games rooms; restaurants and bars. We had no Brazilian money and the club facilities did not encompass foreign exchange. The upper echelons of the fleet had arrived some time before us. They were sprawled round two tables sampling Brazilian beer. We dithered near by. Perhaps it was naïve of us to expect them to offer us a drink, but we hovered in the faint hope that one of them would turn and say: 'Ah, you're from the *Anna Kristina*. Haven't had a beer for ten days. We'll soon put that right.' It was not to be.

They were sitting in an arc looking out to sea. A waiter staggered up with a huge wooden tray laden with tall, one-litre bottles of beer glistening with condensation. Their table was cluttered. He placed it on the one behind them. Andy turned, seized a bottle and topped up a few glasses. He poured carelessly. He didn't tilt the glasses to the bottle. They foamed up.

We looked at each other. Old Bill did a sideways shuffle and snatched a bottle. We followed his example. Heads tilted, Adam's apples throbbed. We put down the bottles gently, eructated and departed. I looked over my shoulder. Andy was doing an impression of Lord Nelson.

We boarded the yacht club's private funicular and ascended the hill. An easy stroll down the opposite slope took us into Barra. It was a pleasant seaside resort. There was nothing to condemn or commend. A few older buildings of no particular architectural merit broke the line of modern, impersonal shops and restaurants facing the sea front. There was nothing to suggest we were in Brazil except for the heat, some palm trees and the odd native taking a siesta on flattened cardboard boxes in shady doorways.

The banks were closed. We had no money. A man in a brown pin-striped suit approached us. He offered to change money. He pulled out a wad as thick as a brick. He gave us 25 per cent above the official exchange rate. Travellers' cheques, sterling, dollars – no problem.

Now we were in business. We went in search of steak and chips. We came across two restaurants side by side, their fronts open to the street. One was plush, wood-panelled with fine, white napery. A waiter in a green waistcoat with brass buttons twirled the prosilient points of his waxed moustache. The other was a fly-blown dump with formica tables. Knick-knacks of the kind you win at Easter fairs cluttered the walls. An emaciated, leering, green-faced Christ had pride of place. I couldn't make out whether it was an El Greco reproduction or simply horrible. A couple of locals snored, heads tilted back and hands clasped on distended stomachs.

'You choose,' Old Bill said. 'It's your birthday.'

'The flies in the posh place are thinner,' I said. We entered the dump. The manager roused himself. He swept the debris off the table with the side of his hand. He gave us a menu and awaited our order, rubbing the sleep from his eyes. The menu was in Portuguese and American so we were able to work it out without too much trouble. Even without the aid of a calculator I soon realised that the most expensive offering was about the price of an ice-lollipop in central London.

'We'll have the steak, chips and all the trimmings – twice,' I said. I'd lost over a stone on the *Anna Kristina*. It took me a while to explain we didn't want two steaks between us but two each. Our host was impressed. He woke up.

We had a banquet. The succulent steaks came with chips, rice, salad, vegetables and baked beans – homemade, real, ethnic baked beans in freshly made tomato sauce. We slugged back beer, wine and local liqueurs. By the time we got to the liqueurs I wasn't in any condition to remember what they were called.

We were there from three until ten. When we got the bill it was so cheap we thought they'd made a mistake. We pointed at the total and fell about laughing. Our host joined our merriment and wound it down a couple of decimal points. We felt guilty. We bought him and the waiter drinks. They joined us at the table. Soon we were swearing everlasting brotherhood. Our host showed us a photo of his sister. We were privileged.

Salo went across the road to buy cigarettes at a stall. He returned complaining he'd been ripped off. He'd paid 3,000 *cruzados* instead of 300 for a pack of twenty. Brazilian money is difficult to work out since the old denomination notes are still in circulation with the new low-denomination notes. Our host flexed his biceps, went across the road and brought Salo back a generous discount.

They wanted to buy us a drink. We wouldn't hear of it. We wanted to buy them a drink. They wouldn't hear of it. Somehow the problem resolved itself.

Eventually we made it to a small, modern hotel a few yards up the road. I got a single room; the others a suite with extra beds.

There was just enough space to edge past the bed. The shower was too small to fall over in. Refreshed, I lay on the bed trying to marshal my thoughts. The room started to revolve. I tried focusing on the fan but it was going in the opposite direction.

I was hanging on to the wall when the telephone rang. A friend wished to see me. Was I receiving guests? Apparently I was. The receptionist sent him up. He wasn't a friend – more of an acquaintance. He needed somewhere to sleep. He couldn't make it back to the ship. He'd be happy to sleep on the floor. I agreed to accommodate him. He passed out quietly.

His presence had a sobering effect. I remembered Old Bill's exhortation: 'You must go to the old part of Bahía.' I consulted a glossy brochure. One hotel in the old quarter stood out – the Luxor Convento do Carmo. I telephoned them straight away. They had vacancies. I telephoned reception and booked an early taxi. Another journey lay ahead – from the suburbs of Salvador to the heart of Bahía de Todos os Santos.

Bahía de Todos os Santos. The very name had seduced me. Old Bill had told me a little about the place but he'd only spent a day there twenty years before on his pilgrimage to collect countries. I had not heard of Bahía before; not many people have. If you look at Brazil in the average atlas you won't find Bahía. What you will find is Salvador. Bahía, once the capital of Brazil, is now the old part of Salvador – the historic core of a modern city which has grown up around it in a vast accretion of concrete.

The taxi driver drove with great panache through the wakening avenues of opulent modern apartment blocks. We passed through streets of office blocks that could have been anywhere in the world. When we entered a spacious square, the Terreiro de Jesús, the change was startling and abrupt. Suddenly we were in the eighteenth century, in a world of cobbled streets, red-tiled houses with wrought-iron balconies and churches. I'd been told that there were 900 churches in Bahía. I could see three in the Terreiro de Jesús, each the size of a cathedral. As we bumped through narrow, cobbled, potholed streets, I caught fleeting glimpses of many more and gained a general impression of baroque splendour restrained by the harmony of classical proportions. I knew that this was a place to walk round slowly. I knew I was going to enjoy it.

The hotel Luxor Convento do Carmo was like a fortress; the masonry radiated a massive, solid presence. The white façade was devoid of decoration except for some subdued relief work framing each iron-barred window. It was a building that looked inwards on itself as had its original inhabitants, the Carmelite nuns. A flight of steps set in a vaulted tunnel led to a central rectangular courtyard edged with arcades of striding arches; movement of stone enclosed cloistered calm. They had resisted the temptation to fill the arcades with boutiques, souvenir shops and beauty salons. The reception was a simple counter lurking in the tall twilight under a massively raftered ceiling. I approached. The supercilious receptionist raised an apprising eyebrow. I was wearing jeans, singlet and a Greek fisherman's hat. I was unshod. I carried my effects in two plastic bags. He looked at me as if I had just walked in off the street. This is a silly expression – I had just walked in. How else should I enter these hallowed walls; descend by hang-glider?

I slid the magic plastic across the polished wood and gave it a snap with my thumb. His eyebrow settled.

'Ah Mester Mainweareng,' he said. 'Welcome to our hotel. Welcome to Salvador.'

'Bahía de Todos os Santos,' I corrected, stressing the last word.

'Just so. Just so,' he agreed.

I was booked in with the minimum of fuss. He gave me a hotel identity card which entitled me to sign for drinks and meals. He slid it across the counter and tried to snap it with his

forefinger. He failed. It did not have the tensile quality of my
dove-hologrammed instant debt inducer. It merely curled and,
like his eyebrow, settled silently.

'Do not lose,' he advised. 'Many bad men out there. If you
lose they will eat for you.'

I ascended to my room on the first floor in a lift hidden away
in an alcove. My escort ushered me reverentially down a long,
silent corridor. It was uncarpeted. The floorboards were two
feet wide and glowed with wax and the rich patina of time.
What Gordon had described as 'musty' I took to be the odour of
sanctity. Here, inside, the masonry exhalted an ancient peace;
the solace of pious contemplation.

My escort unlocked my cell, genuflected and entered. He
showed me how to switch on the television and how to open the
fridge door. Apart from these two modern conveniences the cell
was tastefully furnished with mock antiques, though I doubt if
the nuns had enjoyed the sensuous delight of such a sumptuous
bed. The bathroom was marble from floor to ceiling. The air
conditioning no more than a discreet hiss.

I revelled in the luxury of stillness and silence. I lay on the bed
on top of the cover. The peace that passeth all understanding.
The waters of oblivion closed over me.

The hotel was ideally situated for exploring the surrounding
streets and squares of the old city: the largest concentration of
colonial buildings in the world, nearly 20,000 of them over 250
years old. I did not rush around by taxi or take minibus tours in
an effort to see as much as possible – see everything and see
nothing. I took H. V. Morton's advice, I walked.

Many of the houses were in a state of dilapidation; some were
just shells choked with vegetation and rubble that spilled out on
to the cobbles. Many had been carefully restored and brightly
painted in the pastel shades of blue, pink and yellow so
favoured by the Portuguese. The majority, however, were in
that interesting state of having seen better days; and it was this

that gave the place atmosphere; saved it from being a gentrified museum piece.

The few lace and handicraft shops catering for tourists were well outnumbered by humble bars and shops serving the local population. An air of sleepy decadence prevailed. In some of the rougher side streets the lingering mephitis of parched drains mingled with the pungent scent of cannabis. People sat in windows, motionless, looking out over the sun-baked red tiles. Cats slept on window sills. A transvestite, a grotesque caricature of womanhood, stumbled in high heels over the cobbles. Old ladies in black crossed themselves and genuflected before entering the cool sanctuary of a church. A group of tough-looking children played football in the forecourt, yelling with excitement. An old man came out and pressed a finger to his lips. They nodded and went, pursuing the bouncing object of their worship down the slope of the Ladeira do Carmo. He'd have got an earful in England. I followed at a leisurely pace.

It led me to the Largo do Pelourinho. Pelourinho means pillory. It was here that negro slaves were whipped while ladies watched from wrought-iron balconies; here that they were auctioned from a stone platform where now some local artists displayed their flat, lifeless, hideously coloured renditions of the area.

By the steps of the church of Rosario dos Pretos a black girl in a virginal white lace dress and with a red flower in her hair enquired after my health. I told her I was fine.

'Come home with me,' she said.

I looked blank. I'm a bit slow sometimes. Then I remembered Old Bill telling me that here were the friendliest whores in the world. They expected politeness. I explained I was busy, but how could anyone be too busy? I explained I was tired. In that case what could be more suitable than a quick nap in her bed?

'Tomorrow,' I said. This was the country of *mañana* or,

rather, as the Portuguese say, *amanha*. She understood. Once again honour was saved.

I bumped into her a few more times but tomorrow never came.

In the Rua Portas do Carmo I walked through a small arcade of shops. It led to a small garden where people sat drinking. There was a view of the sea. I turned away. I saw a shape, a sculpture in the shade of a tree; movement in stillness. Shock. A cold wind blew; an interior wind. The leaves hung motionless; black spots in the sky. The air was hot and dense. I waded through an oily translucence.

What I saw brought alive the cold fury of ritualised, institutionalised violence; an act of cruelty captured in the moment for as long as the corruptible steel would last. Fashioned of scrap metal it portrayed a slave being scourged by a hooded figure.

A human ruin sagged against the post held up by chains. His wounds had been cut in the curved metal sheet of his back with a blow torch. Light leaked through instead of blood. The tormentor, welded in the instant of a single purpose, was galvanised by a fluid, accelerating line of energy running up from his outstretched foot, through the straight fling of his arm to reach its climax in the twisted steel rod of the whip. His eyes were black holes drilled in the cowl.

A few hundred yards away the Largo do Pelourinho bustled with life. Here, there was a scar in the air. There was no catharsis.

The next day I went to the museum of the Venerable Third Order of Carmo. There I saw an eighteenth-century image of the crucifixion by the slave sculptor Francis Xavier Chagas, known as 'the goat'. Pagan yet Christian, sensual yet spiritual, it was a glowing amber contradiction. The haggard face of a voluptuary had been quenched of all desire by an inner peace yet the mutilated flesh still craved a caress. The wounds in the straining armpits could have been hacked with an axe. The light coagulated in tendrils of blood composed of 2,000 rubies. It aroused a multiplicity of emotions. It was the work of a mind hovering between earth and heaven; only the hand had been certain. In the churches of Bahía, this city of all saints, there were thousands of images of Calvary; but in that sunlit garden near the Largo do Pelourinho, there was one stark monument to a multitude of calvaries. There, the mind had been certain but the hand had trembled.

I walked to the Terreiro de Jesús. Beneath the trees two young men with superb musculature performed the *capoeira*, a dance fight to the syncopated rhythm of *berimbau* and drums. It was a whirl of feet scything past heads. Slaves had been forbidden to fight so they evolved this dance to settle their disputes. Now it had a less serious intent. I watched for a while and grew bored. Much of it was repetitive and predictable, though it was more interesting than Morris dancing.

I left the shade of the trees and walked to the adjacent Largo do Cruzeiro de São Francisco. It was hardly more than a wide street. At the end were two churches. I passed coffin shops wide open to the sun. I paused outside one. It exhaled the scent of resin, balsam, lacquer, mahogany, polish and teak. The coffins propped against walls were the embodiments of stillness, a stillness enshrined in sunlight. On the pavement children's caskets gaped. Some were hardly large enough to take a magnum of champagne.

As I approached the church of the Third Order of São Francisco the rococo façade seemed to writhe behind a shimmering veil of heat. It was a concatenation of Christian and pagan imagery; an intricate frieze where the corrupted mono-theism of a desert religion struggled to co-exist with animism and the forest deities of Africa. There was a tropical luxury about the carving as if the sculptor had been inspired by the tangled exuberance of the jungle. The ambivalence of this turbulent stone had offended the guardians of the true faith. For years it had lain forgotten behind a thick carapace of plaster. It had only recently been rediscovered and restored. It was well preserved; the plaster had protected it from the elements.

More orthodox, the interior of the adjacent convent church was a luminous gold cavern. I found it impossible to assimilate the wealth of carved detail anointed with gold leaf. I could only sit and let the lambent light pulsate around me.

Bahía is a city steeped in superstition. For every church there must be ten *candomblé* temples. The African slaves had brought their native religions with them. Ironically they were able to hide and transplant their idolatry in the multitude of gaudily painted plaster saints that line the walls of many of the churches. It was amusing to speculate on what dark deity inhabited the insensate plaster of a blue-eyed, blue-cloaked St Francis, or what erotic reveries a cold alabaster Madonna might have aroused, what savage sun burnt in her breast.

This duality of worship was the origin of the hybrid religion now flourishing in the *candomblé* temples. *Candomblé* is not voodoo. To its adherents it is a positive force; its spirits invoked to perform good, not evil. And yet in a shop selling 'religious' accessories I saw some demonic figurines that could only have been conceived for a sinister purpose.

In Bahía the spectrum of faith ranged from the numinous light enclosed in baroque splendour to the dim, anguished sanctity of some humble shrine where old ladies knelt in ashes and pious debris at the Virgin's feet; from the splendour of the image of St Peter of Alcantara to the face of Christ on a plastic clock; from sublime anthem and tired angelus bell to the ululations of one possessed of the spirit rising above the drumming at a *candomblé* ceremony.

I returned to the sanctuary of the hotel. I sat in the cool seclusion of my cell. The evening lay ahead. The telephone purred. The receptionist informed me suspiciously that 'free-ends' were below. I descended. Old Bill, Young Bill, Gary and J. D. awaited me. I hardly recognised J. D. He looked healthy and tanned. Why the hell he goes to sea, I don't know.

We sat beneath the arches and awaited the libation. No bar profaned these hallowed precincts. An acolyte wheeled out a trolleyload of alcoholic and carbonated beverages for our delectation. J. D. had a Coke; the rest of us settled for the pure astringency of gin and tonic. The stars looked down from the black rectangle of sky. The Southern Cross beckoned.

Young Bill, I learnt, had been separated from a high denomination American Express traveller's cheque. He had fallen for the oldest trick in modern history. He had been approached by a peripatetic, black market money exchanger. He had, as instructed, torn the cheque from the folder along the perforated line and passed it over. The money exchanger had taken it into a nearby bank to check on the official exchange rate in order to calculate the additional and unofficial munificence which would accrue to Young Bill. He went in by one door and departed through another. Young Bill waited until the sun reached its zenith before reporting the loss at the American Express office. There he spent the afternoon studying the cold harmonies of Bauhaus furniture.

They were going to 'paint the town red'. A large part of it needed painting. Old Bill wanted me to help them; bring along a can. I declined. I was tired of the endless pursuit. They departed with much hitching up of belts, a girding up of loins for the ordeal ahead.

I retired to my room to enjoy the luxury of solitude. Room service brought me dinner and a bottle of rich Brazilian wine. King Solomon never had it so good.

I hadn't watched television for three months. I switched it on – the news. There were some interesting shots of half bricks bouncing down a street followed by a police baton charge; some minor riot in a town inland. A politician droned his way to a polite applause. I was disappointed. I'd heard they throw shoes at each other over here. Then a bullfight and it was the best bullfight I've ever seen or am ever likely to see. I couldn't make out whether it took place in Spain or one of the neighbouring Latin American countries – but this is how it went.

The matador executed a perfect pass. The crowd applauded. The matador acknowledged their appreciation with four short bows north, south, east and west as the bull careered on across the blazing arena. It skidded to a halt – its forelegs locked, rigid and outstretched, tearing grooves in the dust. It stared myopically at the thick wooden planks. It turned. The matador stood remote; serene; the sun glittering on his finery. Man and beast stared at each other across the aching pool of heat. He shook his *capa*. The bull set off, accelerating rapidly. It connected. The matador cartwheeled over its back – splendour in the dust. The bull performed a three-point turn. The matador ran for it. He was obviously half stunned. He'd lost coordination. This is what probably saved his life. He ran with a peculiar high-stepping gait in a half circle, staggering unpredictably from side to side. Two torreadors drew the bull off. The matador leant against the wooden barrier. He hid his face in his hands. The crowd bayed; a steady roar of execration filled the stadium. An aficionado dropped to the ground beside him and doubled him up with a looping hook to the stomach. Then he kneed him in the face. The torreadors returned. They pummelled the aficionado to the ground. The bull returned. The struggling tangle of limbs untangled – exploded apart. The roar of execration became a howl of amused derision. A storm of thin plastic seat covers filled the air. Cut.

10
Rio and Ronnie

When I returned to the *Anna Kristina* I found some changes. Young Bill, tempted by my praise of the bar and sleeping arrangements, had transferred to the *Amorina*. Hans, the owner, had joined his ship. He'd moved his accountant into my bunk. I moved in with Henrik. And Ricardo, a Brazilian businessman who sold light aircraft, had joined us.

The ten-day sail to Rio seemed to pass in a long reverie of tropical sunlight. We moved like somnambulists through the hot, viscous air. Nobody, if they could help it, made a sudden movement. Deck work was performed lying on our backs in the shade while the paint coagulated in the tins beside us. Even Hans, who was eager to spruce up the ship, moved listlessly among us 'tut-tutting' to himself. Only Ricardo remained unstruck by the heat.

Always immaculate in designer sportswear, he enlivened our prolonged siesta with a refreshing stream of jokes, laughter and snatches of song. He christened me Buffalo Bill because, in a moment of weakness, I'd bought a wide-brimmed leather hat off a street vendor.

'We Brazilians are very clever,' he said fingering my hat. 'Not even the Japanese have a process to make leather look like plastic. We put the leather between hot plates and press it till it comes out shining like this.'

I got my revenge when I found out how he managed to look so cool and dapper.

'Hey, Buffalo Bill,' he called to me a few days later. 'Your hat – it *es* melting.'

'Hello there, Mr Three-showers-a-day. How's your . . .'

'Sssssh, ssssh. You want to get me keel-hauled. It's a fine hat. The shine will keep it from melting.' (We were still restricted to one fresh-water shower a week.)

And when the stomach bug laid low half the ship's company he renamed her the *Anna Latrina*. Every time he said it in front of Hans I winced.

On the night of 25 July we hoved to a few miles north of Rio. At dawn the fleet assembled and sailed in line along Copacabana and Ipanema beaches. The monumental Christ, high on Corcovado, welcomed us with outstretched arms. Sugar Loaf leant out over the sea in obeisance. Few cities have the advantage of such a magnificent natural setting as Rio. Even the *favelas* (shanty towns), clinging to the higher slopes and ridges of the mountains which dominated the city, looked pretty from a distance.

As we sailed back along the Copacabana, Ricardo joined me at the rail. I was studying the grand sweep of hotels that line the beach.

'You are looking for your wife,' he said. 'The Excelsior is there.' He pointed to the northern half of Copacabana. 'Now see the big pink hotel.' I nodded. 'The Excelsior is one, two, three, four to the right.'

'Got it,' I said.

'Now see the line of windows three from the top,' he continued. I strained my eyes and thought I could just about make it out. I've got good long-distance sight. I nodded again.

'Now count one, two, three, four windows from the left.'

'It's just a blur of silver,' I complained.

'No. She is looking out of the window. I can see her plainly. There is a man behind her. He is stroking her hair.'

After I'd chased him three times round the deck I resumed my position at the rail to enjoy the welcoming committee. An armada of small yachts and cabin cruisers sailed out to escort us into the harbour. Many of them bombarded us with cans of excellent Brazilian beer. Rio was going to be all right.

We moored at the passenger terminal near the city centre. I scanned the crowds on the quayside. No sign of Rosamund. Then I heard her calling from the press boat. It pulled alongside. There followed a grand reunion.

The dock guards wouldn't let us through with the typewriter. We plodded back to the ship. I explained the situation to Ricardo.

'I'll fix it,' he said. We plodded back to the gates. A heated but friendly debate ensued. Ricardo berated them in Portuguese. He pointed at the sea. He pointed inland. They clutched their chests. They leant back and held out their hands, fingers splayed, towards us. He pointed at me. He pointed at the sky. They scratched their necks and pulled their ear lobes.

'It's OK now,' Ricardo said. 'You're through.'

'What did you say?'

'I told them you were the greatest writer since Shakespeare. I told them you were a friend of the President. I told them that if they didn't let you through their names would live for ever in your book as a black stain on Brazilian hospitality. The last bit did it.'

The taxi shot off leaving two trenches of molten rubber behind. Red lights were no problem. He was a religious man. He had great faith in the plastic saint dangling from the dashboard. On the Avenida Infante don Henrique, a dual carriageway, we reached 160 kph. The tyres whinnied on the gentle curves. Trees on the central reservation snapped by. One sported a crumpled steel collar. For a moment I thought it was a sculpture until we crackled over a glittering swathe of glass.

'Tsk, tsk, tsk,' our driver tsked, relinquishing the wheel to demonstrate manually the folly of his fellow citizens. We went through a tunnel like an accelerating atom. The overhead lights coalesced into an amber streak. We burst into sunlight and hung a right into the Avenida Copacabana. The Excelsior hotel flashed past. I leant forward and tapped his shoulder. Apologies were conveyed manually. We bucketed over the central reservation and returned.

The Excelsior was a pleasant, comfortable hotel. Our room looked out over the broad sweep of Copacabana beach. I opened the window. Horns tooted merrily. A myriad murmur rose from the mass of humanity in the yellow sand. Hawkers wove through the supine bodies calling their wares. Amber flesh cleaved the blue. Crowds ambled along the wide esplanade patterned with a mosaic of sinuous arabesques. Girls screamed. Skirts billowed. Sugar Loaf tilted at the horizon.

I closed the window. The air conditioning hissed. Soft carpet underfoot. Cans of beer in the fridge glistening with condensation. What more could a man want? I turned to Rosamund.

'Take that dreadful hat off,' she said, 'and have a shower. You stink.'

Rio wasn't going to be all fun. In the book I was still in Tenerife. The only solution was a disciplined routine. I wrote in the morning; joined Rosamund on the beach at noon; took a late lunch in the Italian restaurant in a side street adjacent to the hotel; scribbled perfunctorily in the afternoon; and took dinner in the same Italian restaurant.

Until Rio I'd always hated crowded beaches. But Copacabana wouldn't be Copacabana without the people of Rio – the Cariocas. Lying there in the sun I didn't feel any irritation arising from the territorial imperative. Surprisingly few people felt compelled to blast their slumbering neighbours with the latest cacophony of electronic discords. There were no lunging frisbee freaks and nobody, thank Christ, played cricket. Roped-off areas were set aside for footballers and they did not stray. It was oaf and litter free.

The bottom is the erotic zone in Brazil and the best and most succulent examples are to be viewed on Copacabana; the more fashionable on Ipanema. Nature has democratically endowed office girls with glutei as shapely as their privileged sisters. Only an imbecile would even think of throwing a frisbee when one can laze on the sand and watch what Alberto Lamego described as 'the essence of all the races . . . from the white race, from the black and from the Indian. From Europe, Africa and Asia . . . the universal woman' flaunt her impudent posterior. All day groups of girls parade the strand in bathing costumes scalloped halfway up their backs to show off their major asset.

I made frequent sorties into the pounding surf to cool off. The waves were powerful. I spent a lot of time on my head. Swimming was difficult unless one went out beyond the combers. Few people did. I did once and once only. I was treading water when I felt the cold undertow clutch at my legs. I probably broke the world record hundred metres freestyle getting back between the waves and the shore. One afternoon we watched a helicopter winch to safety two men who'd got into difficulty in the deceptive calm beyond the rising waves.

Of course I didn't stick rigidly to my self-imposed routine. I broke it occasionally to sally forth with Rosamund to see the sights. I was most impressed by the huge concrete statue of Christ on Corcovado. We took the funicular. It rose silently for 2,330 feet up through the cool, leaf-filtered light of the jungle-clad slopes.

The statue is more impressive for its monumentality than any sculptural qualities. Aesthetic considerations apart, the setting and view combine to give Christo Redentor (Christ the Redeemer) a dramatic impact equal to anything I've seen from Borobudor to Neuschwanstein. Those travel writers for the Sunday papers who suffer temporary paralysis of the ventilating system when confronted with far inferior views are advised to give Corcovado a miss unless they're prepared to risk a collapsed lung or worse. The only things I find breathtaking are Gauloises and Javanese cheroots.

I enjoyed Rio. I enjoyed the pace of life and the frenetic race to make and spend money. I even, for a while, enjoyed the traffic. But Rio is not a city to walk in. It sometimes took quarter of an hour to cross a busy thoroughfare. Pedestrians are always in season. The few faded zebra crossings are invitations to commit suicide. The Cariocas themselves have acquired skills enabling them to weave and dodge unscathed through the hurtling torrent of pressed steel. Rio is both exhilarating and exhausting. And although we'd only skated on the icing of the city, I suspected it would not improve by cutting deeper. I preferred the sleepy decadence of Bahía.

Gordon had been to see that other great attraction of Rio, Ronnie Biggs, and had put us in touch with him.

We'd arranged to meet Mr Biggs at eleven-thirty by the dock gates. By noon I'd used up my limited reserves of patience. The sun beat down and bounced off the tar. A humid wind played with dust and litter. The air was acrid with exhaust fumes. The dock guards looked at us suspiciously.

'What's the time?'

'You asked me that a minute ago. Why don't you wear your watch?'

'It's at the bottom of the Atlantic. Got scraped off by a rope. I'll give the bugger another ten minutes. Then I'm off.'

'Is this him?' Rosamund asked. A big man in a silver grey suit emerged from a taxi.

'No, I'll recognise him immediately. Where the hell is he?'

'Gordon told you he'd be late. He didn't turn up at all the first time he'd arranged to meet him.'

'He manages to catch trains on time. What's the . . . there he is.'

Biggs signalled the taxi driver to wait. He was a big man, over six foot. He approached. I stepped towards him. He started to swerve around me. I intercepted and introduced myself. We shook hands with a distinct lack of warmth. He cheered up a bit when I introduced Rosamund.

'You didn't look like a writer,' he said as we got in the taxi. What the hell did he expect, I wondered – somebody with a quill behind his ear wearing a cloak and sitting on a portable tombstone like Richard Le Gallienne.

'But I do now,' I said, 'on closer inspection.'

He turned and laughed. 'Sorry I'm late, I've lost me bird.'

'I'm sorry to hear that,' Rosamund said.

'That parrot cost me a lot. By the way, taken the liberty of booking a table at a seafood restaurant I know. OK with you?' It was OK with us. The restaurant was a tall octagonal building near the waterfront.

'Used to be a fish market,' Biggs explained.

The foyer could have been in a traditional London club. Two venerable old men with ferocious white moustaches sat on a sofa, their hands resting on silver-handled walking sticks. A lift the size of a sentry box transported us to the dining-room.

'A bit posh,' Biggs said, 'but the nosh's all right.'

We were shown a table with a view of the sea. We ordered a bottle of wine to be going on with. Biggs's eyes raked the room. Habit, I supposed. He looked at me over the menu. He had a disconcerting, penetrating stare accentuated by the way his eyelids puckered in the corners.

'The rock oysters are good,' he said. 'How about a dozen each?' Rosamund opted for prawns.

A Welsh accent from the table behind me attracted my attention. I kept turning and staring at the lilting elocutionist. He turned and stared at me. He had long dyed blond hair in the style that went out with flares.

'You're from South Wales,' I said.

'Cardiff,' he said.

'Port Talbot,' I said.

'Know it well,' he said. 'Know it well. Hi there, Ronnie!'

Ronnie nodded, raised an eyebrow and turned away. He looked bored.

'Is there anything I can do for you?' the Welshman asked.

'What?'

'Do you want something?'

'Piss off, you Welsh twit,' Ronnie said with just the right balance of venom and jocularity. He leant forward and spoke quietly. 'He's a drug dealer. I'm not allowed to associate with known criminals. How he gets away with it, I don't know. Tell a lie, I do know. It all depends who you know. That bugger sells the stuff like he's hawking brollies in Oxford Street.'

The oysters arrived. I cast a critical eye over them. They were a bit on the small side. I'd been spoilt in Singapore by giant, jet-flown rock oysters from Sydney. We tipped them back.

'You've had a remarkable run of luck,' I said.

'Yeah. Luck and this,' he said tapping the side of his head. 'Luck in Australia. They were on to me but some daft policeman leaves a file open on his desk. A journalist sees it and it's in the news. Mate of mine phones me up at work and I'm off. Just had time to get home, pick up some things and say bye bye to Charmian. A few hours later there's a regiment outside the house. They'd known where I was for more than twenty-four hours. Then they guard the airports. They'd forgotten about ships. I took a slow boat to Panama. What a bunch. When I think back on it now I could've got away with it if I'd just moved a couple of blocks up the road. Still, here I am and here I'll stay.'

A waitress leant over and spoke quietly in his ear.

'Yeah. Bring 'em over. English couple on holiday,' he explained. 'Want my autograph.'

The waitress ushered them over. They looked as though they'd stepped out of a Giles cartoon. They shuffled forward as if they'd been granted a papal audience. The man actually held his cap to his chest. She fingered her necklace nervously. Ronnie was charming. He'd obviously had lots of practice. He signed

168

bits of paper and serviettes with great panache. I held on to the tablecloth. They trembled with delight.

'Wait till they hear about this at home,' they chanted in unison, backing away. 'Wait till they hear about this at home.' They backed all the way to the door, colliding with tables as they went.

The wine flowed. Ronnie became expansive.

'They've tried to get me out of Brazil three times. Poor old Slipper. I almost felt sorry for him when I saw the picture of him on the plane home sitting by the empty seat where I should've been. And then these fellows tried to kidnap me. Ex-Scots Guards. Big lads, they were. Tried to jump me in the foyer of a nightclub. One got me from behind. Elbowed him in the guts and over the top with him.'

'You're looking fit and well,' I said.

'Had my face re-arranged in Paris in sixty-five. Funny thing plastic surgery. As you grow older you start to look more and more like yourself when you were young. Still, I don't have to hide any more.'

It was nearly four o'clock when we left. There were a lot of empty wine bottles on the table. He invited us back for a few jugs at his place. We took a taxi to Santa Teresa, a quaint old residential district on a hillside – the Hampstead of Rio. We stopped off at his local to get supplies. It was a cross between a grocery store and a bar. Everyone seemed to know him. We had a few beers before setting off up the hill with clinking bags.

'Wanted to walk the last bit,' he said. 'Bloody parrot flew away this morning. Never goes far. No sense of direction. Can't find its way back.'

Halfway up the hill he spotted it. A large red, green and blue bird cavorted in the upper branches of a tree in some wasteground between two houses.

'We'll never get up there,' he said. He threw a small stone into the tree. I picked up half a cobble and hurled it. It passed through the foliage with great velocity. A few leaves spiralled down. Then there was a series of sharp cracks as it bounced along the roof tiles of the house behind.

'Christ Almighty, you'll get me arrested.' We scuttled up the road. We met a slim youth. Ronnie spoke to him in Portuguese.

'He'll get it,' he said. The youth climbed over the wall.

The Biggses' residence, on a steep slope, looked out over red tiled roofs and the haze-shrouded city. It was a pleasant, lived-in house, built some time in the last century, retaining many original features – walls, window frames, floorboards and the like. A swimming pool gaped in the spacious terrace. It was empty except for a crisp carpet of leaves in the deep end.

'Hockney'd have trouble painting this one,' I said.

'It doesn't need painting,' Ronnie said. 'Does it?'

The slim youth appeared at the gate at the top of a steep flight of steps. He bore the multi-hued parrot. It gave me a headache just to look at it. Even nature, it seems, suffers occasional lapses in taste. Ronnie was delighted. He counted out a few sheets in gratitude. The parrot clambered along his shoulders, plucking at his grey curls. He passed it to his son Michael, a dark, handsome, precocious youth.

'What's your favourite group then, Grandad?' he asked me.

'The Sex Pistols and the Amadeus Quartet.' He looked puzzled. 'I don't like the wishy-washy middle-of-the-road stuff,' I explained. 'You know – Cliff Richard and Led Zeppelin.'

'Never heard of the Amadeus bunch,' he said.

'Real shockers,' I said.

'Stop taking the piss,' Ronnie said. 'Let's go and shoot a few frames.'

Michael dragged Rosamund off to the lounge to watch a video-shocker, *Dead-end Drive-in* or something like that. I caught the odd glimpse of it on journeys to the fridge. It started with some soft porn and then plunged into the main theme – gangs of Australian youths kicking orientals to death. It was either so badly made or so surrealistically ambiguous we couldn't make out whether it was a celebration of white supremacy or an indictment of colour prejudice.

Two ranks of gold discs lined one wall of the pool room. Ronnie pointed at them with a pool cue.

'Michael was a pre-teen pop star. They go in for them in a big way over here. I'm well pleased with him. I think he's going to retire soon.'

After four games it was two all. Our shots were becoming more and more erratic. It wasn't a question of skill but who could hold their drink best. We were about equal on both counts. We agreed to call it a day. He was due at the film studio at eleven p.m. He was starring with Steven Berkoff in *Prisoner of Rio*. He thought he'd 'better 'ave a bit of a nod first'.

The night before the fleet sailed for Cape Town we met Ronnie again in the Oba Oba Samba Club. There was a large group of us from the fleet, including Gordon. I won't (because I can't) describe the pelvic gyrations of the female star in the main act. What she did with her anatomy defied the laws of human biology. It was a merry night.

While waiting for the taxi after the show I began to feel cantankerous. I addressed myself to an elderly Australian woman who'd shown an excess of sloppy adulation for our hero.

'Nobody's been wearing a trench to the grave of the guy they bashed on the head.'

'Up yours,' she replied.

11
Rio to Cape Town

We sailed out of Rio with mixed feelings. We were certainly sad to leave but, at the same time, looked forward to sailing as a fleet. To achieve this, the Commodore and Captains, after several lengthy meetings, had thrashed out a plan which they hoped would ensure we stayed together. We were to anchor for the night off a nearby island. The next day the new trainees would be taught the rudiments of sail-handling before we committed ourselves to the wilderness of the South Atlantic. Unlike the previous leg, the journey would not be broken by visits to exotic ports like Bahía and Cape Verde. There was nowhere to stop.

But, oh how naïve we were on the *Amorina*. The wind, though light, was blowing in the right direction. The Captains of the smaller ships succumbed to its promise and went with it. The *Søren Larsen* and the *Tucker Thompson* surged ahead, boring into the horizon. The *Anna Kristina* raced up from astern and passed us not a hundred yards away. John, Mons and Henrik waved. This was to be the last I saw of Henrik, but I didn't know it then.

The plan was abandoned. The fleet began to disintegrate. The proclamations of unity and brotherhood at sea had all been so much rodomontade. And in reply to the tedious and sometimes acrimonious arguments that later raged in Cape Town about who left whom, I would simply state this – 200 years ago our predecessors, without satellite navigation, without radio com-

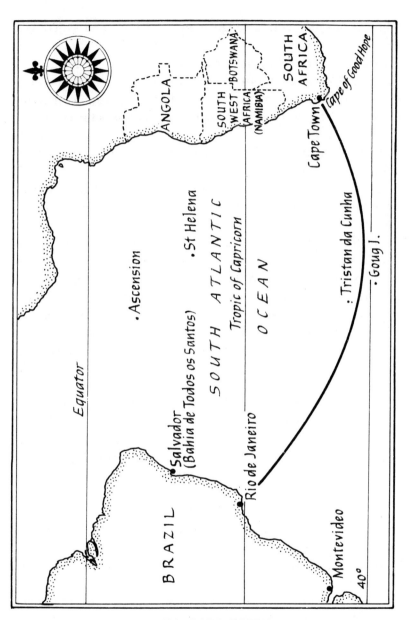

RIO TO CAPE TOWN

munication and without engines as a backup, had sailed as a fleet.

And so, as the *Amorina* made slow but stately progress, I watched Rio recede in our wake. The lineaments of the colossal statue of Christ, arms outstretched in a gesture conferring infinite mercy, hope and benediction on the sinners below, coalesced into a stark silhouette – a gaunt crucifix on a desolate Golgotha. Sugar Loaf darkened and tilted until it was no more than a charred stump.

Our Svanen stayed with us for four days and then slipped away over the horizon. The *Bounty* shadowed us on the rim of the world.

On the ninth day we heard over the radio that the *Bounty* was anxious to sail with us. Could we slow down? We were glad to. We reduced speed by taking down the topsails. She passed us in the night, motor-sailing, and drew ahead. To put up more sail in the rushing darkness would have incurred unnecessary risk. We radioed her watch officer. He replied that he'd no authority to slow down. He refused to wake Captain Small. We felt betrayed. By dawn she was a smudge seven miles away. Then nothing.

We were alone in one of the world's greatest wastes, far from the shipping lanes.

And yet not quite alone. As if sensing our bereavement, three wandering albatrosses appeared out of the limpid fastnesses of the southern latitudes. They circled the *Amorina* in long, languid spirals, their eyes fixed on the waves below. For 2,000 miles they wove an invisible, protective skein around us.

They were masters of the wind. They changed course by spilling the air out of their wings with only a hint of a tilt. They passed beneath the bowsprit inches from the waves and then, following the contour of the rising swell, soared upwards until they were level with the royals, banked and sank in elegant parabolas behind the stern. Sometimes, as if overcome by their own momentum, they swung out, out and away towards the horizon, but they always returned. And sometimes, when executing a more violent change of direction, they hung motionless at the apex of the turn as if pinned to the sky, their shadows stamped on the sea below. Mesmerised by their gyrations I watched them for hours.

I'm not superstitious but in those mighty seas where one looked up at the waves, they seemed like guardian angels.

In reality they had come to scavenge. There was an abundance of waste. All the breakfast, lunch and dinner scraps were thrown overboard. And in the intervals between meals, food preparation in the galley ensured a steady supply of eggshells, potato peel, fatty offcuts, carrot tops and so on.

I took great pleasure in feeding them. I would go to the bow and decant a pail of scraps. Then I would rush to the stern and be rewarded by seeing them settle in the floating mess within ten feet of the ship. It became an obsession. The dinner scraps were thrown overboard in the dark. I didn't know how well albatrosses could see at night so I hoarded the leftovers in plastic buckets. Suzanne, the cook, a Bessie Bunter with a Rabelaisian sense of humour, found this amusing. She re-christened me, with heavy irony, Mr Nice Guy. This puzzled some of my shipmates whose brains were on the same rung of the evolutionary ladder as the barnacles that clung to the hull. I had established, I can't think why, a reputation for being sarcastic, cantankerous and savage-tongued in proportion to the rate at which the atmosphere infiltrated the inverted gin bottle behind the bar.

The albatrosses, much to their disgust, were soon joined by a mixed flock of Pintado petrels (Cape pigeons) and white-chinned petrels. Their smaller cousins, though less elegant in flight, were nimbler and quicker to the scraps.

The white-chinned petrels were the clowns of the ocean. With rigid, outstretched legs and apricot webfeet splayed, they came into land flapping wildly and, as soon as their heels hit the water, ran frantically over the surface like old ladies afraid of getting their petticoats wet. Quite often their timing went drastically wrong and they would plunge beak first into the side of a wave and surface with beads of mercury dancing on their oily, black feathers.

The albatrosses, disdaining such antics, approached in a long curve before arching their wings and sinking with ponderous dignity into the mêlée below. Once in the fray they would lose their sang-froid and, with gaping beaks and hoarse squawks, drive the petrels off.

Walther disapproved. The bellicose behaviour of our avian comrades upset the fragile scheme of his watery Utopia. He rationalised. 'You should not feed zem. You are making zem like humans fighting over all zis trash. Vithout you zey vould not make var,' he complained. 'Zey are beautiful circling the ship.'

'So you expect them to grace the skies nourished by some sort of spiritual vapour?'

'Vat?'

'With nothing to eat.'

'Zey find food in ze sea. Schools of little fish. Big fish vich have died. Squid.'

'Of course! Must make all the difference to their table manners when they find a decomposing dolphin. I suppose they form a queue. I can just imagine it. "I say, after you old boy." – "No, no, be my guest." – "You're too kind." – "Think nothing of it." Really Walther.'

He stalked off. Later that afternoon I found that Suzanne had cut the rind and about three inches of fat off a huge side of bacon. I took a two-foot knife and started to carve it into ribbons. It was a long process. Suzanne hated interlopers in the galley when she was working.

'You're in my way,' she said.

'I'd be in your way in the Gobi desert.' It took her a few seconds to work this one out. Then she shrieked with laughter and threw a carrot at me. After that we got on like a Hindu funeral; the ones those spoilsports the British put a stop to.

I cut the pork ribbons into pieces the size of dominoes and, filling a bucket, threw them overboard. There was more than enough to go round and the albatrosses and petrels dined in harmony on the ample bosom of the swell.

Now that we were alone, Walther and Sven made a decision about something they had long been contemplating. They would take the *Amorina* further south, ostensibly in search of stronger winds. In fact, their real motive was to visit Tristan da Cunha, the remotest inhabited island in the world, 1,300 miles south of St Helena, 1,800 miles east of Uruguay and 1,500 west of the Cape of Good Hope. This was to be our consolation prize for not sailing with the fleet. And so we sailed to Cape Town in a sweeping arc that took us 600 miles south of the other ships.

It was a journey that gave us a sense of achievement and pride. And more importantly it gave the *Amorina* the standing and respect that she'd hitherto been denied. Often sneered at and dismissed as the 'hospital ship' or the 'floating hotel' for her relative comforts – comforts soon nullified by stormy weather – she sailed through seas which would have made life a nightmare on the smaller vessels. I learnt later that they would have been in danger of breaking up under the constant battering the *Amorina* received. As it was the *Bounty*, a hundred miles north of us, would radio a few days later to say that she was retreating further north to calmer seas. Some of her trainees were in great distress, finding life impossible in the relentless turbulence that went on day after day, night after night. I could well imagine their suffering. The *Bounty*, with her rounded hull and blunt prow, would roll on wet grass. But the *Amorina*, with her huge sail area and raked bow, came into her own in the powerful winds that blew over the heaving desert, larger than the Sahara, surrounding Tristan da Cunha. And so we diverged, edging southeastwards towards that mote in the eye of the wind.

*   *   *

I had changed. I felt at home on the ship. I no longer regarded her as I had on the Tenerife to Rio leg, as a prison which could sink. The demands of the *Anna Kristina* had broken me in. I now took for granted what the new trainees, including Rosamund, found alien and disturbing.

Rough seas apart, one had to contend with deranged sleep patterns; toilets which bubbled and stank; shower cubicle floors awash with effluence; meals which were often a jostling, cursing shambles; drenched clothes at five in the morning and the irritating peccadillos of one's shipmates. Some 'floating hotel' this. And yet, despite these discomforts, the *Amorina* was a happy ship.

The tolerant, easy-going attitude of the Swedes, combined with the twenty-four-hour facility of the bar, made it a ship of revelry. There were parties, planned and spontaneous; parties that went on long into the night so that those coming on watch at four a.m. would find an exhausted rearguard lying semi-comatose in the debris of inverted ashtrays, smashed glasses and spilt wine.

Walther had given Lindo a free passage to Cape Town on condition he ran the bar. This was a cunning move for, as Walther had anticipated, Lindo's bar bill reduced substantially the extent of his generosity.

It was on this leg that I got to like Peter Doc. He'd calmed down a bit. Walther had made him a watch officer and a temporary crew member. He was good at his job. He was also a good instructor; he was patient and precise. He taught me how to steer.

On the Portsmouth to Tenerife leg I'd been given the helm, told the compass course and left to get on with it. My instructor (who shall remain nameless) had neglected to inform me of certain 'steering aids' such as the dial above the window which showed the helmsman the rudder angle to port, to starboard and when it was dead amidships. I was prone to over-steering

16 John Sorensen, Captain of the *Anna Kristina*, with the author

17 *Anna Kristina* sailing out of Rio

18–19 Tristan da Cunha, the remotest inhabited island in the world

20   The Lord Milner Hotel in Matjiesfontein

21   The author and his wife, Rosamund, enjoying a pre-dinner soak

22 Oasis of Victorian elegance in the Karoo

23 Suzanne, the cook, with the author

25 Gordon Carvosso and the author with Table Mountain in the background

26   Unfurling the sails on the *Amorina*

27   *Amorina* under full sail

28 Sailing into the sunset

29 The grand welcome in Sydney Harbour

and then over-correcting: writing my signature in the sea, as Walther put it.

It would have been helpful to know the angle of the rudder and when it was amidships. On the *Anna Kristina* it had been easy to tell by looking at the rudder arm through the wooden grating beneath one's feet. Like a horizontal pendulum, it swung to and fro at the turn of the wheel. The *Amorina's* power-assisted wheel enclosed in the bridge up front far from the rudder was very woolly and unresponsive by comparison.

The second week Rosamund and I changed to Peter Doc's eight-to-twelve watch. After a few days I noticed that she was a lot better at steering than me. This irked. When I took the helm people sniggered. This also irked though it gave me some satisfaction when their sniggers often became cries of alarm as the sails whipped and cracked and the ship tottered dramatically on the crest of a twenty-foot swell.

'God, damn and blast,' Sven would shout. 'Are you trying to kill us all? Where are you going?' And throughout the ship the general cry of, 'Who's on the helm? Who's on the helm?' would arise to the sound of pots and pans bouncing around the galley.

On the morning of the tenth day I was watching Rosamund steering with the aplomb of a veteran sailor.

'What's she got that I haven't?' I asked Peter Doc.

'Intelligence!' he replied, rather too predictably.

'It's just a bloody wheel,' I grumbled. 'You turn it one way or the other. I managed all right on the *Anna Kristina*.'

'There's more to it than that. You have to keep an eye on the rudder and wind gauges. You have to anticipate and concentrate. You don't.'

'Rudder gauge?'

Peter pointed to a dial above the window.

'I thought that was the temperature gauge.'

'You might have noticed that the needle moves even with the engine off. Anyway temperature gauges don't swing back and forth like that.'

'I thought it was a busted temperature gauge.' And I had. The starboard degrees were marked on a green arc and the port on a red arc.

When it was my turn to take the helm Peter stepped in. He taught me how to steer properly in about five minutes.

'When you take over don't just grab the wheel. Leave it a moment to see which way the ship's pulling.'

The wheel turned lazily to port. The rudder gauge showed an angle of ten degrees to port. Peter corrected until the rudder angle was about five degrees to starboard, held it a moment and then let the needle slip amidships. After this simple lesson my steering improved rapidly and within half an hour I was as proficient as anyone else with the exception of Gordon and the professional crew. Knowing the function of the rudder gauge was a great help. Pity somebody hadn't told me about it before.

Sailing to Tristan da Cunha was to prove the most exhausting part of the whole voyage. The swell had been building up steadily. Eventually it reached a height of thirty feet from trough to crest. It was relentless. It was mesmerising. It went on twenty-four hours a day for nine days. Rampart after heaving grey rampart swept across the ocean. No sooner had the *Amorina* dropped into a trough than she would start to climb the glacis of the next looming escarpment. She would tilt sickeningly as the slope steepened; sink deep into the convex brow until the sea sluiced along the deck; rise and stagger across the crest, the masts describing huge arcs in the sky; totter on the edge of the opposite slope before slithering down into the following trough. Sometimes the bowsprit bored into the side of the swell. Then the sea would burst over the prow in a white explosion and pour along the deck in a dark emerald torrent veined with bubbling grey tentacles of foam. Sometimes a rogue wave crashed into the side and flung a semi-translucent vault over the boat deck to drench those sheltering in its lee.

Despite these conditions I had no trouble sleeping. The

problem was the nature of the sleep itself. It did not refresh or revitalise. Lars had provided Rosamund with a sheet of plywood to jam between the mattress and the side of the bunk. Thus she could sleep without fear of being hurled to the floor. I had no such safety device. I would wake with aching shoulders and arms. So strong was my instinct for self-preservation that, even in sleep, I braced myself between the wall and the low lip of the bunk.

On 22 August the midnight watch heard over the ship's radio the tragic news that somebody on the *Anna Kristina* had fallen overboard. The *Trade Wind*, *Tucker Thompson* and *Søren Larsen* had converged with the *Anna Kristina* to search the area. We were too far south to join them. The next day we learnt it was Henrik. The search had been called off.

I don't like writing about things I haven't witnessed but this sad event calls for more than a bald statement of fact. When I rejoined the *Anna Kristina* for a final leg from Fremantle to Sydney, John, the Captain, solved my dilemma. He gave me permission to print his account of Henrik's death which he'd written for the Court of Inquiry. Here it is in full, together with Suzanne Phillips's statement:

Anna Kristina, 23.08.87

The Circumstances of the Death of Henrik Bak Nielsen

During the night watch 00–04 22.08 of which Henrik was the watch leader, an attempt was made to set the 'lee sail' as an outer jib. Henrik was leading the work. Abigail Heath and Ricardo B. Neto participated and Suzanne Phillips was at the helm.

The weather: NE 5/5, overcast, moderate visibility, the ship's course was 140° true.

Whilst the sail was being hoisted, Henrik was leaning over the side to gather the violently flapping sheets in order to make fast on the pinrail. The ship heeled and Henrik was pulled over the side.

This happened at approximately 01.05 hours and the ship was doing five knots. Henrik, still holding the sheet, was dragged alongside some seconds.

I was woken up by the helmsman and managed to get on the deck before Henrik let go. The rudder was put hard into the wind, both the life buoys were thrown and one of the lights was seen flickering shortly after.

By this time more people were on deck. I asked Salo van de Vooren to pull in the log line. Henrik was holding on to it but let go after some seconds.

The sails came down, and I called PANPAN on the VHF, noted the position (31°21'S 15°52'W) according to the Sat. Nav., and that last fix was two hours old.

The *Trade Wind* answered my PANPAN, they were approximately seven miles to the leeward side – time 01.10 hours.

MANOEUVRE:

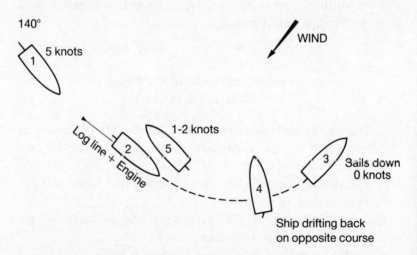

1) Sails flown:– mizzen, main, stay sail, inner jib.

The ship came around to the opposite course with the engine on slow speed and the aldis and masthead light on as search lights. Henrik was suddenly observed at the port quarter ten metres away.

Johan Brox instantly took a coil of rope from the pinrail and dived into the water in Henrik's direction. At the same time I gave full throttle astern but had to give up because Johan was just astern. At this time Henrik was out of sight.

When we saw him, he was without a life buoy and was screaming in panic and flapping his arms, his voice was full of water.

The rudder, at the same time as Johan was pulled back on board, was put hard to starboard and the engine on full throttle ahead.

I turned the ship so that the wind was on the beam and continued to turn to go down wind to the position where Henrik was last seen.

Henrik was not sighted after this but some believe they heard him.

We continued with short opposite courses. The full visibility with the masthead light, aldis light and flashlights was twenty to thirty metres to port and ten metres to starboard. The darkness was intensified by the dense air humidity.

The *Trade Wind* arrived at the search area at approximately 03.00 hours, at which time I was still convinced that we were close to the area where the accident occurred. The life buoys were never sighted again.

The *Trade Wind* and the *Anna Kristina* continued on parallel courses and changing courses and stopped many times when suspected observations were reported.

The *Søren Larsen* and the *Tucker Thompson* joined us at around 06.00 hours. A systematic search was organised over an extreme area covering four miles width, six miles length, two miles to each side of the position where the incident occurred and six miles to lee.

Daylight came at 06.00 hours as a relief. I still had hopes.

The incident position was 31°21′S and 15°48′W after later satellite positions.

The search continued all day with the participation of all four ships and covered all down to twelve miles lee of the incident position. Much was observed but no Henrik or life buoys were seen.

Half an hour after sunset the search was called off; this was a decision agreed upon by all the ships' Captains.

Henrik had by this time been in the water for eighteen hours; his clothing consisted of jeans, rubber boots, sweater and anorak. The water temperature was fourteen degrees.

The information given in this report, compiled by Captain John Sorensen, has been fully confirmed by the entire ship's company on the *Anna Kristina*.

Captain John Sorensen   Johan Brox
                                                                          Witness

To whom it may concern:

On the early morning of 22 August, I was on watch with Henrik Nielson – the watch leader, Abigail Heath – crew member, and Ricardo B. Neto – trainee. About thirty minutes after our watch began at 12.00 a.m., Henrik decided we would put up the raffee sail on the outer jib line. Abigail and Ricardo went to assist Henrik and I was told to take the helm. It was a dark night and, from the helm, I could not see the other crew. We were steering 110° by the compass. The ship was keeping course well with maximal variation only between 105°–110°. I heard a sail flapping in the bow and Henrik shout to 'pull the rope' – a moment of silence – then I heard Abigail scream. I immediately got John Sorensen – the Captain – who was on deck in a second. As John came on deck, I saw Henrik floating by the starboard aft side. John threw him a life buoy and took the helm. Henrik disappeared quickly in the darkness. I ran forward down the fore companionway and awakened the rest of the crew – most, however, were already awake by now and on their way to the deck.

We lowered the sails – by now John had the ship turned back to where we thought Henrik would be. Within moments, we did see him. I saw him directly behind the ship for just a few seconds – maybe fifteen yards away. At this time, Johan was also in the water. However, he had a rope and was quickly pulled back on board. We continued searching. A few times after the last sighting, some of us thought we heard him – but we were not sure. We never sighted him again.

Suzanne Phillips

Henrik's death made us realise that this was not simply a re-enactment voyage; a sort of maritime history play performed for the most part to a largely indifferent and invisible audience. Apart from the welcomes and sendoffs we enjoyed at each port, we were on our own in the middle of the ocean with all the attendant dangers. The sea, the waves and the wind were real. The ship was not a stage and we were not actors. We were sailing on a voyage in its own right.

After two days' sailing from Tristan da Cunha the wind dropped to no more than a light breeze. The sails sagged. The ship wallowed awkwardly on a decreasing swell making little or no progress.

We were in radio contact with the island. We learnt that the sea and weather conditions there were mild enough to permit landing parties and would possibly, but only possibly, prevail for two or three days. I suggested to Sven that we get the engine on and motor straight for the island.

'Ve are here to sail and sail ve vill,' he said smacking his fist into the palm of his hand. 'A strong vind vill come tomorrow. It vill get us there.' I knew better than to argue; it only made him more stubborn.

He was right about the strong wind; it came the next day. Nevertheless, in my opinion, he'd made the wrong decision. With a strong wind came a rising swell which diminished our chances of getting ashore. We'd wasted twenty-four hours bobbing about aimlessly to satisfy an old salt's absurd prejudice against the internal combustion engine. We had lost, as I had feared, an opportunity to land on an island which few people ever see, let alone set foot upon.

Tristan da Cunha, named after the Portuguese admiral who discovered the island in 1506, has a limited and a somewhat eccentric history. It was explored by the Dutch in 1643 and, more than a hundred years later, by the French in 1767. Neither nation was sufficiently impressed to raise a flag on its bleak eminence.

In 1811 an American adventurer, Jonathan Lambert, declared himself sole proprietor and with two companions attempted to settle the island on a permanent basis. He planned to sell seal oil and skins to the few passing ships. However, his ambitions foundered and the island was abandoned.

Paranoia, engendered by Napoleon's escape from Elba, incited the British to send a detachment of troops and artillery to take formal possession in 1816. This military expedition was justified on the apprehension that the French might use the island as a base to launch a raid to free Napoleon imprisoned on St Helena 1,200 miles to the north. The military withdrew in 1817 but a Scot, Corporal William Glass, his wife and children and two seamen were granted permission to remain. Over the years they were joined by shipwrecked mariners, whalers and sealers, the ancestors of some of the present inhabitants.

After twenty days' sailing we came upon Tristan da Cunha at dawn on 28 August. Rising abruptly 6,760 feet out of the ocean it was an impressive sight; but here in the slate-grey turmoil of these remote latitudes far from the shipping lanes, it inspired a sense of awe over and above mere physical presence.

A heavy mantle of cloud oozing tentacles of vapour into the gulches scarring the precipitous slopes obscured the volcanic cone, so that the island resembled a grey Ayers Rock in a desert of shifting grey dunes. And although grey predominated, it was a greyness of many subtle gradations of tone that seeped into each other or separated in a constant liquid flux. Near vertical planes of rock seamed with fissures, inked in with wet shadows and luminous moss, glinted coldly through a pale web of moisture suspended from the long, nacreous cloud on the summit. The sky behind, lit by the subdued radiance of an invisible sun, glowed like the inner surface of an abalone shell. The waves obliterated themselves in a continuous explosion of foam along cliffs which in some places rose sheer for 2,000 feet. The settlement of Edinburgh, a cluster of white houses, crouched on a slanting green shelf four miles by half a mile wide.

How could people live in such a place? After a weekend in the Chilterns I'm itching for London. And yet nearly 300 people did live there and, by all accounts, happily. In 1961 a volcanic eruption forced the evacuation of the entire population to Britain but two years later all but a few had returned to set up home again on this stark rock in the South Atlantic. No doubt a strong community spirit overcame any sense of physical remoteness and, in human terms, the islanders were probably less isolated than the residents of many a tower block in England.

On the bridge a dialogue in the form of question and answer was taking place over the ship's radio with Alan Swain, the island's postmaster. We learnt that there was a pub; a disco every Saturday night; a school; a hospital; and that they'd watched *Dallas* the previous night on cable television. Apart from sea birds and the rock hopper penguin, there were three indigenous birds: a finch, a brown thrush and the 'Island Hen', similar to an English moorhen. Only one species of tree grew there: a buckthorn (*Phylica nitida*) which had the merit of burning brightly even when green. There was no crime though 'rowdiness' was not unknown. Stamps and the succulent tails of rock lobsters from the cold, unpolluted waters were the main source of revenue. I could go on but facts such as these don't evoke much of a sense of place. One would have to live there for at least a year to discover what life was really like on the island. Perhaps somebody – an outsider – should. I'm sure there'd be a book in it.

Weeks later in Cape Town I was able to get hold of a copy of the *Tristan Times*. It contained the usual parochially introspective material ranging from 'Craft Shop News' to a recipe for 'Potato Bread'. However, I would like to reproduce, almost in full, two news items which, to me, seem to bring the island alive.

RATTING DAY

The annual mass hunting of rats and mice took place on Monday 22 June. The day itself was windy with occasional heavy showers. In spite of the weather, a significant percentage of the population participated in killing rodents. The tails were counted in the evening with the assistance of the Chief Islander. The results of the day's activities by team were as follows: Second Watron, 148 tails; Coolers, 192 tails; Below-the-Hill, 197 tails; Farm, 44 tails; Bill's Hill, 24 tails; Red Body Hill, 30 tails; Old Pieces, 22 tails. Total for the day, 657 tails.

The prizes were presented in the evening in the Prince Philip Hall. The presentation was well attended in spite of not having a dance afterwards. Prizes were given for the top three highest catches per man, the longest tail (the Farm team) and the booby prize of a rat-catching stick (complete with dead rats) for the lowest catch per man.

FATTING TRIP

On 24 April, two longboats, the *Union Castle* and the *Stirling Castle*, sailed in uncertain weather on the annual fatting trip to Nightingale Island. Three days later they were joined by five further boats, bringing to the island a total of sixty-seven islanders. Sharing the twenty-seven huts, everyone quickly fell into the routine of collecting petrel meat and oil, a task that was completed in five days.

Although the weather remained generally calm and fine, the wind failed to move round to the right quarter for the journey home. The men consequently took the opportunity to repair the huts which had been unused and neglected for nearly a year. The days went by and still no possibility arose of making the return voyage. After twelve days food parcels from Tristan arrived opportunely on *Hekla* which had commenced fishing off the island. Finally, on 18 May, after twenty-five days, the wind veered to allow the welcome launching of the longboats and a homeward sail to Tristan.

I also obtained a local map of the island. The names of the beaches and other physical features seemed straight out of a children's adventure story. Here are just a few: Ridge-where-the-goat-jump-off; Deadman's Bay; Down-where-the-minister-landed-his-things; Slippery Bluff; Soggy Plain; Washout Gulch; The ponds-up-the-east'ard; Cave Hill Gulch; Joey's Garden and Seal Bay.

The wind strengthened and with it went the last faint hope that we might get ashore. For two hours we'd been drifting in the island's shadow held to by the jib and stay sails. But this was the wind we needed. The main and square sails were hauled aloft, the yardarms braced and we set our course for Cape Town. Soon we were doing seven knots. The black bulk of the island loomed for an hour behind a curtain of rain before dissolving in a ruined sky. That feeling of isolation engendered by the desolate wastes of the South Atlantic returned. But the albatrosses and petrels stayed with us. Riding the wind they circled the ship tirelessly, maintaining, as we liked to think, a ceaseless vigil. I continued to feed them.

By now even Walther had taken to calling me Mr Nice Guy. I considered this bad for my image. I decided to put a stop to it. I'd read in a book on the history of square-riggers that the albatross is easily tamed, being quite happy to flop about the deck if fed regularly. The book also described how to make an albatross trap. I resolved, in the interests of natural science of course, to make one and put it to the test.

I hoped to catch one albatross in particular. Unlike its companions it had no brown markings but was a pure, unsullied white. It was also the biggest. Each wing was the size of a water-ski. They were all masters of the sky making the maximum use of the air currents in order to expend the minimum of energy as they sustained perpetual motion over thousands of miles day and night. Occasionally, perhaps once in a circuit, they were forced to break the elegance of their serene parabolas with an awkward flap to adjust their flight path. But this giant could complete gyre after gyre without disturbing the equilibrium of its poise by lapsing into the indignity of self-propulsion. And when it alighted on a floating mess of scraps the others made way for this monarch of the wind.

I estimated its wing span to be about twelve feet. The general consensus was ten feet. I think I was right. I later read in the introduction to a book on ocean birds that people tend to underestimate the size of sea birds when there is nothing to judge them against except a shifting grey chaos. It's much easier, for example, to assess the size of a heron in a reedbed or a starling on a TV aerial.

I went down to the engine-room to make a trap. It was a straightforward task. I cut a rectangle six inches by four from an aluminium sheet and put it in the vice. I hacksawed out a narrow V-shaped slot and drilled two holes, one in each arm, to facilitate the attachment of fishing line. According to the book one simply inserted a piece of meat, preferably pork, in the apex of the V and trailed the contraption behind the ship. In theory the albatross should strike at the pork and get its hooked beak stuck in the cleft. It all seemed quite feasible to me. They were greedy birds. In the mêlée over scraps they displayed a total lack of culinary discrimination, pecking up anything, even teabags and grease-proof paper. Pork fat and bacon rind sent them into a squawking, hissing hysteria of excitement.

I was just filing smooth the cut edges when Walther arrived. He hovered over my shoulder tutting and clucking, the usual prelude to a bout of moral indignation.

'Vat are you doink?' He knew very well what I was up to. Unfortunately I'd aired my intentions in the bar. His spies were everywhere. I ignored him.

'Vat vill you be doink vith zis metal?'

'I've been commissioned to construct a mobile sculpture by the Tate.'

'Vat is Tate?'

'It's a charitable organisation. They buy up piles of bricks, off-cuts, torn canvas, scrap metal . . .'

'You are making a bird trap. I know. It is bad luck to kill ze albatross. You should know zis from ze famous English poem about ze senile sailor. You vant I hang a dead bird round your neck?'

'Who said anything about killing an albatross? I just want to catch one. Keep it as a pet for a few days. There's no harm in that.'

'Zis device vill kill ze bird. How vould you like to be dragged

through ze vaves beak first. It might suffocate or break its neck.
I am forbidding zis crazy plan. Zere are people on board giffing
donations to Greenpeace. Zey vill be upset.'

I agreed to abandon my plan. I was scared of being
bludgeoned to death by a horde of ecomaniacs. Walther had a
point. It would, at the very least, be a traumatic experience for
such a large bird to be hauled by the beak through the
waves and up the side of the ship – or so I thought at the
time.

But something happened a few days later to make me doubt
the nervous sensitivity and physical fragility of these birds.
Shortly after leaving Rio, Lars had attached a trailing fishing line
some 200 yards long to the stern. The 'finny tribe' had ignored
the spinning, flashy metal lure for so long that we'd forgotten it.
Then one of those clowns of the sea, a white-chinned petrel,
collided with the line and somehow contrived to entangle a
wing. It was being towed upside down through the waves.
Disaster. Famines in Ethiopia paled into insignificance.
Scandinavians suffered nervous prostration at the sight. The
line was tied to the top bar of the stern rail about twenty feet
above the surging waves. It would have to be pulled in to free
the creature. After a debate it was decided that to minimise the
beast's ordeal somebody should cut short its ascent by grabbing
it as it passed one of the large square portholes in the bar. I was
that person.

Lars hauled away and I waited until the flapping, shrieking,
coal-black demon was level with the porthole. I knew immediately that I'd been right in my first estimation of the size of the
albatross. I'd calculated a petrel's wing span to be about three
and a half feet but when this hissing, beak-snapping smaller
brother appeared in the porthole I could see that it was nearly
five feet from wing tip to wing tip. I reached for it. My hand
nearly disappeared into a stretched pink maw. I wrapped a bar
towel round its beak. As I cut away the line its wings buffeted
me about the face. It dropped free but hardly had its feet hit the

water than it rose on an air current to resume circling the ship as if nothing had happened. It had shown no sign of trauma or mild shock. It hadn't even settled on the water to compose itself. The mechanics of pure instinct had dictated an immediate resumption of the endless cycle. Within seconds I couldn't tell it apart from its twenty or so companions. The incident gave credence to the stories of sailors catching and keeping them as pets. It was obvious that it would take a lot more than a brief tow through the waves to injure one of these birds. They were all muscle, bone, sinew and quill.

A week from Cape Town I got a headache. This was no ordinary headache but a relentless, uninterrupted pain that the analgesics only partially relieved. It was accompanied by an intermittent fever. I could tell by the way I felt that this was no mundane illness such as flu. Bjorn, the chief engineer, was also stricken with exactly the same symptoms. Thus Peter Doc was forced to take my grumbles seriously and not attribute them to self-indulgence.

It turned out that Bjorn and I were the only two on board who hadn't taken malaria pills on the previous leg before reaching Brazil where the disease was widespread. That we had malaria was only a hypothesis based on this significant coincidence and the bouts of fever. We would have to wait until Cape Town for blood tests to provide conclusive evidence.

I was dubious about the malaria theory: I couldn't remember being bitten, or rather punctured, by a mosquito in Brazil. After years of living in the tropics I'd come to the conclusion that mosquitoes were allergic to me. Those desperate enough to ignore the foul exhalations of my polluted blood fell off after the first sip with an outraged whine and spiralled out of control to an agonised death. No. I was sure it wasn't malaria. As it turned out, after tests in Cape Town, Bjorn and I had acquired something much more exotic.

A few days from South Africa Sven underwent a sudden conversion as dramatic as that of Saul on the road to Damascus.

We'd run out of fresh fruit and vegetables, and, more significantly, steak and potatoes. Sven, like me, was a red meat and spud man.

I was in the wheelhouse that memorable afternoon and witnessed the old Viking's transmogrification from first glimmer to final illumination. We'd had a good run from Tristan da Cunha averaging six to seven knots for a week in strong westerly winds. Now the sodden sails hung heavy and limp. Sven was showing symptoms of suppressed agitation. He was pulling his mouth into a thin, hard line by thrusting his chin forward aggressively. He muttered darkly in Swedish. Gordon, at the wheel, whistled 'A Life on the Ocean Wave' lento. Walther, hunched over the chart table, pretended to be engrossed by the pattern of currents off the Cape of Good Hope.

Sven went out on deck for the third time in ten minutes and, standing legs astride, arms akimbo, glared at the sky. The sails steamed. His grey eyes flashed in the watery sunlight. He stepped back in and continued pacing, his hands clenching and unclenching. I lounged in the doorway exhaling languid blue coils of cigarette smoke into the still air. A pencil snapped with a sharp crack. Sven hurled the pieces to the floor. I knew what was bothering him. I considered offering him some ball bearings but thought better of it. He probably wouldn't have got the allusion anyway.

'We'll get a parking ticket at this rate,' I said provocatively.

'Vat?' he grated.

'Parking ticket. You know. We've been on double yellow lines for an hour.'

He turned away. He picked up a pencil and started to flex it between his thick fingers.

'Where's Bjorn?' he grumbled. 'Tell him to get the engine on.'

'Bjorn is sleeping. He's ill,' Walther said.

'Ill? Ill! No vonder he is ill. Pasta! Pasta! Pasta! Nothing but bastard *pasta*!' he spat. He pronounced 'pasta' with such a

194

plosive virulence he made it sound horribly obscene. '*Pasta!*' he raved beating his stomach with his fists. 'How can a man live on pasta? Wake Bjorn or get Lars to start the engine. Pasta basta. Basta pasta.'

Walther went in search of Lars. Gordon whistled melodiously. I watched the pencil arc alarmingly between Sven's fingers. The engine rumbled into life.

'Come on. Come on,' Sven grumbled even though he knew it would take half an hour to warm the engine up.

I took a turn at the wheel. Gordon went to make us tea. Without wind, except for the occasional feeble gust, it was a difficult task and somewhat nerve-wracking with Sven in such a mood. It was all I could do to keep the bowsprit pointing in the general direction of Africa. I was very relieved when the engine tone changed as the power went through to the propeller. It made steering a lot easier. But Sven still paced the bridge. He was on his third pencil.

'Vy are ve not going faster?' he asked. Walther explained that the ship was under half power to conserve fuel.

'Fuel!' Sven raged. 'Fuel. To hell vith saving fuel. It is fuel for men zat ve need. Put ze bloody machine full on. Pasta! Pasta!'

The pitch of the engine rose to a resonant throb like the one in my head. Soon we were bashing our way through a rising swell at eight knots. Waves crashed over the bow and foamed along the deck. The fickle wind picked up. The seas increased. For a moment I thought Sven would give orders to cut the engine but I was wrong. The pasta diet of the last few days had overcome his aversion to motor-sailing.

'More sail. More sail. Put up more sail,' he shrieked. 'Pasta. Pasta.' Walther went out to supervise the setting of the top sails. Shouts rang out as willing hands climbed the shrouds. The wind strengthened. Spray lashed the wheelhouse. Pots and pans clanged in the galley behind us. Suzanne cursed eloquently and foully.

'Motor-sailing is goot,' Sven announced. 'Soon ve vill be

having potatoes and steak. Potatoes and steak. Pasta. Faster. Basta, pasta. Potatoes and steak. Goddamn pasta.' The *Amorina* surged forward and Sven's eyes shone with a beatific vision. I spun the wheel like one inspired and skewered hallucinatory steaks with the questing bowsprit.

On the Mauritius to Fremantle leg when Sven suffered another bout of the 'we'll sail or nothing' psychosis, Suzanne and I were to exploit his pastaphobia with a Machiavellian cunning.

On the morning of the thirty-second day out of Rio I woke late. The ship's motion was gentle. The porthole was a blue disc. I gobbled back a handful of painkillers and went on deck for a cigarette. We had arrived. The magnificent amphitheatre of Table Mountain, colossal in a cloudless sky, dwarfed the city below. Cameras clicked like crickets.

But we could not dock. Instead we would have to wait to make a formal entry in line with the rest of the fleet scheduled for the next day, 10 September. They had been enjoying barbecues on the beach for the last two days at Saldanha Bay, a small fishing port north of Cape Town. We dropped anchor a few miles out off Robben Island.

Sven got in radio contact with the First Fleet Re-enactment Company office. He ordered supplies of steaks, potatoes and fresh vegetables to be sent out by launch at the company's expense.

They replied it was impossible. Surely we could wait until tomorrow. Sven told them we couldn't wait. They replied we would have to wait. Sven insisted we wouldn't wait.

'Get Suzanne,' he snarled. 'I'll make a list of everything we need. Now listen good,' he said returning to the radio phone. 'If I do not have supplies within two hours I vill bring ze ship into port to get our own supplies.'

'You can't,' the radio wailed.

'Can't! Vy can't I?'

'You'll spoil the grand entry tomorrow. Everything's arranged.

The press. TV cameras. Civic reception.' He smiled evilly. He knew he had them.

'OK. I am raising ze anchor now and ve are coming into port.' The radio hissed. I could imagine the hullabaloo in the office. Suzanne's bulk filled the door. Sven opened a notebook on his lap and felt around for a pencil.

'Pencil,' he shouted. 'Vy can I never find a pencil ven I need von? Pencil! Get me a pencil.'

'Pencils?' the radio bleated. 'Anything you want.'

I gave him a felt-tip. Suzanne took the phone and reeled off a list of supplies. Sven wrote it down and made them repeat the order.

'Vithin two hours,' he threatened, 'or you vill be seeing us at ze dockside zis afternoon.'

The First Fleet Re-enactment Company excelled themselves. Within the specified time a launch chugged out laden with the fruits of that beloved country, from fillet steaks to pineapples to crates of Castle beer. And potatoes, of course. Suzanne handed out flat ingots of chocolate and tubs of yoghurt. We gorged ourselves. My headache reached its zenith. Bjorn sat in the sun by the anchor winch clutching his brow. He looked as rough as I felt.

12

South African Sojourn

Though we were anchored a few miles off-shore, Table Mountain dominated. We ignored Robben Island and paid only brief attention to the wreck of a colossal Japanese supertanker lying, broken-backed, on a sandbank, the waves surging through a hole in its side larger than a double-decker bus.

Sugar Loaf and the 120-foot concrete Christ on Corcovado dispensing futile benediction over the seething hive of Rio had impressed me; but the austere grandeur of Table Mountain was imbued with a symbolic significance over and above any visual impact. Towering over what is essentially a European city, it suggested the fortress mentality of the Afrikaner and, at the same time, proclaimed an ancient right that must inevitably vanquish the alien power below. Above all its stark monumental defiance declared 'no compromise'. Of course it was just a rock.

We knew the fleet would receive a grand reception and a rapturous welcome in Cape Town. South Africa, ostracised as it was from most international cultural and sporting events, would, we anticipated, take full advantage of our visit. There had been some vague talk about leaving Cape Town out of the itinerary but this would have undermined the concept of the voyage being a re-enactment and done nothing to further the cause of the oppressed.

The welcome we received as we sailed into the harbour exceeded our expectations. A host of yachts sailed out to escort us in. The breakwater, the piers and wharfs were thronged with packed ranks of people standing shoulder to shoulder. There were speeches, presentations, bouquets of wild flowers for the ladies, a black jazz band, a Malay bagpipe band and much mutual congratulation. And, although like most people I disapprove of the regime, only a witless fanatic could have hardened his heart to the pleasure our visit gave to both blacks and whites.

We took a room in the Heerengracht, a five-star hotel in the city centre. It could have been in any major city. The décor was modern international. Only ostrich steaks on the menu suggested that we were in South Africa. But it was comfortable and the service excellent.

Yet certain things surprised me. White waiters worked alongside their black counterparts. Roughly half the clientele were black. Black businessmen in pin-striped suits winced when I entered the lift. Well, I hadn't had a shower for a week and was attired in salt-encrusted jeans, cut-away T-shirt and Taiwanese thongs. Apartheid, it appeared, was not admitted through its anodised aluminium portals. Mammon was the great leveller. And this intermingling also took place outside the privileged precincts of the Heerengracht. Blacks, whites and coloureds mixed freely and unselfconsciously in the humbler bars and restaurants. TV documentaries portraying a rigid demarcation between blacks and whites in every facet of daily life had influenced my expectations. I was not aware of any racial tension but then this was cosmopolitan Cape Town and I had a permanent headache.

I spent a lot of time contemplating the ceiling or watching the house video. I did take short walks in the neighbouring streets and sallied forth most evenings to those functions where the alcohol was free. There was a limit to how many painkillers I could take even with my liberal interpretation of the instructions on the bottle. Alcohol also brought temporary relief.

After a pleasant evening at a reception in the Royal Cape

Yacht Club adjacent to the wharf where the fleet was moored, Rosamund and I paid a visit to the *Amorina*. In the bar a few stalwarts paid homage to Bacchus. There was an air of subdued inebriation. Young Bill grinned amiably. He always looked the same no matter how much he'd taken aboard. Lindsey, a young Australian girl, sat giggling to herself in one of the large square portholes. Lindo and Suzanne had drunk themselves into that curious state of near physical paralysis accompanied by a ponderous lucidity.

'I'm not an alcoholic,' Lindo informed the nodding congregation from behind the counter. He gave each syllable equal stress. 'No!' he stated, wagging his finger like the arm of a metronome, 'I'm not an alcoholic but an alcoholist. An al-co-hol-ist!' Suzanne nodded sagely. Young Bill smiled encouragingly. Lindsey giggled. I ordered a gin and tonic.

'I have done much research. I know what I like. Pernod with everything. Tonight I have had pernod with everything. With brandy. With gin. With vodka. With Cointreau. With dram – dram – dram. With rum both amber and white. With whisky. With . . .' He turned and stared at the bottles. 'With Benedictine. With Tía María.'

Lindsey giggled and belched. She put her hand to her mouth. She fell backwards. Her feet hovered in the porthole. She disappeared. There was a splash followed by a brief silence as we admired her dramatic exit.

'Save her,' Lindo shouted. Young Bill did a Douglas Fairbanks and dived through the porthole. It was not a pleasant or easy task. The oily water was covered with a noxious layer of litter and scum; and Lindsey was not inclined to be saved. After a struggle he managed to get her to a wooden pontoon and, after another, more prolonged struggle, she was carried, protesting, down to her cabin to be subdued and sanitised.

On the sixth day in Cape Town I ceased procrastinating and took myself and my headache to the seaman's clinic. The doctor was very interested to hear I was from the *Amorina*. This simple piece of information enabled him to make an instant diagnosis; though he did take a blood sample which he was sure would confirm his opinion. He told me that Bjorn, who had exactly the same symptoms, had been in hospital for four days. Tests had revealed he had brucellosis, an obscure disease caught from drinking unpasteurised milk, not an uncommon hazard in Brazil. It all fitted. I don't usually drink milk but in Bahía and Rio I'd guzzled back gallons of the muck in the hope of regaining the weight I'd lost on the *Anna Kristina*. I also learnt that the disease, once contracted, was prolonged and exacerbated by drinking even pasteurised milk and eating dairy products such as butter and cheese. This explained why my headache often reached its zenith shortly after breakfast. The Heerengracht put on a sumptuous buffet for breakfast which included a generous choice of yoghurts.

Armed with antibiotics, assured by the prognosis that the headache would gradually diminish if I avoided milk and its by-products, and free from the delusion I had a brain tumour, I went to Budget Car Rental and acquired a vehicle.

That night we went for drinks with a group of local journalists. One of them, and I won't mention his name just in case, was working, as far as he was able within the constraints of the law, to further black rights and bring an end to apartheid. When I expressed surprise at the absence of 'white only' park benches, public toilets, cafés and bars, he told me that such obvious manifestations of apartheid had largely disappeared. He conceded that the recent reforms were not just 'cosmetic' as the furious reaction of the right-wing hardliners demonstrated. Anyway it would be difficult to simulate the goodwill that existed between the people, whatever their colour, in what he called the 'middle-ground'.

Despite the reforms which had generated greater social interaction, he was pessimistic for the government was, counter-productively, pursuing a policy of increasing residential segregation. The blacks, while free to mix with whites, were nevertheless expected to live in dormitory towns. The policy was spawning a host of mini Sowetos; breeding grounds for crime and terrorism. What the government saw as containment was backfiring. He estimated there would be a blood-bath within twenty years.

We also discussed less serious matters. I told them we were going on tour the next day. When I mentioned we were thinking of visiting Bloemfontein they clutched their brows and fell about laughing. The name had attracted me. It conjured up a vision of dignified old Dutch houses, fountains and flowery squares. Apparently, it was, in reality, a concrete eyesore where the inhabitants got their kicks from driving round and round the roundabout on Sunday mornings.

They told us where to go, where not to go and drew up a rough itinerary. They were very keen for us to go to Matjiesfontein, about two hours' drive north of Cape Town. They stressed we should stay in the Lord Milner Hotel, take a tie and be there before six o'clock. We were intrigued.

We set off early the next morning. Since it was only 150 miles to Matjiesfontein, we took a circuitous route through the Stellenbosch wine region. It reminded me a bit of the Tyrol. Majestic rocky crags cut into a cold, pastel blue sky above pine-clad slopes and manicured vineyards. The air was diamond hard and slightly chill. Summer here was just beginning. It was a picturesque landscape of chocolate-box mountains and carefully cultivated valleys dotted with white-washed farmhouses, solid and restrained except for the occasional flourish of a rounded gable. But to me it wasn't Africa.

We pressed on to Matjiesfontein. We rejoined the N1, the main road to Johannesburg, and entered a vast area of semi-desert known as the Great Karoo. It was a wilderness of rust-coloured rock, low scrub and *kopjes* (small hills), many of them flat-topped, resembling miniature Table Mountains. It was a harsh, forbidding landscape. I imagined the Boers toiling across with their ox-drawn wagons. We whizzed along the grey ribbon of road so fast that we nearly missed the sign to Matjiesfontein, which turned out to be a small cluster of white buildings looking lost and forlorn in surrounding desolation.

A line of venerable Victorian buildings faced a railway halt. This was it. The road petered out in the scrub of Karoo. It was like a mirage. I half expected the place to shimmer and fade away. I could feel the emptiness seeping in. But the Lord Milner Hotel, a symmetrical building with a central tower and a pair of castellated wing turrets pulled together by a spacious wrought-iron terrace, was solid enough. An Italianate fountain of four graduated stone basins tinkled discreetly in the forecourt.

The receptionist in her wood-panelled office seemed a bit frosty. She reminded me of the stereotyped English prep school headmistress, all tweeds and sensible shoes. She thawed a little when I gave our address as the *Amorina*, First Fleet Reenactment, Wharf 11.

'We have two rooms left. One has twin beds, bathroom ensuite and the advantage of a balcony.' She paused. We waited. She continued reluctantly. 'The other has a double bed, bathroom ensuite with twin adjacent baths but no balcony. Both are fifty-eight Rand per day inclusive.' I opted for the novelty of twin adjacent baths.

She handed us an information booklet and two bus tickets.

'The bus will leave for a tour of the town at six sharp.' I thought I detected a glimmer of amusement in her eyes.

Our accommodation was splendid, consisting of a hall-cum-dressing-room, bedroom and a bathroom so large that a more accurate description would have been bathroom with bedroom ensuite. The room itself glowed with highly polished antique furniture. I decided to skip the bus tour and enjoy, instead, Victorian comfort and luxury. From what I'd seen of the place you could walk round it in five minutes.

I lay on the bed and idly read the bus ticket.

NOR ANY DROP TO DRINK

Matjiesfontein Omnibus Company

Standard Conditions of Touring

Glasses are not transferrable.
Spillages strictly forbidden.
Stray cows may not be milked at stages.
Padkos may be taken along provided the
driver is not fed.
The throwing of bones from the upper deck
is strictly forbidden.
Spontaneous *Tickey Draais* when the bus
exceeds 5 miles per hour is prohibited.

I decided to go after all. I glanced at the information sheet. 'Jacket and tie', underlined in red and black, were required for dinner. Ladies were to be 'smart'. We were ordered 'to be seated by eight-fifteen p.m.'. I was gratified to note that 'no dogs or children under ten' were allowed. I thought the latter rule a little liberal. I'd have made it twenty-one.

At five to six a series of bugle blasts summoned us to the forecourt to await the bus. The Union Jack and the South African flag flying from the end towers were hauled down with due ceremony. A red, open-topped, double-decker bus trundled up accompanied by a final demented bugle blast and shuddered to a halt. Victorian music-hall favourites blared from a stereo in the cab. The manager sat behind the wheel staring grimly ahead. One of the porters, in claret-coloured jacket, sash and fez, clipped our tickets. We went upstairs. The seats were bare metal frames stripped of upholstery. We stood. The bell tinkled and we were off to the strains of 'Roll out the Barrel'. We rumbled to the end of the street and bumped about a hundred yards into the Karoo. We stopped and treated the wilderness to a defiant blast of 'Two Lovely Black Eyes'. We bumped back to the street and, roaring past the hotel at ten miles per hour, reached the other end of town in just under a minute. Once again we ventured a hundred yards into the Karoo, stopped and entertained the scrub with a hearty rendition of 'All the Nice Girls Love a Sailor'. Then we returned to the hotel to the more subdued strains of 'If You Were the Only Girl in the World'.

Before changing for dinner we enjoyed a long soak, head to toe, in the capacious, cast-iron adjacent bathtubs. It was a civilised interlude. It induced a feeling of goodwill and, among other things, amicable if inconsequential conversation. It struck me that many a marriage on the verge of breakdown through a failure to communicate could be saved if the antagonists were given the opportunity to lie, head to toe, in hot water and have a natter through a miasma of steam. All marriage-counselling bureaux should henceforth offer such a facility. Local councils should give grants to subsidise the installation of the dual bathtub system. Parliament should rush through a bill making it law that all new houses should have them and thus ensure a new era of domestic harmony. And note that sharing a bath is no substitute. It invariably leads to heated arguments about who should have their back to the taps.

So mellow did I feel that for the first time in twenty years my body clock failed to go off. I left Rosamund wallowing in foam and sprinted to the Lairds Arms, a pub attached to the north wing. (It was really part of the hotel.) I sat at the bar, savouring a Castle, and contemplated an arsenal of bullets and shells, most of them relics of the Boer War when the British had established a Remount Camp of 10,000 men and 20,000 horse at Matjiesfontein. The Karoo round about is still strewn with rusty bully beef tins preserved by the dry air. The walls were decorated with prints, sepia photographs of cricket teams and the usual bric-à-brac associated with the ambience of the traditional English country pub. A fire dutifully blazed.

A tall, gaunt English colonel (he may have been a general) tottered to the bar. He sported quizzical, tufted eyebrows, cropped white hair and a no-nonsense, straight-line, clipped white moustache. His watery blue eyes focused on my beard and then took in my white leather shoes. He sighed and shook his head. He'd probably dropped a few bully beef tins out there in the Karoo. He ordered two large whiskies. The barman offered to add water.

'I've been pouring my own water for eighty-five years and I'm not going to stop now,' he grated, reaching for the flask with a huge, blue-veined, shaking talon. He slopped about half a pint on the bar and a thimbleful in the whisky. He took a dog-leg route back to his wife. She had a brow like the Eiger, a jaw like a snowplough and a stare that would make the thorns drop out of a cactus. In the good old days she'd have been worth a regiment of Gurkhas. The barman stood to attention until he'd reached his seat.

Vulcanised rubber shrieked on tar. A group of tough-looking Afrikaner youths in sports jackets, cavalry twills and Oxford brogues bounced in. Their raucous shouts died to a murmur under the radioactive gaze of the colonel and his wife. A pear-shaped businessman oozed in accompanied by a ravaged, simpering ex-beauty who could hardly raise a hand for the weight of precious stones.

At seven-thirty the bugle blared. The colonel and his wife tipped back their whisky and stalked out. The Afrikaner youths became raucous again. They slammed their glasses down when they ordered beer. They had eight each in about thirty minutes. They left. Engines howled as they drove off into the night. I speculated. Were they the sons of local farmers? Each farm out here was about twenty miles apart. They weren't passing through – the barman knew them well. The nearest town was twenty-five miles away. What a life. Rosamund came to collect me.

The dining-room was gloomy, the atmosphere funereal. I could just about hear the sound of maceration through the steady clinking of cutlery. A sudden laugh would have brought the chandeliers down. It was a sacred place.

The head waiter presided from behind a lectern by the door.

He interrogated us. He led us to a small table lost in the shades of a Stygian gloom. I realised that the waitresses would need radar to find us there. For once I was not going to be put upon by a flunkey even if he was wearing a dinner jacket. I protested. He relocated us at a table under half a ton of crystal.

When I saw the menu I could understand why the place wasn't ringing with conversation. It was a strictly on with the nosebag, heads-down establishment. Dinner was a set ten courses terminating with coffee and candied peel – a good few sabre cuts above your After Eights, what! At Rand 15.50 (£4.30) a head it was a bargain banquet. You didn't waste time talking – you got on with it. I ordered two bottles of their most expensive red wine, loosened my tie and belt and set to. Black waitresses in black dresses with frilly white pinafores moved like phantoms between the tables. They deftly removed empty plates and replaced them with laden plates. The chandelier above shivered. Once it tintinnabulated icily as someone with heavy tread went past.

It was an excellent meal. Quality as well as quantity. Somebody out at the back knew how to cook. The average London restaurant would have trouble reproducing just one of the courses. By the end I was exhausted. I wiped the sweat off my brow. I forwent candied peel. I had two double Benedictines instead. This caused some mild consternation but they solved the problem by serving them in sherry glasses. I don't know why it is considered *de rigueur* in England to serve the amber ichor in glass thimbles. The Spanish serve it in goblets and the French are happy to dispense it in galvanised buckets on request.

We were the last to leave. I felt like a python that had swallowed a pig. We took a stroll through the four inter-connected lounges. They were beautifully furnished with genuine antiques. Mahogany and rosewood glowed. Cut glass and crystal refracted light. Mirrors shone. Chaste marble exhaled coolness. Intricately patterned tiled floors gleamed. Carpets did whatever they do. Silence and stillness. The colonel

NOR ANY DROP TO DRINK

Matjiesfontein Village

★★ TYYY

<u>R15.50</u>   <u>17.09.87</u>

<u>DINNER</u>

PATé MAISON

* * *

BOONTJIESOP

FRENCH ONION SOUP

* * *

CAPE MALAY PICKLED FISH

FILLET OF HAKE MEUNIERE

* * *

MUSHROOM CRêPES

* * *

GRILLED KAROO LAMB CHOP - MINT BUTTER

DAUPHINOISE POTATOES

* * *

ROAST SIRLOIN OF BEEF - HORSERADISH SAUCE

YORKSHIRE PUDDING   ROAST POTATOES

GREEN BEANS   SAVOURY RICE

CAULIFLOWER IN WHITE SAUCE

* * *

PATATS   SOUSBOONTJIES   SALAD

* * *

DESSERT BUFFET

* * *

CHEESE BOARD

* * *

CONA COFFEE   CANDIED PEEL

* * *

LH LANZERAC HOTELS

208

and his wife sat reading. I felt reckless. I gave them a burst on the Welsh harp as we left. They smiled and wished us good night. We returned to our Victorian boudoir. I sank into feather-bedded, quilted oblivion and arose to a lucid, clear-headed dawn. My headache had gone.

I went for a stroll in the garden. It was semi-wild. Restoration was still in progress. The air was crisp. The rough lawn squeaked beneath my lissom, unclerical tread. I left a trail in the argent gossamer. The astringent scent of shrubs and scrub tickled my nostrils. A solitary duck towed a chevron along the glittering waters of a huge stone tank. Green cohorts of cactus brandishing spiky clubs poured through breaches in the fence. Beyond, the flat summits of *kopjes* hovered above a tenuous film of mist which shrivelled and disintegrated under the rising sun. Soon a hard crystalline light encapsulated the landscape.

We decided to stay another night and planned a round trip through the mountain passes of the Grootwartberge. We left the main road at Lainsburg and climbed into a barren landscape of ravines, precipices and long, desolate escarpments. Iron-red rocks seemed to burn with the heat in which they were cast. Pale green filaments of vegetation traced the beds of dried-up watercourses down narrow ochre valleys. Eagles drifted on invisible thermals under aching blue skies.

We drove along unmetalled tracks trailing a magnificent plume of white dust. For over an hour we didn't see a single car. A troop of baboons crossed the road in front of us. We stopped. They stopped. When I got out they fled.

We reached the top of a pass. We were alone. The air was so clear we could see for ever. The stillness was palpable. The silence hissed. I closed the car door gently. To have slammed it would have shattered the whole fragile edifice. We were at the centre of a diamond.

We drove on to Oudtshoorn, a small town in an ostrich farming region. We brought three ostrich eggs – empty ones.

They syphon them out. One will make scrambled eggs for ten people.

After some difficulty we found the road to the Swartberg pass. A few miles out of town we rounded a bend. The road sloped down to a bridge over a small river. On the opposite hillside was a straggle of shacks. A crowd milled about in the road. It looked like a celebration. I slowed to a crawl. I stopped just over the bridge. It wasn't a celebration.

A middle-aged man, his face a mask of blood, staggered along the grass verge. A woman ran in front of the car shouting and gesticulating. A gang of teenagers danced around the reeling man. One of them, from less than six feet, threw a stone the size of half a brick into his face. I heard the bone crack. His knees buckled slowly and his body skewed sideways. I didn't wait to see more. I accelerated away.

What should I have done? Got out of the car and tried the big white *bwana* routine? Had the woman been shouting abuse or screaming for help? Was the victim her husband? She'd sounded hostile to me. But a few days later something happened which made me doubt my immediate assessment of the incident.

We pulled up in a village so Rosamund could take photographs of the children. As she was focusing a black Sophie Tucker started bellowing. At first I thought she was denouncing us in apocalyptic terms but it turned out she was ordering them to move closer, wipe their noses and generally compose themselves in a military fashion. By the time she'd finished they looked as though they were on parade.

We drove on into the emptiness and climbed the rugged heights of another mountain range. There were no more villages. From the head of the pass we looked down at an umber plain. A pall of smoke, miles long and hundreds of feet high, followed a livid, flickering ribbon of flame. Above, the wind soughed along crags deaf to the 'still, sad music of humanity'. But perhaps Wordsworth would have heard 'low breathings coming after' him. Edmund Burke might have described the place as sublime. It gave me the willies. My stomach rumbled. A ten-course meal called.

From Matjiesfontein we headed for Kimberley to see the Big Hole. It was a 480-mile drive but on the empty South African roads we made good time, reaching speeds of 110 m.p.h. For the first half of the journey the road traversed the sweeping undulations of the Great Karoo. We enjoyed the sense of space but the scenery was unremarkable. It would not be facetious to say that once you've seen one *kopje* you've seen 'em all. But there was a certain indefinable atmosphere engendered by the feeling of remoteness, the limpid absences, vast skies and the rocky, uncompromising wastes.

The Karoo gave way to a dusty yellow plain so flat we could see the curve of the earth. For the last seventy miles the road ran parallel to a railway line. Racing steam trains proved a welcome diversion. We beat them easily. I sometimes slowed up to enjoy the raw power, thunder, smoke, steam and hammering pistons of the locomotives often coupled together.

The Big Hole at Kimberley was a big hole. I was vaguely disappointed. It was not as vertiginously deep as those bird's-eye photographs in old school textbooks had led me to expect. And what I'd taken to be the Stygian entrance to profound, illimitable depths was a still, black pond. The guidebook informed me that '22.5 million metric tons of ground was excavated to produce 2,722 kg (14.5 million carats) of diamonds'. The surrounding museum, a replica of the mining settlement encompassing the church with all its original furnishings to a bar complete with rollicking drinking songs on tape, made the journey worthwhile.

We hurtled on eastwards to the Royal Natal National Park, a mere 350 miles. This sort of travelling, rushing from tourist hole to beauty spot, was against all my notions of how it should be done. But we wanted to see an elephant and so we continued our reckless pursuit of the noble, untamed pachyderm which has never tasted a doughnut or performed cumbersome gymnastics for the delectation of breadsnatchers.

I would have been happy to spend the short time available wining and dining at Matjiesfontein. There I could have explored the Little Karoo on foot, turned over stones, observed the minutiae of nature and worked up an appetite at the same time. And to those who say Matjiesfontein is not Africa but merely an anachronism, an outpost of colonial splendour and privilege, a senescent symbol of centuries of white rule entering a long overdue terminal phase, I say this. It is. But it is also living history. Whether you approve or disapprove, go there and experience the last vestiges of an Empire preserved, ironically, by the white tribe who fought that Empire in a long and bitter war. Go before it is too late. Tread where Cecil Rhodes and Olive Schreiner trod. Her cottage has been preserved. Hear ghosts in the ringing clarity of sunlight. See those who are about to become ghosts. The Karoo will always be there.

There were no elephants at the Royal National Park. It was small, minute compared with Kruger Park. Its *raison d'être* was not wildlife but scenery.

We were lucky to get the last vacant room; the Park Hotel was hosting a bowls tournament. This was a bonus. Once outside the immediate environs of the hotel we had the walks to ourselves.

We climbed the foothills, mountains by English standards, in the vast horse-shoe escarpment of the Drakensberg. The path wound up steep grassy slopes between gaunt outcrops of rock. We saw baboons and once a small antelope broke cover and bounded away. At the top of a ridge we viewed the grand sweep of the natural amphitheatre glowing in the late afternoon sun, radiating a golden light that lapped on the yellow grass around us.

On the way down we met a group of rangers; one white, ten

black. They all carried shotguns. They'd been hunting packs of dogs from the surrounding villages that enter the reserve to prey on the small deer. It made me think how precarious must be the Afrikaners' hold over the population – based as much on bluff as force. I thought of the isolated towns we'd passed through. I remembered the sight of a white woman pushing a pram down a wide sunlit street apparently oblivious of the hundreds of blacks around her.

Shadows filled the amphitheatre. The evening sun set the enclosing escarpment on fire.

We hadn't time to go north to Kruger Park. We'd almost given up hope of seeing an elephant when Rosamund spotted on the map the Addo Elephant National Park near Port Elizabeth. It was ideally situated. We could take it in and continue back to Cape Town along the Garden Route.

It was raining when we arrived two days later at the Addo Elephant Park. We went to the rangers' centre to get a map. We discovered this was the first significant day of rainfall for eighteen months. Somebody had seen forty elephants at the main waterhole that morning but that was before the rain had started.

The Addo elephant is slightly smaller than its counterpart that roams the great plains. Some 90 per cent of the park is covered with Spekboon – a stunted tree about ten feet in height. The succulent leaves and stems, which have the capacity to regenerate quickly, provide the elephant with its main source of food.

After an hour of driving along muddy tracks in a steady but fine rain we'd seen a few large tortoises, kudu and red hartebeest. We'd seen half an elephant – the back half. The front and more dramatic half was buried deep in thick bush. It ignored my foul exhortations. I felt like getting out and throwing rocks at it. The waterhole was, of course, deserted.

I drove on getting more and more irritable. It was like going to Egypt and finding the pyramids were on loan to Disneyland.

213

We stopped on some high ground and looked out over the gently undulating Spekboonveld glistening green in the pale rain and scarred with patches of red earth.

'They've got to be down there somewhere,' I said.

'Do you think we should?' Rosamund said. The track dropped sharply down a precipitous slope. It was a torrent of red, bubbling water.

'We'll get down all right,' I said. 'Getting back up may be a problem.' According to the map this was the only way in and out of this area of the reserve. We decided to risk it.

The car careered down the slope, sideways for the last half after I'd stupidly applied the brakes. I drove on skidding through patches of thick mud. Suddenly we came upon steaming mounds of elephant droppings. Branches torn from the Spekboon littered the track. Some of the trees had been snapped off mid-height. Much of the bush had been trampled flat. It looked as though a Panzer division had just preceded us.

We rounded a bend. Two adolescent elephants were coming towards us. We stopped. They stopped. They swung their heads from side to side, then crashed off into the bush.

We drove on expectantly. We came to a clearing where the bush had been devastated. A mother and her baby blocked the track a few feet ahead. They turned off to the left and stopped a few yards into the scrub. The mother seemed confused and agitated. Rosamund was fiddling frantically with her camera.

'The baby's half hidden,' she bleated.

'Take one of him,' I said, pointing to a magnificent bull with a full set of ivories about fifty feet away on the right-hand side of the road. We had a good view of him unobscured by bush. I wound down the window and leant back. Rosamund leant across.

'Hurry up, for Christ's sake, before he runs away.' She takes so long to take a photo you need a haircut by the time she's finished.

The bull swung his head from side to side.

'I wish he'd keep still,' Rosamund said.

'That's a warning signal,' I said. 'But he won't do anything. They always do that.'

Then he started swinging his whole body from side to side, pivoting on his back legs.

'He's working himself up into a right lather,' I said, beginning to doubt what I'd read in the book about elephant behaviour.

He advanced a few paces and stopped. He flared his ears. He pointed his rigid, trembling trunk straight at us. This was an unmistakable gesture of hostility and intent to commit GBH.

'That'll make a good one,' Rosamund said, frantically refocusing.

Suddenly I realised the cause of his rage. We'd cut the mother and baby off from the herd. She was still dithering about in the scrub a few yards to our left. I'd thought elephants were intelligent creatures. All she had to do was loop round us.

By now the bull was lumbering towards us, gathering momentum. This was no display of male *braggadocio*.

'Suffering Jesus! He means it,' I yodelled.

The front wheels scrabbled ineffectually, splattering the side windows with gobbets of red mud. I trod on the accelerator. It took a few long seconds for the tyres to wear away the mud and gain some traction on the shale below. We accelerated away, slithering sideways, the engine racing and whining as the tyres intermittently lost their grip. For one nasty moment Jumbo's tusks were nearly boring holes in the back window. It wasn't until I'd got into third gear that he dropped behind.

'I thought they were supposed to swerve away at the last minute,' Rosamund said.

'If I'd waited till the last minute he'd have tipped this Japanese biscuit tin upside down and trampled it till we oozed out of the key holes like cranberry sauce.'

'Oh shut up.'

We saw a few more elephants tearing branches off the Spekboon but we didn't linger. I took a quarter-of-a-mile run at the hill and hit the lower slope at 75 m.p.h. Even so we only just made it to the top.

I stopped the car on the brow of the hill. We looked back over the rain-shrouded Spekboonveld where the elephants' backs protruded through the glistening vegetation like granite boulders. I've been caught in two riots, nearly drowned twice, stranded on a coral reef, stung by a Portuguese man-of-war, struck by lightning, wrecked two cars, lost in the Malaysian jungle and the passenger on a cargo ship that caught fire in the Indian Ocean. This was another one for the list. I reached for a cigarette.

'And when are you going to give that up?' Rosamund asked.

'When I've finished the book.' But I didn't say which one.

We returned to Cape Town via the Garden Route along a spectacular coastline.

13

To Mauritius Across the Indian Ocean

When Handbag Bill came on board at Cape Town, Foul-Mouthed Fred was so amazed he forgot to swear. In fact he was rendered speechless for three days – not that Fred was capable of anything approaching the accepted definition of speech. His normal mode of communication consisted of grunts and roars of rage or pleasure liberally interpolated with four-letter words. On the day we sailed he showed signs of recovery.

'Bloody poofta,' he snarled and spat in the sea instead of on the deck.

Bill was so outrageously camp I thought he was in for a rough time. I was wrong. He was so uninhibited and disarmingly direct that he soon endeared himself to everyone on the ship. Even Fred gradually came round, though it was ten days before he deigned to sit, somewhat uncomfortably, at the same table as Bill.

We were supposed to set sail on Saturday 26 September but the wind was from the wrong direction. It would have blown us back to Rio via Tristan da Cunha. There wasn't much we could do about it except hang around the ship waiting for the wind to change. But Bill was delighted, as I discovered in my first conversation with him.

'This will give me time to finish my shopping. Now I'll be able to take back the toilet-roll holder.'

'Toilet-roll holder?'

'And exchange it for a tissue-paper dispenser.'

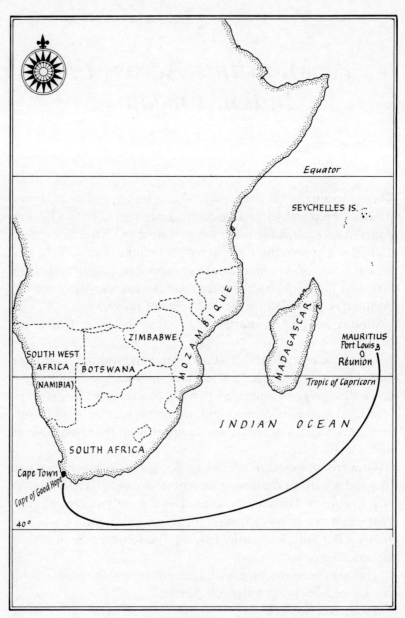

CAPE TOWN TO MAURITIUS

'Tissue-paper dispenser?'

'Is there an echo around here?'

'Echo?'

'There it goes again. Now don't get flustered, dear. It's just my way. After all, how were you to know? Let me explain. When I came aboard on a recce there wasn't a toilet-roll holder in the loo. The thought of my personalised, patterned paper rolling about the floor was too much. So I took myself off and bought one. When I got back I found that some sweetie had put one up. I suppose I could have two. One port. One starboard.'

'I hear you've brought a lot of luggage.'

'Just a few essentials, like an anti-snoring pillow. Not for me, of course, but I never know who I might end up sleeping with. I suppose I have been a bit naughty. I didn't dare bring it on in the day. I skulked on in the dead of night. With three porters. Three! Imagine that.'

'Three porters?'

'There it goes again. Must be Table Mountain. I'm going to take an inventory. I may have overlooked something. Come and see my things. They might amuse you. Bring a notebook and your secretary.'

'I haven't got one.'

'You type it all yourself? No wonder your fingernails are in such a state. Who's the beautiful girl you're always with, then?'

'That's Rosamund, my wife.'

'But you're so affectionate all the time. I didn't dream you were married. Where is she? This is the first time I've seen you without her.'

'She's climbing Table Mountain with Jonathan King and a few of the others.'

'And you're down here flirting with me. Come and look at my things. I promise to be good.'

Bill hadn't been exaggerating. It was a miracle he'd managed with three porters. He was in a four-berth cabin. Luckily for him one bunk was vacant. He had utilised every cubic inch of space and had commandeered nearly all the available drawers.

'I always cope somehow,' he said, pulling open a drawer beneath a lower bunk and removing it completely.

'You see there's all this space underneath. Runs the length of the bunk. Makes a nice little wine cellar. Champagne, dear!'

From then on I could hardly keep up with him. The cabin was almost an Aladdin's cave. Although I scribbled away frantically I missed many items.

'A witch's mask,' he began, producing it with a flourish and then throwing it carelessly aside.

'What on earth for?'

'For parties, of course. I never travel unless I'm fully equipped for parties. Look! I've brought an Arab's headgear; streamers; invitation cards; Hallowe'en cards; artificial cobwebs; balloons; rolls and rolls of crêpe paper; a white dinner jacket; a selection of bow ties; lots and lots of . . .'

'What's that?' I asked, pointing at a strange-looking gadget.

'That's an electric acupuncture machine. It's not working very well. I must get it serviced in London. I'll just have to make do with my massage equipment. Look at this. It's a back massager. Very phallic. These two balls rotate. Good for the spine. I'll have to train somebody to use it. I've brought lots of massage equipment. Couldn't bring my jacuzzi, though. They wouldn't let me on the plane with it.'

He pulled open another drawer crammed with packets.

'This is my lucky dip. What have we here? I can never remember what I've brought.' He selected an envelope and poured the contents on to a bunk.

'Ah! Bookmarks.'

'Bookmarks!' I exclaimed. There were at least a hundred.

'I must get that mountain removed.'

'Why do you need so many bookmarks?'

'I don't. I give them away. Just little presents. Then people will think of me when they're reading a boring book. I hope you're going to put me in your book. I've always wanted to be famous.'

'No.'

'No!' He looked startled.

'There's that echo again,' I said.

'You are a tease. What else have I got? Let me see. Sew-on badges; reflective stickers; coasters for the bar; cards for all occasions; cocktail umbrellas; my own wine bottle labels and . . . let's go on to another drawer. Keep some surprises for later. This is just part of my larder. Birch tea for my gout. Avocado salad dressing. Can't go anywhere without it. Chrome Tai Chi balls. They're in the wrong drawer. Ah! A jar of Umeboshi plums. They counteract acidity. I'm glad I didn't forget that. Now where are the jelly beans? I shall throw a wobbler if I've left them in the taxi. I always like to leave a little something if the driver's been nice. This time I was positively festooned. Festooned! A kilo of jelly beans!'

I refrained from exclaiming. Bill rummaged frantically.

'Ah, here they are. Now what did I leave in the taxi? I hope it was something compromising. What else have I got? Clothes pegs. A night mask in case I meet a shy lone stranger. Thirty tins of sparkling apple juice. Cards. Monopoly. Fifteen litres of assorted fruit juice. Crystal key-rings for people who've been sweet. Japanese tooth powder made from egg-plant ash and sea salt. Here, you'd better have that.'

He was right. Cigarette smoke, Coca-Cola and red wine had taken their toll.

'Matching towels. My own pillow. Five kilos of nuts. I hope you're taking all this down.'

On 28 September, after a two-day delay caused by southeasterly gales, we sailed out of Cape Town Harbour escorted by an armada of yachts. Apart from the few unscheduled visits to Porto Santo, Cape Verde and Bahía, this leg to Mauritius was to be the first significant deviation from the original route of the

First Fleet. They had sailed nonstop to Botany Bay on an arduous, two-month, gale-lashed final leg. Ignorant of the then undiscovered Bass Strait, they had sailed deep into the Roaring Forties on a course that took them south of Tasmania before turning north up the east coast of Australia.

The Re-enactment Fleet was, however, to break the final stage of this epic voyage into three legs. There were sound commercial reasons behind this decision. The last two legs would be, and, in fact, turned out to be the most popular, especially with Australians. Thus historical accuracy was sacrificed for the extra revenue to be gained by a higher turnover of paying trainees.

When we gained the open sea Walther called a general meeting to deliver his usual introductory talk. He sat at the end of the mess beside the ship's mascot, a polar bear with a Greenpeace badge pinned to its chest. Handbag Bill lounged in the doorway cradling his travelling companion, a blue-grey koala. We were to be treated to two monologues.

'Ve vill be von big happy floating family,' Walther instructed. 'Zere are now forty-eight people on board, ze highest number yet. Zere vill haf to be two sittings for lunch and dinner. Ve vill haf to be patient like ze bear here vich never complains.'

'Oh dear,' Handbag Bill began. 'I can't speak for Kenny the Koala. He doesn't like other bears, especially polar bears. He likes to be the centre of attention. If he'd known there was going to be competition he wouldn't have come.'

Walther ignored him and, without pausing, continued his own monologue.

'Ve haf three thousand nautical miles to Mauritius. It vill be ze experience of a lifetime. I vant you all to make ze most of it. You vill enjoy yourselves.'

'This is the first time Kenny's left home. He didn't mind the flight. The stewardesses were so sweet to him. But how he's going to stand up to the rigours of such a long sea voyage I don't know.'

'Ve all must pull together as ve pull on ze ropes. Ve must verk as a team. Ve are all needing each other.'

'Perhaps I should have brought Benny instead.' Handbag Bill passed round a photo of a big brown bear slumped on a sofa. 'He's a very experienced traveller. Trouble was he was beginning to enjoy being body-searched by the customs. I was getting very jealous. They did the most intimate things to him.'

'Cabin doors are not to be locked. Veather side doors are to be kept shut. Safety harness is to be vorn up ze rigging.'

The ship was now rolling about twenty degrees from side to side. The audience started to thin out as many of the new trainees turned green. Some went below and did not re-emerge for three days.

'I hope you don't go that colour, Kenny. It doesn't go with any of the clothes I've brought. I'd better take you out for some fresh air.'

'Ven ve get off ze continental shelf ze vaves vill be further apart and zen ze motion vill not be so violent. Zey bunch up in zese shallow vaters.'

The winds were unfavourable. For over a week we were obliged to motor-sail or simply motor to make any progress. If you have a strong wind and a big swell rolling up from astern or even from an angle of forty-five degrees, the motion of the ship, although dramatic, settles into a predictable rhythm; and sailing under such conditions can be an exhilarating experience. What we now underwent was quite the opposite. The winds were contrary and the *Amorina* was forced to motor into oncoming waves. There was no rhythm; no glorious rise and fall on a twenty-foot swell under full sail. Instead the ship bucked, slewed and jolted through the sea's attrition in an effort to meet an artificially imposed schedule. In the old days of sail, without an engine as a backup, they would have either heaved to or run with the wind.

There were casualties. Early in the morning of the third day in a heavy southwesterly swell, strengthening wind and increasing sea, Margaret tottered out of the mess door weatherside and into the galley leaving both doors open. A rogue wave slammed into the ship and the top three feet burst over the deck. It doesn't sound much but the rounded crown of this wave was thirty feet across so a considerable tonnage of water was dumped on the deck and found its way into the bowels of the ship. The galley was swamped. Margaret was found floating in two feet of water with pots and pans bobbing around her head. Plug sockets sizzled and sparked before the fuses blew. Luckily they were situated high up the walls near the ceiling otherwise she'd have been electrocuted.

Water poured into the mess, cascaded down the companionway and flooded the dry store beneath, to be known, from then on, as the 'wet' store.

Heather, an elderly South African lady, was flung head first into the rail and sustained a wound to her forehead that needed eight stitches. Suzanne broke a finger in the galley. Keith, a young bank manager from Hampshire, was hurled from his bunk, bounced off a chest of drawers and landed in Foul-Mouthed Fred's bunk, which, fortunately for him, was vacant at the time.

The anchors pounded against the bow. The incessant booming drove Sven out of his forward cabin. He exercised his Captain's prerogative and commandeered the bar to sleep in. He kicked us out at midnight and locked the door. It was a tough week.

By the end of the week the swell eased as the wind fell from a high of force nine to a miserable force one. Conditions improved but we were behind schedule and, more seriously, had used up too much fuel in this early stage of the leg. What we needed was a strong southwesterly to drive us in a long loop northeast to Mauritius. The wind continued to be fickle, veering from northwest to southsoutheast to westsouthwest. By the tenth day Walther and Sven were forced to acknowledge that things were not going according to plan.

The day started well, bright and sunny. Three killer whales, their muscular backs arching out of the water, raced purposefully towards the *Amorina* like fighter planes intercepting a lumbering bomber. They kept pace with us for a few minutes and then, either having satisfied their curiosity or finding the ship inedible, peeled away in search of other prey.

Walther was delighted. No. That's an understatement. He was enraptured. His eyes twinkled. The corner of his mouth tugged into a smile.

'Vales,' he whimpered. His hands twitched. I thought he was going to start dribbling.

Late that day I heard a rumour that we were short of fuel. I went straight to the wheelhouse. The atmosphere was tense. Walther was plucking nervously at his beard. This was a bad sign. Sven kept pushing his chin forward until his mouth was a straight hard line. This was even worse. They looked up. Their eyes flicked away. Not even a grunt of acknowledgement. Bjorn, the chief engineer, smiled placidly and nodded.

The radio crackled. Sven snatched the phone off its cradle.

'*Amorina. Amorina. Bounty* calling. Do you read me?' It was Captain Small.

'*Bounty. Bounty. Amorina* reading you loud and clear.' Sven dispensed with his usual time-wasting effusions.

'How many two-hundred-litre oil drums have you got?' Captain Small asked. 'Over.'

Sven looked at Walther. Walther looked at Bjorn. Bjorn looked out of the window. 'One,' he said. I knew the one. They used it as an ashtray in the engine-room.

'Oh shit,' said Walther. He actually clutched his brow. It was the first time I'd heard him use a scatalogical expletive.

'We have one. Over,' Sven said, grating his teeth.

Captain Small seemed surprised to hear this singular piece of information.

'We have a number,' Captain Small said cagily, 'but they're full of lubricating oil. I think we could rustle up four twenty-five-litre containers. Three hundred litres a trip. Call me back when you've worked out your requirements. Over.'

Calculators were reached for, punched, shaken and hurled in disgust back on the chart table. Like the ship's torches, they were repositories for long-defunct batteries.

They looked expectantly at Bjorn. His lips moved silently. Bjorn was immensely unflappable. He knew his job. What this crowd on the bridge did, did not do, or undid, did not disturb his equanimity. The vagaries of the wind and waves did not worry him. His sole concern was the engine. A finer machine never felt the tickle of a feather duster in the Science Museum. The Germans had commandeered it when they invaded Norway and installed it as a generator on an airfield. After the war the Norwegians had sold it to the Swedes. The Swedes had installed it on the *Amorina* and probably hoped never to see the like of it again.

'It will take thirty trips in the rescue boat,' said Bjorn, presenting them with the harsh reality rather than an abstraction. Sven stretched his mouth. Walther dropped the beard hair he'd been contemplating. There was what's commonly known as a pregnant silence before Sven radioed this last snippet of information to the *Bounty*. Captain Small, after another silence during which we could almost hear the rattling of abaci, eventually spoke.

'I think we could spare nine thousand litres. Thirty trips. The transfer will take at least two days.' This, as it turned out, was a very optimistic prognostication.

'They should be able to spare nine thousand litres,' said Bjorn. 'Easily. The *Bounty* can carry ninety tons of fuel to our twenty.'

After this the conversation became incomprehensible. Charts were pored over. Books on navigation were consulted. Sextants were brandished. When Sven started throwing pencils around I retreated to the deck.

I stood beside Peter Simpson-Jones who had been listening at the door.

'How we got this far I'll never know,' he said. A pencil whizzed past his ear and disappeared over the rail. He didn't flinch. I lit a cigarette. Peter craned his neck, straining to hear. He was an ex-naval man, the owner of two ocean-going yachts and a very experienced sailor. I knew that we were short of fuel but all the talk about longitude and latitude had confused me. I asked him to elucidate – to reduce the situation to the essentials.

'We're in trouble,' he said. That much I already knew from the ragged state of Walther's beard. Peter marshalled his thoughts.

'We're ten days out of Cape Town. We've travelled nine hundred and eighty miles – most of it motoring because the winds haven't behaved as they should. We have two thousand three hundred miles to go by the planned route. We have nine days' fuel left. Got that? We have three options.'

'Hang on. I'll get my notebook.' Peter was a valuable source of information and had the ability to unravel even Walther's more convoluted statements.

'We have three options,' he resumed. 'One: to continue further south in the hope of finding more favourable winds. We're only about one degree from the Roaring Forties. But I'm afraid they're not roaring. They're asleep.

'Two: make for Port Dauphin in South Madagascar, one thousand eight hundred miles away, and hope that we can refuel there. Dicey. There's a civil war on there.

'Number three is the one I favour. Motor northeast to Durban. It's only five hundred and forty miles as the crow flies. Refuel and then proceed direct to Mauritius. That's the only fail-safe option.'

'I thought using the engine was anathema to you dedicated sailors.'

'It is. But I have a plane to catch on 28 November. I have to

be in London on the twenty-ninth. There's a Channel Tunnel
Committee meeting. I'm the linguistic co-ordinator.'

'So you don't think we're going to make it to Mauritius on
time.'

'We could. But not at this rate. Depends what decision they
make. They can be relied upon to make the wrong one.'

The commotion in the wheelhouse died down. Sven emerged.

'I'm going below to change,' he announced portentously.
Bjorn emerged, lighting a cigarette. We looked at him. He
shrugged.

'They've made a decision. They've decided to discuss it
further. Sven's going over to the *Bounty* to talk to Captain
Small face to face.'

'More time wasted,' Peter groaned.

Half an hour later Sven was back on deck in full regalia.
Sunlight glinted on his epaulettes. He marched towards the
stern. He stopped. His body stiffened. His hands clenched and
unclenched. The rescue boat still hung from its davits. Sven
exploded.

'Who is ze von not getting ready ze rubber duck when I am
putting on ze uniform. Time vasting incomp . . . incomp . . .
in . . .' He reverted to Swedish. First time I've understood
Swedish. Walther came out of the wheelhouse. He went back in
faster than a stoat up a drainpipe.

It was mid-afternoon when Sven returned. He looked happy –
too happy.

'He's had a few,' somebody remarked as he struggled up the
ladder.

'Ve are going to follow ze *Bounty*,' he announced. 'Ve vill sail
more south to find ze big winds. But first ve vill get fuel from ze
beautiful, beautiful *Bounty*. Captain Small is a fine man. A real
English gentleman.'

'Oh God,' said Peter, 'we'll end up at the South Pole.'

Bjorn and Petra took the dinghy over to the *Bounty* on a trial run with the 200-litre drum lashed in the centre. Diesel was pumped down into the drum from the deck of the *Bounty*. They returned, battling through six-foot waves. The fuel was then pumped, with great difficulty, up to the inlet on the boat deck. The whole operation took forty minutes but, as they gained experience, they reckoned that they could reduce it by five to ten minutes. They managed another run before darkness.

The next day the wind came. Much rubbing of hands and baring of teeth. The day after the wind went. More pencils hit the waves. Then the fun began. They decided to spend the day refuelling.

A team was scraped together. I say 'scraped' because it certainly wasn't organised. People who just happened to be wandering by were asked to perform certain tasks. Two were put in charge of the bow and stern lines of the dinghy. Another was assigned the job of holding the fuel line (the fire hose) in the inlet. I was given the important task of lowering the electric pump on a rope to the dinghy. I then had to pay the rope out or draw it in as the fuel drum rose and fell with the waves. I also had to prevent the electric cable from becoming tangled and contend with the fuel line which hung down from the boat deck above. Peter Doc and Lars took the dinghy on the first run. It went slowly but well.

The next run was entrusted to Foul-Mouthed Fred. Another Australian, Gordon, who had joined at Cape Town, volunteered to assist Fred.

'Forty fucking minutes,' snarled Fred. 'I'll fucking do it a lot fucking quicker. Fuck me if I don't.' Nobody took up his offer. And off they went in a welter of spray.

Fred clipped perhaps one minute off the journey there and back. The process of pumping the diesel in and out of the drum could not be shortened. However, time could be saved by the efficiency of the reception team. As Fred manoeuvred the dinghy alongside the *Amorina*, Gordon threw up the bow line. Claire failed to catch it. It fell in the sea. Fred got very excited as he saw his record slipping away. For all his skill and courage, the savagery of his language was counter-productive. It only flustered people and generated an air of hysteria. Eventually the dinghy was secured fore and aft.

I lowered the pump. Fred grabbed it with one hand and held it on top of the drum. He had to hold on with the other. Likewise Gordon, who had to insert the suction tube and then prime and start the pump. They had done well to complete the run in just over forty minutes. In calm seas it would have been a difficult operation. In these conditions, soaked in spray and working one-handed in a bucking rubber dinghy slippery with diesel oil, it was hazardous. But Fred was determined to beat the forty-minute record. He set off again, his monotonous oaths rising above the laboured whine of the outboard motor.

He failed again to break the time. No sooner had the bow line been attached on his return than it tore through the rubber mounting bracket. Fred frantically tried to re-start the outboard motor as the dinghy turned side-on and started to drift back at an increasing speed. The person in charge of the aft line had secured it and wandered off, thinking that his job was done. It was only Ian's quick thinking and grasp of Fred's predicament that averted disaster. He rushed to the aft line and cast it off. What would have happened to the heavily laden dinghy when the aft line snapped tight in rough seas at four and a half knots, we dreaded to think. It took twenty minutes to re-attach the bow line.

By the time Fred set off on his third, final and most disastrous attempt to break the record, he was rabid. His incoherent cursing attained the dithyrambic fury of a pagan chant at a human sacrifice.

I will never be sure what happened then, since Fred has been remarkably reticent about the matter. The bow and aft lines had been secured without incident. I had lowered the pump. Gordon had inserted the suction pipe and was trying to start the pump when Fred fell into the sea. He was lucky. He managed to grasp the rubber tyre that had been hung over the side to prevent the dinghy from banging into the side of the ship.

We all leant over the rail and admired Fred as he was towed through the waves, his face a mask of concentration. At least a minute passed before it dawned on us that the situation was potentially very serious. People rushed about waving their arms. Somebody suggested lowering a rope and went off in search of one.

I was the most experienced person there. What to do? I couldn't let go of the rope because the electric cable was wrapped around Fred's leg. If Fred went, the pump would go with him.

'Tell them on the bridge,' I yelled. 'Tell them to slow the engine.'

Walther and Sven emerged. Like us, they seemed temporarily mesmerised by the sight of Fred being towed through the southern latitudes of the Indian Ocean.

'He's in the water! He's in the water!' Sven shouted.

'Man overboard!' Walther bellowed.

They rushed back to the bridge to cut the engine. And got jammed in the door.

In the meantime Fred saved himself through brute strength. After various contortions he extricated his leg. Then he let go with one hand, and, reaching back, seized the rope ladder. It doesn't sound much of an achievement but in those seas it took determination and guts.

Once on deck Fred went berserk. He stripped to his underpants and prepared to get back on the dinghy. I suspect that this was a gesture — an act of bravado.

'Go below and get dry clothes,' Sven ordered diplomatically. 'Ve don't vant you catching cold.'

'Ah you can stuff the fucking job,' snarled Fred, and retired. This, for Fred, was a most graceful way of acknowledging he'd had enough.

Sven was visibly relieved. He stood arms akimbo, looking

pleased with himself. A squat plastic twenty-five-litre drum slid between the rails. It crashed to the deck beside him and ruptured. A fountain of diesel oil enveloped him.

'*Feta!*' he spat and kicked it up in the air. He followed Fred below to change.

Bogdan the Brave and Rick, a South African, took over. They had just finished pumping up the fuel and were preparing to leave when Sven reappeared in full uniform.

'I'm going over to ze beautiful *Bounty*,' he announced. 'I can take maybe three or four trainees with me for a visit. Ve are going to do an exchange for ze afternoon.'

'I don't believe it,' said Peter. 'Pleasure trips at a time like this.'

Rosamund and Eve decided to go. Margaret wanted to as well but common sense prevailed. Peter Doc forbade it. One had to have good timing and agility to negotiate the rope ladder.

The dinghy received its human cargo without mishap. The lines were cast off. Bogdan caught the stern line and started the motor. Rick missed the bow line. It fell into the sea. It passed under the dinghy. The motor spluttered.

'Put it in neutral, you fucking idiot,' Fred yelled.

It was too late. The bow line was wrapped around the propeller. The motor died completely. The dinghy turned sideways into a wave.

'I'm piss-wet already,' raged Sven.

We watched, fascinated, as the dinghy drifted away and passed behind the ship. We rushed to the stern. Sven's curses grew fainter and fainter. Rosamund and Eve looked forlorn and vulnerable as they rose on the crest of a wave and then disappeared into a trough. I waved to Rosamund. She waved back. Bogdan had cantilevered the motor out of the water and was struggling to unravel the rope. I was only slightly worried. I had great faith in Bogdan. Unlike Fred, he didn't get excited when things went wrong. Peter consoled me.

'Think nothing of it, dear boy,' he said. 'Neptune is probably so amused by the antics of these clowns that he's decided to be merciful. Pleasure trips to the *Bounty* indeed.' He shook his head and stalked off.

Bogdan and Rick returned with a load of fuel and four trainees from the *Bounty*. Everything went smoothly. We'd perfected the routine. The pump whirred contentedly.

'It's all going well,' observed Peter Doc, tempting fate.

The fumes grew stronger. A warm, sticky fluid soaked the back of my T-shirt. A stream of diesel oil ran across the deck and bubbled along the scuppers. I turned. Gallons of fuel were cascading down the wall of the mess. The fellow in charge of holding the hose in the inlet had gone for lunch. The hose had extracted itself. I went below to change.

We were about ten days from Mauritius when I decided that the rigours of the watch system were not conducive to writing. It wasn't the lack of sleep that prevented me from writing – I can do with four hours a night – but the disruptive nature of the working hours themselves. Twelve to four, eight to twelve and so on. Something had to be done. After all, as one of the few people going the whole way, I had, by now, done my share of watches. Besides, I was supposed to be writing a book. What I needed was a return to the normal pattern of life – a routine. I ambushed Walther on the deck and broached the subject with my usual tact and diplomacy.

'Hey Walther, I want to talk to you,' I said, prodding his nascent potbelly.

'I'm busy,' he replied, and hurried off. When it came to special requests Walther was telepathic.

'You're always busy, so now will be as good a time as any,' I said as I pursued him across the foredeck.

'Vat you vant?'

'I vant – sorry – I want to be excused watches. I want time off to write.'

'Ach, you poor thing. Everyone else is writing. Vy not you? It is easy to write. I myself haf written a wery amusing piece about ze freezers turned into bison.'

'Bison?'

'Ya! Bison! Ze freezers come loose in ze storm. Zey stampede and attack our friend Gordon in ze dark hours. Zey hurl zemselves upon him and pin him to the floor. I make ze corners of ze freezers into horns. A wery goot pun like yourself is always making. Ze Swedish for corner is also meaning a horn.'

'Yeah, yeah. Very amusing. Now come on, Walther. I'm being serious. I haven't written a word for three weeks. I can't be expected to do two jobs. Writing a book isn't easy.'

'No, no and von final no!'

'I'll take to drink,' I said.

Walther exploded. He doubled up. He clutched his stomach. He clawed at the air. He banged the wall. He clung to a rope. He took off his glasses and wiped his eyes. He replaced his glasses and looked at me. Then he went through the whole process again.

'Take to trink,' he gasped. 'Ven are you not trinking? Your bar bill last leg vas enough to pay ze whole crew and I do not joke vith you.'

'I haven't paid it yet,' I said meaningfully. Walther relented.

'Suzanne needs help in ze galley. Ze hours vill be regular. I vill see vat I can do.' And with that he stalked off.

I smiled inwardly. This was the result I'd anticipated. Suzanne and I had hatched a plot. Over many gins and tonics in the bar I'd explained my predicament. She had sympathised and had come up with a solution. She needed some help in the galley, 'some' being the operative word. What she really wanted was a companion. It was lonely work. She admitted this freely. Of course people called in but she found them irritating. They usually prefaced their visits with some inanity like 'What's for lunch?' as sixty sausages sizzled on the huge hotplate beneath their noses. There's no reply to such a question.

Later that day Walther brought me the good news.

'I haf talked vith Suzanne. You are to vork in ze galley from ten till noon and from four till six, seven days a week. Short hours. No more getting up in ze middle of ze night. Ve giff you a trial veek. Zen if you are goot you can help her for ze whole of ze next leg. And von more thing. I don't vant to see you in the bar in ze afternoons. I haf granted zis favour for you to write ze grand vork on zis our epic voyage. You go to your cabin and write. I vill inspect your vork. Understood!'

'*Jawohl Sturmbannführer!*' I snapped, crashing to attention.

'You are now a galley slave,' he said ominously. 'Behave like von.'

I'd got what I'd wanted but I felt uneasy. I knew that somehow I'd been outmanoeuvred.

The next day I reported dutifully for work at dead on ten. The galley was about ten feet by six from wall to wall. Subtract the space taken up by the fridge, cooker, sink and work surfaces and the floor area was reduced to about six by four. Insert Suzanne and there wasn't much room left for me.

She was sitting in the corner with both feet in the stainless-steel sink. The sea was still very rough and the ship was listing about fifteen degrees. This was her way of hanging on.

'Well, what do you want me to do?' I asked, eager to show willing.

'Nothing much. There isn't much to do but don't tell Walther. Just try to look busy. You can close the door for a start,' she said, lighting a cigarette. 'Walther knows I smoke in here but likes me to be – how you say?'

'Discreet,' I proffered.

'Discreet.' She repeated it a few times. 'Good. You can teach me English.'

'But your English is excellent. All you Swedes speak English remarkably well.'

'I'm not Swedish. My father is Estonian and my mother is –'

Walther appeared in the doorway. Suzanne blew smoke at the ceiling.

'It is goot that you are at vork on time but vy you hang around talking?'

'We're discussing the lunch menu, Walther,' I said.

'Hah. Tinned ham and salad again, I haf no doubt.' He closed the door with a bang.

'Good idea,' Suzanne said. 'I was wondering what to do. You'll find a big tin of ham in the cool room and bring up three cabbages. Here's your shopping bag.' She handed me a plastic potato sack. 'And move the cornflakes around,' she called after me.

'Where to?' I asked, pausing in the doorway.

'Anywhere,' she said, clutching her brow. 'Just try to look busy. Walther will be watching you for the first few days. Moving cornflakes will not strain you. I want you to appear — how you say?'

'Diligent,' I replied as I departed.

After I'd done the 'shopping' I went to the dry store to move the cornflakes around. It was, by the ship's standards, a gourmet's goldmine. I found all sorts of odd tins of esculent material in the darker recesses; odd in the strict sense that they were not one of a pair and even odder because they were the lost brethren of packs of twenty-four. I removed the odd tin of salmon, pâté and crabmeat to my cabin for personal consumption. I salved my conscience with the thought that one tin of crabmeat wouldn't go far divided by forty-two.

I was re-locating a carton of cornflakes when Walther's face appeared pressed against the glass of the single window embedded in the steel wall. I acknowledged him with a friendly thumbs-up gesture. He looked pained. Then I remembered that, according to Suzanne, in Sweden, or, at least, in the Gothenberg region, this gesture did not have the same benevolent connotations as it had when performed by a Roman emperor or a London taxi driver. In Gothenberg it means insert digit into appropriate nether orifice and rotate. Walther vanished.

I've always been the master of the social gaffe, trivial or spectacular. Once at a dinner party I inadvertently offended the hostess by asking if the *gaspacho* was tinned. It was an innocent question meant as a compliment. All my friends' attempts at the dish had proved lukewarm disasters. I had therefore assumed that a good *gaspacho* couldn't be had outside the metropolitan area of Madrid and that her *tour de force* could not possibly be homemade. Tortuous logic. She was offended. She made it known visibly and volubly. Luckily she was an acquaintance whose patronage I was not sad to lose.

Now for the gaffe spectacular. This occurred at a party. It was a good party. The wine tasted pleasantly expensive. It was also pleasant to stand in the toilet and contemplate a Braque. Anyway, to save the editorial lead, I was wandering about in a state of mild euphoria when a sharp burning sensation at my fingertips told me it was time to relinquish my cigarette. I was standing beside what appeared to be a lump of driftwood masquerading as an ashtray. I extinguished my cigarette thereon. There was a polite uproar – it was a Henry Moore. And they weren't mollified when I suggested that a Black and Decker sander would easily remove the minuscule burn mark.

When I returned to the galley Suzanne was putting the finishing touches to the cabbage salad. She poured a tin of fruit salad over it. The cold ham was bolstered with salami and assorted cheeses.

'I'll cook the buggers a proper meal for dinner,' she said. 'Get four joints of beef out of the port-side freezer and bring up a bag of potatoes.'

And so ended my morning duties. I was on to a good number, as they say at British Leyland. Or so I thought.

*   *   *

That afternoon the wind strengthened and the swell rose. We were under full sail in an effort to catch up with the rest of the fleet. They were two days ahead of us.

By five o'clock conditions in the galley were appalling. With the oven full on in a belated attempt to defrost the huge joints of beef, with three huge cooking pots steaming on the stove, and with Suzanne radiating palpable waves of body heat, the atmosphere was so thick I felt like a tadpole in custard. Add to this the twenty-five-degree list, the violent jolting, the occasional splashes of scalding water, the cigarette smoke, the floor slippery with grease and the mind-bludgeoning cacophony of Frank Zappa pouring at full volume from the radio-cassette suspended from the fire-sprinkler, and you have an approximation of the medieval conception of hell.

'Do we have to listen to this anarchic drivel?' I snarled, as the radio dealt me a severe blow behind the ear.

'Put what you like on,' Suzanne said, 'but I want noise, lots of noise.'

I removed the Zappa cassette. A ringing silence gradually gave way to the sound of the wind moaning in the broken air extractor and the intrusive, almost mocking, hissing and splashing of the waves. Then I appreciated her desire for a constant barrage of electric, artificial noise. It was an essential gesture of defiance against this sweltering, steaming, crazily tilting private hell of hers. I put on the Rolling Stones. The first track turned out to be 'Nineteenth Nervous Breakdown'. The air pulsed to the steady but crude rhythm of our choice.

'Watch out!' she shrieked above the din. She prised open the oven door with a bare foot. A blast of hot air and steam billowed out as she extracted a three-foot-long stainless steel tray, radiant with heat. Two joints of beef oozed and spluttered in a mess of bubbling scum-pocked water. She poured this away into a cooking pot. She didn't use oven gloves but two thin damp dish cloths. Her hands, wrists and feet were covered in scar tissue and livid red weals. A large unhealed burn glowed on her forearm. She hacked at a joint with a carving knife. The core was still frozen solid. She took a cleaver and bludgeoned it in half. She hurled the tray back in the oven and kicked the door shut.

'Fucking hell!' she snarled, mopping her sweat-streaming brow with a dish cloth. 'I should've stayed in Gothenberg.'

Suddenly the ship lurched violently and I found myself drowning in her massive embrace.

'Geroff,' I honked, surfacing for air between the heaving swell of her breasts. 'Geroff, I'm a happily married man.'

We staggered apart, reaching for the grab handles. Pots clanged. Knives and cleavers shot along the floor. Scalding water slopped down the side of the cooker. Throughout the ship the usual cry went up. 'Who's on the helm? Who's on the helm?' It only took a momentary lapse in concentration to let the ship wander off course and throw everyone off balance.

'You needn't worry,' Suzanne said. 'I don't take learners to bed. Not for internal use. I only like men over forty-five. They know most of the tricks and I teach them a few new ones.' That put me in my place for three years.

Then she told me stories about her experiences as head chef at an exclusive gay club in Gothenberg. Kraft Ebbing would have written a treatise on what one of the scullions did to the mince.

And then came the wind. The ship came alive. The insensate metal tingled. The shrouds and lines hummed. Shouts. More sail was hauled aloft. The jib sails above the questing bowsprit curved into taut white blades. The square sails unfurled and bloomed from lower forecourse to dizzy royal. The huge mainsail on its thirty-foot boom swung out over the emerald waves. Top sails, stay sails and mizzen – all blossomed to harness this great exhalation of energy from over the horizon. And the swell, in harmony with the wind, rolled up from behind in cadence after cadence of long, gentle undulations.

It was a perfect wind. It blew in a smooth, steady continuum and for a week we followed the tilting, black pagoda of the *Bounty*. We arrived at Mauritius in time for Peter Simpson-Jones to catch his plane. He'd bet Sven a case of champagne we wouldn't make it. It was a bet he was glad to have lost. And so were we. Sven shared his spoil.

I found Mauritius a disappointment. Perhaps I've been spoilt by spending so many years in the Far East; spoilt by driving along the palm-fringed beaches on the east coast of Malaysia, deserted except for monkeys and wild pigs; spoilt by the islands of Rawa, Tioman and Sri Lanka in off-season.

Mauritius was, paradoxically, both overdeveloped and under-developed. Modern, impersonal, international hotels catering mainly for package tours lined the best beaches. Outside these enclaves of expensive and antiseptic luxury, the villages were shabby and poor. The central mountain range was craggily dramatic but the surrounding countryside was a melancholy waste of sugarcane fields dotted with grim piles of black basalt cleared from the soil. Port Louis was a dusty, traffic-choked shambles of crumbling pavements. It dies at seven in the evening to the sound of clanging metal shutters, bars and chains. I counted eleven padlocks on one shop door. Nevertheless we enjoyed a pleasant if unmemorable week in a modern hotel on the beach at Flic en Flac. The people were friendly and, if anything, a little over-eager to please. The security men in their kiosk at the hotel gate interrogated me every day. 'Was I enjoying myself? How did I like the island, beach, food, hotel room, climate, etc?' My polite replies, lacking Gallic effusive-ness, failed to convince them. By the end of the week they were frantic. I took to scaling the twelve-foot fence to avoid their attentions and the embarrassment of telling white lies. They caught me one afternoon and led me to the gate muttering commiserations. They obviously thought I was quite mad. I felt a pang of guilt when we left. As the taxi drove away they stood in the white, dusty road waving forlornly.

14

Mauritius to Fremantle

After seven months at sea, including ports of call, I wasn't looking forward to the next leg. I was impatient to get to Australia. The prospect of another month on the ocean did not excite me.

After waving to Rosamund until she blended into the fading quayside I went to the bar. Suzanne bought me a large gin and tonic. We sat there glumly. We could hear Walther instructing a group of new trainees.

An Australian girl entered carrying a guitar. She asked if we minded. We politely invited her to go ahead. She curled up in the corner in a semi-foetal position and gave us the benefit of her repertoire.

She commenced very aptly with 'Blowing in the Wind'. Her voice was thin, hard and shrill like chalk being scraped across a blackboard. Every time she missed a note she said, 'Whoops, sorry'. She apologised a lot. By the time she was into her third number and her thirty-third 'Whoops, sorry' I began to analyse the situation. Would she do this at home? How long would her local pub put up with the free entertainment before bankruptcy and the bailiffs came knocking at the door? I realised that many people embark on such a voyage with the 'romantic' notion that if they have even the most rudimentary knowledge (skill is the wrong word) of the guitar or spittle filter, they will immediately be surrounded by an appreciative audience of hearty seamates. Damn Hollywood. Remember *Twenty Thousand Leagues*

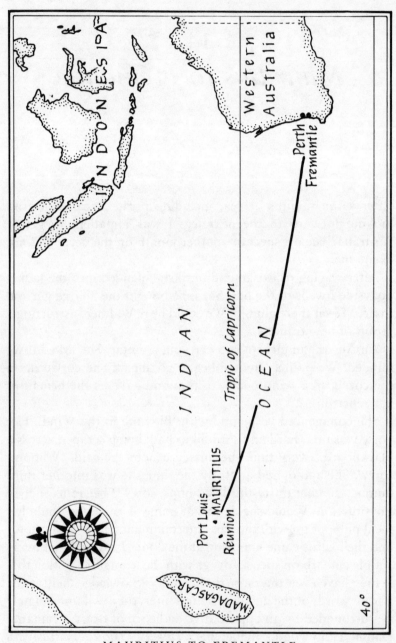

MAURITIUS TO FREMANTLE

under the Sea and Kirk Douglas singing 'It's a Whale of a Tale and a Tale of a Whale'? And on a ship the amateur minstrel has a twofold advantage over performing on land – a captive audience and a generally high increase in the boredom threshold.

By the fifth number I'd begun to twitch. Suzanne recognised the danger signals. She went behind the counter and put on a U2 tape. A barrage of sound sent shock waves through the ship. What'shername got the hint.

I was now a full-time scullion. The job, like most, had its perks and drawbacks. The main drawback was Suzanne. She was a bad influence. She used a lot of red wine in the cooking, or, to be more accurate, while cooking. I was dispatched to the bar every other day to commandeer a five-litre box of wine for 'cooking'. She started early. I, having more experience and having learnt from the folly of a misspent youth, had, in recent years, stuck religiously to the six o'clock rule, Sundays exempt. (It was only after I'd started this enlightened regime that I started to suffer hangovers – they hadn't had a chance to catch up with me before.) I suffered a relapse.

The perks of being a full galley slave were a special diet, regular hours and a good night's sleep. I fell into a routine from which I rarely deviated. I rose at five in the morning and went to the bar to enjoy the best two hours of the day when it was free from the 'ACDC turn-it-up brigade' and the 'turn-it-down South Pacific geriatric gang'. Suzanne and I took a two-hour breakfast of black coffee, Coca-Cola and cigarettes. We listened to music uninterrupted by inconsequential chatter interspersed with shrieks that passed for social intercourse. Somebody had left behind a collection of classical favourites housed in the slots of a neat plastic carry case. We played Handel, Mozart, Wagner, Beethoven and Johnny Clegg at concert-hall volume. We always started and finished the session with the crisp, plangent chords of Handel's 'Messiah'. It was a wonderful two hours that left me mentally cleansed but shaking from caffeine and nicotine poisoning. Suzanne returned to her bunk at seven to sleep out the breakfast chaos.

A week out of Mauritius we came upon something that wasn't on the map. The *Søren Larsen*, some miles ahead, radioed that they'd spotted an unidentified object on the radar. We altered course to investigate.

A gaunt steel pylon rose above the horizon. Sven was puzzled. There were no oil fields in the area. When we got nearer we saw that it rose from the deck of a ship, the *Sedco/BP 471*.

Radio contact was established. The sea was calm enough to allow an exchange of visits. The rescue boat ferried us across in groups.

It wasn't an oil exploration ship as we'd first thought but a floating research station funded by American universities. We were taken on a guided tour of laboratories for analysing geological specimens from the ocean bed. We saw the cinema, gymnasium, library and dining-hall.

They were very efficient. Our tour ended in a small lecture theatre where we were invited to attend an explanation of their aims in layman's terms. The young lecturer waited patiently for us to compose ourselves.

'We are not here drilling for oil,' he began. 'Our aim is pure scientific research into the geological nature of the earth's mantle. The ship and the drill are kept over the target by fourteen propellers – thrusters, we call them. They are controlled by an acoustic beacon on the ocean bed linked to computers which constantly monitor the effect of the wind, waves and currents and instantly initiate the necessary adjustments.' He paused. We all nodded sagely.

'At present,' he continued, 'we are investigating ocean plate tectonics. The ship is drilling into an eighteen-thousand-foot deep fault three and a half times the size of the Grand Canyon created by two plates grinding past each other in opposite directions.' He paused again. Some of us conveyed our awe by emitting prolonged brays. Satisfied, he resumed.

'Why, I hear you ask (we all looked at each other), do we drill into a deep fault when we could reach the earth's mantle in much shallower water?' Hushed expectation.

'The answer is this. Drill bits are expensive. From five to ten thousand dollars each, depending on the number of diamonds.' More brays of awe.

'A fault exposes deeper layers of the earth's mantle. Thus we can drill straight into them without the expense and time wasted by boring down through the upper layers.' Digestive silence.

'We were the first to discover a fossilised magma chamber. A fossilised magma chamber! Imagine that.' The sound of head-scratching while we tried to imagine.

From then on he lost us. His eyes glazed over and he continued without pause about abyssal peridotites; gabbroic and ultramific rocks; pelagic ooze; curvilinear bathymetric trends; Schlumberger logging tools; lithoporosity and un-supported base-rock spud-ins. I was very impressed by the sound of pelagic ooze.

He was forced to cut short his eulogy on submarine geology. The next group was waiting in the doorway. He sighed. We trooped out as they trooped in.

'We are not here drilling for oil,' I heard him begin again. I wondered what the 'BP' stood for in the ship's somewhat functional name. I should have asked.

Back on the *Amorina* I found the bar full of scientists and technicians. The *Sedco/BP 471* was a dry ship. They were getting it down themselves as fast as they could. I fought my way through the scrummage to the counter. The 'Dazzla' was serving.

'I'll have a double pelagic ooze,' I said.

The 'Dazzla's' presence lent the fleet an authentic touch. He was an ex-convict. He was more than happy for everyone to know he'd robbed a bank, served his time and was now going as straight as the Foster's would allow. He was tall and gaunt.

High living, I supposed, rather than time, had 'delved' the 'parallels' in his brow and cheeks. Although he was younger than me, I found solace in his ravaged face: I looked younger than him. His brown eyes smouldered like an underground peat-bog fire.

He served me a gin and tonic before resuming what he liked doing best – talking about himself. He had a fresh audience.

'Yeah. Where was I?'

'On the beach,' an Igneous Petrologist prompted.

'Yeah, I was walking along the beach minding my own business. Gin and mango juice coming up, luv. I broke this branch off this tree, see, and this guy walking his dog says he'll report me. Report me! "If you report me," I said, "I'll cut your dog's fucking head off." He got the message. Was it guava juice or mango juice, luv?'

The assembled Paleomagnetists, Paleontologists, Geochemists and Downhole Hydrogeophysicists ordered more beer.

'Got a farm now,' the 'Dazzla' continued as he passed round the stubbies. 'Raise a few cattle. Snakes are a problem. I hunt them. With a gun. With a two-two. I use a two-two to give 'em a chance. You've got to get 'em first time through the head. Or they'll get you. And there's jumping adders. They'll kill a horseman. Jump right up and bite his leg. Yeah. I hunt them. With a gun. With a two-two. This dog kept coming on my land. I told the owner. I told him I don't know how many times. I told him, "If your fucking dog comes on my land again I'll . . ." Whisky and Coke, vodka and orange, four beers coming up.'

Midway to Fremantle, after days of sailing and motor-sailing, the main drama of the leg occurred – a confrontation between the smokers and non-smokers. Except for the bar and engine-room, all indoor areas were designated 'no smoking'. The non-smokers, or rather a vocal minority of non-smokers, did not like this arrangement. They spent some time lobbying Sven to ban smoking in the bar and exile smokers to the deck. We smokers did not take much notice (we were too busy smoking) until they presented us with a *fait accompli*. Sven, an ex-smoker, capitulated to their wish. A hullabaloo blew up. Sven found himself caught in a vicious crossfire. He tried to compromise. The bar would be a non-smoking area on alternate days. This was a daft idea. It did nothing to mollify the extremists – the 'Dazzla' and myself for the smokers and a watery-eyed, white-wine-drinking Englishman for the *South Pacific*, wallpaper music, turn-it-down sect.

'If anyone tells me to stop smoking I'll stub my fag out in his earhole. Except for Sven and crew, of course,' the 'Dazzla' fumed. I believed him.

I did some research. I consulted the bar bill book. I was outraged. It appeared that the vocal minority hardly drank at all – even soft drinks. Many of their names proudly headed a blank page. Watery-eyes, who, incidentally, liked his classical music Mantovanified and provided with a beat he could tap his Hush Puppies to, was the single exception. He'd shifted a few crates of white wine. The others read Jeffrey Archer novels in the bar. They could do that in the mess.

I bombarded Walther and Sven with statistics. I told them my bar bill for one week was four times the sum total of all the non-smokers' for the last two weeks. This was true if you left Watery-eyes out of the calculation. They were impressed but remained adamant – no smoking every other day. I showed them the 'Dazzla's' bar bill. They were even more impressed but remained impervious to justice and logic. I threatened to give up drinking. That got Walther worried for a while but he was incapable of any prolonged willing suspension of disbelief. I retired defeated.

The deadline approached. I was sitting in the bar the night before the first non-smoking day was due to be implemented.

'What's all this fuss about smoking?' Bjorn asked. He spent so much time in the engine-room he was out of touch with internal politics. I explained. He listened quietly, nodding occasionally. He was a heavy smoker. I waited for the enraged denouncement of the opposition.

'I see,' he said, stubbing out his cigarette. He got up and left. Five minutes later he was back.

'It's all over,' he said. 'No more crap about no smoking in the bar.'

Our expression begged an explanation.

'I went to Sven. I told him I spend a lot of time in the engine-room. It's hot and noisy down there. I told him if I couldn't come to the bar and relax with a drink and cigarette I'd resign immediately and leave at Fremantle. No more problems.'

The trouble with this leg was that it was too easy. No towering, relentless swell swept across the ocean; no wave burst over the bow; no gale howled through the rigging; nobody was flung from their bunk in the middle of the night or fell down the companionway or had hot food tipped in their lap. It was all too tame. If 'Watery-eyes' had been on the ship when we went to Tristan da Cunha, he wouldn't have worried about a whiff of smoke. There was nothing to distract people from the petty preoccupations that plague them on land. And before you challenge the implicit dismissal of passive smoking as a petty preoccupation, let me say this. The air is so clean at sea that after a few days of leaving port my smoker's cough disappeared. But, more to the point, the smoking dispute was only one of many. I chose to write about it because it concerned me personally. The other symptoms arising from too many people in too confined a space on an uneventful leg are too trivial and tedious to relate. I longed for a storm – even a hurricane.

In the middle of the third week it soon became apparent the *Amorina* was behind schedule. There was a lot of radio communication between the ship and the First Fleet Company executives ashore. It was especially important that on our first landfall in Australia the ships should sail in to port together as a fleet. A grand reception was to be held in our honour. The press, television and film cameras were awaiting our arrival. The mayor was dusting down his robes.

Sven told them we'd arrive a few days behind the other ships. That did it. The atmosphere sizzled with heated exchanges. At the time we were sailing along at five to six knots in a fair breeze. The company suggested we motor-sail. Sven thought we'd done enough motor-sailing already. He started his 'Ve are here to sail' routine. The company ordered him to motor-sail. He launched into his pencil-snapping, 'Nobody hundreds of miles away is going to tell me how to sail my vessel' act. The airways were clogged with threats and counter-threats. Contracts were quoted. Small print was closely scrutinised. Polysyllabic words like 'obligation' and 'responsibility' strained the transmitters.

'Obligation! I haf obligations to my trainees. They haf paid to sail and sail they shall,' Sven raved, smashing the phone down. He changed into full uniform and paced the deck muttering imprecations at the horizon. This was a bad omen. It meant he was in his 'I'll go down with the ship before I change my mind' mood.

It hadn't occurred to him that many of us didn't relish the thought of extra days at sea simply to avoid motor-sailing. It was estimated we could be up to five days behind schedule at our present speed. Something had to be done.

The solution was simple – pasta. Suzanne and I made our plans carefully. Sven was no fool.

There were one and a half sacks of potatoes left. I put the full sack at the back of the narrow cool store and hid it behind cabbages, pumpkins and boxes of fruit. I rearranged the chest freezers, burying the excellent South African fillet steak under fishfingers and bags of hideously-coloured mixed vegetables.

That evening we served spaghetti bolognaise. We had made the sauce as minceless as we dared. When Sven came to the hatch I gave him a wobbling mound of spaghetti topped with a spoonful of sauce. He pulled his mouth into a thin, hard line until his lips were like a stretched elastic band. His eyes were bleak.

'More sauce,' he said, shoving his plate towards me. I dribbled a bit more on. He shuffled away muttering in Swedish.

We didn't overdo it. The next evening we served fishfingers with lashings of chips. Sven looked at the fishfingers with mild distaste and ordered extra chips.

On the third evening we dished up macaroni in a bland white sauce with processed peas scattered over the surface. When Sven saw it he stiffened. His face looked as if it had been hewn out of an iceberg. He walked away, stopped and came back.

'Vy ve haf pasta twice in three days? Vonce a veek is enough.'

We feigned embarrassment, mumbled apologies and tried to look convincingly worried. We succeeded.

'Vat are ve having tomorrow?'

We looked at each other. Suzanne wiped the sweat off her brow with the back of her arm. It had been a hot day and we'd boiled the macaroni until it was obscenely flaccid.

'Pasta,' she replied.

'Pasta? *Pasta!*'

'Yah. Pasta. Maybe with fishfingers. I don't know yet.'

'I vant potatoes and meat,' Sven said in quiet, even tones you could have sharpened a knife on.

'We're short of potatoes,' I explained. 'Maybe enough left for two more meals. One probably. No steak left either.'

'So much has gone off,' Suzanne said before he could accuse her of mismanagement. 'Very bad-quality supplies from Mauritius.' This was true. Sven had seen us throwing overboard the stinking so-called fresh tuna fish the first day out.

He spun on his heels and marched to the mess. I watched him spear a slimy white tube. He contemplated it with disgust. Less than a minute later he was out on the deck scraping his plate over the rail.

Later that evening I saw him poking around in the freezers. I'd left the near-empty potato sack near the door of the cool store. That would be his next stop. Things were going to plan.

The following morning we were motor-sailing. Sven was back in shorts, shirt and sandals. As the days passed the wind increased but the engines were kept full on. We made excellent progress, very rarely dropping below eleven knots. At one point we hit twelve point nine knots. Calculations were made. If we could keep up a speed of ten knots we'd be off Rottnest Island the night before we were due to make the grand entry to Fremantle.

Sven got carried away by the excitement of this race against time. He didn't comment on the gradual reappearance of potatoes and fillet steak. He stood in the wheelhouse, legs astride and arms akimbo, his gleaming eyes flicking from the horizon to the liquid crystal speed gauge. The company was happy; Sven was happy; Suzanne and I were happy; everybody was happy; even Watery-eyes grinned happily through a blue veil of smoke.

But the divine ether did not remain silent for long. A journalist on the *Bounty* had picked up the tangled threads of the dispute between the *Amorina* and the First Fleet Company. He had also heard the 'Dazzla' read over the radio a petition requesting the company fix a realistic date to accommodate the possible late arrival of the *Amorina*. This petition had been signed and backed by all the trainees except myself. I like to stand well back out of range of the half-bricks to get an overall view.

To be fair to Sven, the company had brought forward the date of arrival, put it back, then brought it forward again. On the other hand, nobody seemed to consider the plight of the media awaiting our arrival on a specified date or the cost of keeping helicopters, camera crews and assorted parasites on stand-by. The journalist transmitted a coherent, articulate report to his paper, exposing the commercial pressures on the Captains of the slower ships to meet nearly impossible deadlines. An article was duly published. The First Fleet Company was enraged. The ship's radio started to hiss, sizzle, pop and crackle. Aerials melted. The airwaves started to silt up. Contracts were exposed to the light of day again and pored over until the edges of the paper began to curl. Captains, it transpired, were not allowed to express opinions to the press and were held responsible for any views transmitted from their ships.

A carefully worded general reprimand from the highest echelon was radioed to the Captains of the fleet. I transcribed it for Sven and typed it up. As far as I could make out they had him knocked up solid. He couldn't quite fathom the deeper implications of the message. He asked me to explain.

'Don't rock the boat,' I translated, 'or you've had it.'

And there was more to come. The Australian police had received a tip-off that there were drugs on the fleet. We were warned to expect a full customs search with sniffer dogs before we could dock.

'It's because I read out the petition,' the 'Dazzla' complained. 'They [the first Fleet Executives] must have fed my name into the computers and come up with my criminal record. They [the First Fleet Executives and the police] are out to get me. I want an independent witness with me when they [the customs] search my cabin. They'll try to frame me – plant drugs or something.' It appeared a lot of people were out to get the 'Dazzla'.

And even I made a small contribution to clogging the airwaves. It's a complicated story but I'll try to keep it simple.

I shared a cabin with Young Bill. He was the ideal cabin mate. I could, on the rare occasions when inspired, write without fear of interruption. Merely to say he slept a lot does nothing to convey the single-minded dedication with which he pursued this harmless pastime. He hibernated. There was only one season in his life – an endless winter of content. He emerged occasionally, like a squirrel from a dray, to microwave a snack of cheese on toast. (He invariably missed breakfast and lunch.)

He basked in his bunk with a beatific smile on his face. I could see that he didn't sink into oblivion but actively enjoyed his long journeys across the astral plain. Once, after an uninterrupted stretch of eighteen hours, he woke and stared at me blearily.

'Where am I?' he asked.

'We'll be landing in Heathrow in an hour,' I replied.

'Oh good,' he said, and fell back into the deep arms of Morpheus.

But nothing is perfect. There was one drawback in sharing a cabin with him. He had so many clothes we could hardly move. It was like living in a boutique. He'd even attached nets to the ceiling to accommodate his garments. The ample residue was piled on the floor. One day I counted fourteen pairs of shorts.

He'd restocked his wardrobe in Mauritius but wouldn't throw his old clothes away. I nagged him. I implored him to get rid of them but to no avail. Finally I tried persuasion by example.

'Look Bill,' I said, 'this is what you do.' I took two pairs of jeans and a shirt from my own limited wardrobe. I went up on deck. He dutifully followed. I threw them over the rail into the darkness.

'There. Now wasn't that easy? Why can't you do that, you stupid pillock?'

He shrugged and grinned amiably. Then my heart missed a beat. I felt my back pocket. Nothing but a comb. I was down the companionway in two strides. I ransacked my drawer. I looked in my wellies. I shuffled through my papers. I tore my bunk apart, although I knew it was useless. They were gone. I always keep my credit cards in my back pocket. My magic plastic had been consigned to the waves of the South Indian Ocean. I had no money. What would I do in Fremantle? And so, to pick up the tenuous thread of my narrative, that was how I came to add my voice to the babel in the ether.

I radio-telephoned Rosamund. This was a complicated

procedure involving a relay station in Australia and a satellite. It took two hours to get through. After the usual preliminaries and mutual endearments I got to the point.

'I've lost my credit cards.'

'Have you looked everywhere?'

'Of course I've looked everywhere.'

'Are you sure?'

'Of course I'm sure.' Rosamund became suspicious. I'm very rarely sure of anything.

'How can you be so sure you've lost them?'

'Because I threw them overboard,' I said, becoming increasingly irritated.

'You threw them overboard?'

'Yes. That's what I said. O for ostrich. V for velocipede. E for elephant. R for rage. Overbloodyboard.'

'Why did you do that?'

'It was an accident. I didn't mean to. I can't explain now.'

'Are you all right?'

'Of course I'm all right. Listen. This phone call is costing a fortune. I want you to ring VISA and get them to send a replacement to Fremantle. Got that?'

'What have you been doing? How can you throw your credit cards overboard by accident?'

And so it went on. Walther sat on the bench beside me, shaking and groaning with mirth, his head buried in his arms. Peter Doc sobbed in the doorway. Young Bill had gone to bed.

We arrived off the north coast of Rottnest Island on the evening of 11 December. A customs launch butted out to us through the jolting waves. They had difficulty getting aboard. They really meant business. There were about ten of them.

'Where's the dogs then?' I asked.

'Couldn't bring 'em, mate. They'd get seasick in this.'

They split up in pairs and started a systematic search. By the time they reached our cabin their enthusiasm was waning. They looked tiredly at the mounds of clothes. They poked about in a desultory fashion. They soon gave up.

Fremantle surprised me perhaps because I was not anticipating anything special. Years ago a friend from Perth, who had considered Fremantle a mere suburb rather than a separate entity, had dismissed it as a 'backwater smelling of fish where you need to speak Yugoslav'. It has since benefited from a comprehensive face-lift when it hosted with Perth the America's Cup.

It was a pleasant city to walk round (the traffic subdued) with the provincial air of an English county town. Well-preserved Victorian buildings predominated in the central area. Many had spacious wrought-iron balconies. No one building stood out but the overall effect of patterned brickwork, stucco, stained glass, intricate wrought iron, pillars, porticos and pediments would have made John Betjeman feel at home. But the cloudless skies, temperature in the high thirties and the dry air was far from English.

The constant juxtaposition of the familiar and unfamiliar created a strange dream-like atmosphere. Blinding sunlight in a dignified Victorian Street. The tanned clientele wearing shorts in a bar of richly glowing mahogany, brass and engraved mirrors. But the essential difference was – the natives were friendly.

They were friendly in such a natural, effortless and un-assuming way that I didn't notice it until I started to think about it.

They didn't introduce themselves or start pumping your hand. They simply included you in the conversation as if you'd always been there or drew you into whatever debate was raging. They made disconcerting remarks about their fellow habitués which were difficult to respond to without a detailed knowledge of the subject's private, domestic and public life.

'Fred's bought a dag' (clotted wool on a sheep's bum), my

neighbour said as if we'd known each other since National Service.

'Yeah,' I replied.

'I told him.'

'Yeah.'

'He spends more time under it than in it.'

'Yeah.'

'The only good bit's the bung bar' (contraption for warding off kangaroos that goes 'bung' when you hit one).

'Sad about Ken's wife.'

'Yeah.'

'He's going to miss her.'

'Yeah.'

'She used to drive him everywhere.'

I realised that the friendly English pub is a myth. What you really have are groups of friends sharing a room and if a stranger walks in he walks out a stranger. Strangers are not allowed in small-town Australian pubs. Sydney was different.

I decided to sail on the *Søren Larsen*, the flagship, for the final leg to Sydney. Those going the whole way could choose rather than be allocated a ship. With some trepidation I went to the fleet office. Claire, the purser, was overworked and usually at the centre of a crowd of trainees making impossible demands.

I was astonished. She was alone at her desk. As usual she was smoking, taking short nervous puffs and looking from side to side as if she expected a war party of Comanches to appear on the horizon. She greeted my request with understandable cynicism. I'd been going to change to the *Søren Larsen* at Mauritius but changed my mind at the last minute. This had involved her in extra paperwork and awkward berth rearrangements.

'Are you sure this time?' she asked, shuffling papers.

'Absolutely positive.'

She sniffed, sighed, squinted at me through cigarette smoke and entered my name in the appropriate column.

I wandered back to the Esplanade Hotel through quiet, sunny side streets. A group of First Fleet bigwigs, Captains, owners and executives clogged the doorway. I waited for them to untangle themselves. Hans, the owner of the *Anna Kristina*, approached me. He looked agitated.

'I'd like to talk to you,' he said. This sounded ominous. 'I'll buy you a beer.' Several people within earshot swayed as if they were about to faint.

We went to the bar. I sat down and waited expectantly. What had I done to deserve this treatment? I was on good terms with his son Salo but I hadn't saved his life. Hans buying me a beer. Hans buying anyone a beer. Neurons ricocheted off each other.

He returned bearing two beers. There was an awkward silence.

'Cheers!' I said, saluting him with my glass.

'I hear the book's been sold. Bloomsbury and Penguin.' I nodded. There was another pause before he got to the point.

'I'd like you to go on the *Anna Kristina* again.'

I looked amazed. I was amazed. Most ship owners and Captains dreaded having me aboard.

'Why?' I asked, wiping the froth off my nose.

'When you were on the ship before there were problems. Problems with food. Problems with . . . we were inexperienced. No doubt you wrote about these . . . ah . . . problems,' he said, nodding significantly. I nodded significantly back, hiding behind a long pull at my cigarette.

'Well things have changed. Improvements have been made. I've installed a big freezer. Extra storage space for food has been constructed. A new cooker is being fitted right now. No more problems. I'd like you to see for yourself. Experience the new *Anna Kristina*.'

I thought of Claire. The Comanches were gathering on the skyline. What Hans didn't know was that I liked the ship and her crew. Food problems apart, I would be happy to sail on her again. I thought of Mons.

Hans took my reflective silence as a rejection. I decided to exploit the situation. I pushed my empty glass towards him. By the time he returned I knew what I wanted.

'What do you say?' he asked anxiously.

'It's difficult to write at sea. The watch system . . . so disruptive. Difficult to concentrate. Difficult to get into the rhythm of writing.'

'I'll fix that for you,' he said, leaning forward eagerly. 'I'll fix it with John. You won't have to do watches. You'll be free to write when you want. Sleep all night. Pull a rope when you feel like it.'

'You realise, of course, that your kind offer won't influence what I write.' He looked genuinely insulted.

'I'm asking you back because things are really better. No more catering problems. The only favour I ask is you sail on her again. Write what you have to write.'

'It's a deal,' I said. We shook hands. Hans leant back happily. I thought of Claire. The Comanches were pounding down the slope.

'Let me buy you a drink,' I said.

'No, no. Thank you very much. I've got to get back to the ship. So much to do.'

'You'll be passing the office,' I said. 'You wouldn't mind popping in and telling Claire.'

15

Sailing to Sydney

I joined the *Anna Kristina* a few hours before the fleet was due to sail. I picked my way through sacks of vegetables and boxes of fruit cluttering the deck.

Mons was hopping on the spot. Beside him a cheap radio-cassette emitted a horrible wailing noise backed by a rhythm like somebody endlessly stirring a cup of tea.

'Didn't know you were into post-structuralist music,' I said.

'No, no,' he replied still hopping. 'I've been recording aborigine music.' He had, I learnt, been walkabout. He had also acquired startling blond dreadlocks.

'I hope you're not going to play that fucking row for the next three weeks.'

'Wunnerful, wunnerful,' he moaned. I could see he was going into a trance.

I found John. He confirmed my agreement with Hans. I was excused watches. He also offered me the use of his cabin to write in. This was an unexpected bonus.

Helga, a tough-looking Australian girl of German origin, was dipping fruit in a solution of bleach and water. She ordered me to rinse them and store them in two large water-tight chests bolted to the deck in front of the anchor winch – one of Hans's improvements. It took two hours to clear the deck and stow everything away.

Below there was a new chest freezer disguised by a casing of pine planks; and a new stove. We were going to be all right for food. I'd been allocated my old bunk in the bone rack near the

259

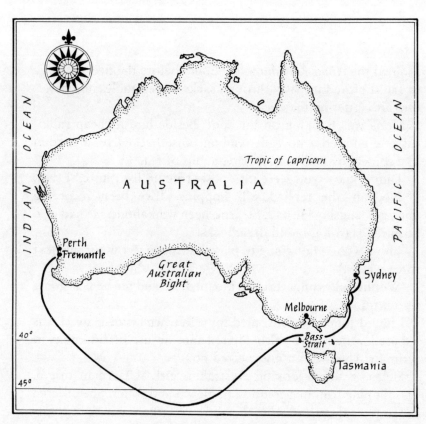

FREMANTLE TO SYDNEY

engine-room and the door to the companionway. The previous occupant had attached black plastic rubbish bags to the ceiling, or rather the underside of the deck, to catch the drips. Lying flat on my back they hung to within two inches of my nose.

The usual crowds waved us off as we sailed out of the harbour. Once out of the lee of Rottnest Island the sea increased. The ship, under full sail and with the motor on, crashed through the short waves at a good eight knots.

'Why the motor?' I asked John.

'The plan is to get down south as quickly as possible. Get down into the Forties. Pick up the big winds. They'll drive us across the Australian Bight. I'm using fuel now precisely because we haven't got enough to risk pottering about near the coast. The longest route is often the fastest.'

We went to the radio kiosk which doubled up as the chart room. John spread out a map.

'We've got to get past Cape Leeuwin before we can turn east anyway, but the winds here are not reliable,' he said, drawing his finger along the empty coastline. 'That's the Nullarbor Plain. Eight hundred miles of desert. There's nothing there. Look what it says here. Stratified cliffs of four to six hundred feet. No towns. Nowhere to refuel. We've got to get big winds. We've got to go down here,' he said, stabbing his finger between the fortieth and fiftieth parallels. 'Then we'll sweep across the Bight and curve in towards the Bass Strait. It's going to be interesting. You're going to experience some real sailing.' Whenever professional sailors talk of 'real sailing' they mean it's going to be cold, wet, rough, extremely uncomfortable and, above all, dangerous.

By late afternoon Rottnest and the rest of the fleet had faded astern. The swell had risen to well over ten feet. The sun shone fitfully through wind-torn holes in the scudding clouds. The sea was a lurid, bottle-green tumult flecked with grey. A lot of the new trainees were displaying the same colours. There was a lot of vomiting. One by one, most of them disappeared below.

John was right. The further south we went the stronger the wind but also the rougher the sea. At latitude forty-five degrees the temperature dropped to ten degrees. Add to this the wind chill factor and it was extremely cold after the high thirties of Fremantle. There I'd bought two pairs of shorts and suntan lotion in anticipation of a long but sunny haul. But we sailed, really sailed, sometimes covering 200 miles in twenty-four hours. However, although it was exhilarating and satisfying to know we were making such good progress, there's a limit to how long one can watch the sea rush by, so I often took refuge in John's cabin.

This was situated in the stern just in front of the helm. To enter one descended a perpendicular ladder. The cabin was about eight foot by eight. A wide bunk ran the length of one wall. Shelves and cupboards lined the others. Hans had preserved the original features. John explained the functional nature of the design. Two portholes set in the wall facing the bow gave him a view of the length of the deck and enabled him to monitor the trim of the sails and the angle of the yard arms. Through a glass dome in the centre of the flat roof he could keep an eye on weather conditions. The Captain is always on duty.

I spent a lot of time there wedged behind the small, fixed table, trying to write. I didn't get much done. It's difficult to concentrate or write with any degree of fluency when the page is rising and falling and the trappings of one's trade – pens, cigarettes, matches and ashtrays – need constant supervision. I read a lot instead, hiding such gems as Spillane's *The Big Kill* or *Art, Science and Human Progress* under the pad whenever John 'dropped in'. A peculiar range of books accumulates on ships.

On New Year's Eve we were to have a treat. Katrina produced a pair of frozen turkeys. Ian, an intense young man with piercing eyes, was the cook for the day. (Hans's improvements had not run to employing a full-time cook.) He set about the task with his usual energy and application. He was going to do the full works – roast potatoes, three veg and stuffing. As the afternoon wore on he became more and more harassed. Sam, a businessman, watched him balefully. It was not done to offer advice to the cook of the day.

'Watching him cook is a time-and-motion expert's nightmare,' he muttered under his breath. 'The only thing he's got right is to get the turkey in first. He's boiled the sprouts to rags and hasn't peeled the spuds yet.'

At that very moment the oven door burst open. Both turkeys shot out. They bounded round the mess with Ian in pursuit. He cornered one and grabbed it. He dropped it quickly. It was still sizzling. Eventually, with the aid of a greasy tea towel, he rounded them up. They had been well basted in bilge water. I was more amused by his language than by the incident. There is always more entertainment value in listening to someone curse whose normal mode of speech is unadorned with quaint Old English verbs used as adjectives.

'Get back in there you illegitimate, copulating, hirsute female orifices,' he snarled, kicking the oven door shut.

Despite the problems and the fact that the turkeys escaped again, it turned out to be a tolerable meal for those who got the surface cuts. Deeper in, the half-cooked flesh was pink. The stuffing came, with much apology, as the dessert.

Afterwards we sat round drinking red wine. I was looking forward to an evening of traditional revelry when suddenly Monotonous Morris burst in. His face was tight with barely contained fury. The relieving watch had lingered too long over the meal. He'd spent an extra half an hour on the helm.

'We've saved you some turkey,' Helga said, producing a plate of pink flesh. 'There's plenty of veg left.'

Morris took it without a word and tipped it into the waste barrel. He went straight to his bunk and lay there staring at the deck planks.

Monotonous Morris had earned the alliterative appendage for his ability to deliver lengthy and tedious monologues. He was ready to pontificate on each subject from military history to Indian architecture. He had a *Reader's Digest* mind; he could hit the nail hard on the head and bend it. He had at his disposal an anecdote for every occasion, though, to be fair to him, he often prefaced them with, 'When a friend of mine was shark-fishing, pot-holing, tobogganing down Everest . . .' He was, he claimed, an ex-member of the Israeli secret service.

It was not to be a night of revelry. Many of the trainees were still stricken with seasickness. I left them pale, listless and withdrawn. When not on watch they took refuge in sleep.

Sam drank himself into a state of mumbling incoherence and retired early. John and I broached a five-litre box of passable Australian red. It was going to be a quiet, uneventful New Year's Eve – or so I thought.

Just after eight somebody, I forget who, clattered down the companionway shouting that the tiller had broken. Drinks were abandoned.

At first I found the news rather alarming. I didn't expect the ship to sink but I did have visions of us careering out of control at the mercy of the wind to the South Pole.

It's on such occasions that one can witness in operation the qualities which make a good Captain. John gave orders quickly with a quiet authority. The wooden gratings were lifted to expose the tiller arm. The chains were disconnected and the arm lashed tight so we ran with the wind. The yard arms were adjusted and braced. Then the steering mechanism cowling was removed to reveal the cause of the problem. A cast-iron cogwheel, eighteen inches in diameter, had shattered. It was a vital part of the transmission between the tiller arm and a smaller cog on the steel shaft running from the centre of the wheel. There was no spare. It had been cast at the turn of the century. We would have to wait until Botany Bay to have a new one made up.

The lashing of the tiller arm was a temporary measure. We were safe enough as long as the wind remained steady and the fifteen-foot swell continued to march up from behind in neat, orderly ranks. Nobody mentioned what would happen if the wind suddenly veered or if a line of swell broke rank and sent a freak wave crashing into the side. It did occur to me.

We had to regain the steering. John came up with various solutions. The simplest emergency measure was to trail a wooden beam on two ropes astern. By shortening one rope or the other one could create a 'drag' that would provide a very crude form of steering. It was not suitable in such a swell. There was always the risk of the beam being hurled over the stern.

John opted for the more complicated but, in the end, most effective remedy which entailed regaining the use of the wheel itself.

Johan started the generator and brought up the electric drill. Two blocks (pulleys) were fixed on the rail either side of the wheel and two more were attached directly below on the deck. A rope was then wound three times round the wheel shaft, passed through the blocks and attached to the tiller arm. Success depended on whether or not the rope would grip on the steel shaft.

It took six hours to complete the makeshift steering system. At two in the morning John went to the helm. He turned the wheel. The rope gripped. It worked. In fact some of us preferred it to the original system. Without the spring-loaded chains it seemed tighter and the rudder more responsive. I think John was as surprised as the rest of us at the successful outcome. For the last hour, although outwardly calm, he'd forsaken his pipe and, instead, smoked a large number of my cigarettes. This had worried me more than the fact that the ship was hurtling southwards hurried along by an endless succession of glinting, black ridges. The wind and waves had rushed us into 1988. We had not paused to toast the advent of the new year.

I usually got up early but on that first day of 1988 I woke late. Above the sound of the waves gurgling along the hull and the cosy, domestic clatter of cutlery, I could hear Monotonous Morris droning on about Exocets. Breakfast is a good time to deliver monologues – people are less inclined to interrupt or offer an opinion.

'You're on watch in ten minutes,' Helga said. Morris went up in flames.

'Don't you give me orders,' he screamed, 'or I'll break your fucking jaw.'

It was not what he said but the venom of the delivery which caused me to sit up abruptly, cracking my head on the planks above. Silence. The companionway door slammed. The clinking of cutlery resumed.

'I was only reminding him,' Helga said faintly.

Living at close quarters in such a confined space as the *Anna Kristina* would prove, on land, a strain. Imagine twenty people sharing a living space less than twenty feet by ten where six of them slept in cavities in the wall and the rest in cramped cubicles leading off. Put in this space a large table, two stoves, storage cabinets, work surfaces and a sink. Provide them with a single handbasin and restrict them to one shower a week. Make them take turns to cook for the others and wash up. Wake them every other night at four a.m. and midnight. Knead and pound dough at three in the morning and set a generator snarling and rattling at four-thirty. And so on. Then Morris's outburst would not seem strange. But at sea, paradoxically, it seemed very strange indeed.

At sea, whether bobbing about in mid-Atlantic or crossing the Australian Bight, one becomes blessed with a great reservoir of tolerance for the habits and idiosyncrasies of one's fellow travellers. I noticed it in myself and in others. People put up with me and I put up with behaviour that, on land, would have involved me in numerous altercations. Grumbling about food apart, my new-found tolerance and patience surprised me. At first I thought I'd caught some sinister disease that renders one apathetic and indifferent to human folly. At home my patience span can only be measured in micro-seconds. Smart young ladies in cloaks (funny how they always wear cloaks) who generate supermarket queues by laboriously writing cheques, stub first, for ninety-nine pence, send me into a murderous frenzy. And as for people who manage to choose the one unpriced tin out of a thousand – bring back the rack! But at sea I was content to listen to imbecilic conversations and put up with certifiable behaviour.

What was up with Morris then? We knew he had a low opinion of women in general and Helga in particular. Was it because they were taller than him and she a bad cook and German to boot? But even I had refrained from mocking her cooking after seeing the hurt look on her face after I'd called the grey sludge she'd served up Stalag Stew. We never found out what was bothering Morris but from that morning on, in Helga's presence, he radiated palpable waves of animosity which, unfortunately for both of them, culminated in an ugly incident at Botany Bay.

Towards the end of the second week, as we neared the Bass Strait, the sea decreased and the sky cleared. Bare breasts and the fumes of Ambre Solaire heralded the sun. The wind eased but we still made a good six knots. A school of dolphins joined us. We crowded to the bow to watch them power along in the glassy pressure wave. Watching wasn't enough for Mons. He wanted contact. He clambered along the bowsprit and hung from the chain beneath. His heels clipped the waves. The dolphins were quick to spot a game. One by one they surged forward beneath his feet, slicing the air between his ankles with their dorsal fins.

John came forward. He watched for a while, puffing ruminatively on his pipe.

'Get back here, you silly bastard,' he shouted.

'Wunnerful, wunnerful,' Mons gibbered as the dolphins queued up to cleave his dangling feet.

'Get back here now. That's an order. We don't want another . . .' Reluctantly Mons obeyed.

'Bloody fool,' John grumbled. 'More accidents happen on the bowsprit than any other part of a ship. People very rarely fall from the rigging. The height keeps them alert to danger. But on the bowsprit . . . they treat it like a playground. They relax. They fool around . . . then along comes the big wave and they're gone. And if you fall the ship goes right over you.'

After the rigours of crossing the Bight we enjoyed a few idyllic days of glorious sunshine. But was this the calm before the storm? The Bass Strait is a notorious shipping hazard. The weather can change in minutes from a 'seraphic calm' to a 'howling storm'. The First Fleet, unaware of this shorter but more perilous route, had sailed south of Tasmania before turning north. Matthew Flinders and George Bass discovered the strait in the late 1790s and it was first charted by HMS *Beagle*.

When I looked at the charts they did nothing to inspire confidence. From what I could see it appeared to be a marine obstacle course: Skull Rock; Black Pyramid; Sea Elephant Reef; Squally Cove; Waterwitch Reef; Judgement Rock; Devil's Tower; Cape Farewell; and so on.

I turned to the pilot book. It was no more encouraging. It stated that the channel south of King Island 'is obstructed by many dangers and should not be used except in emergency, unless local knowledge is available'. We took the less exciting route, the north channel. The *Trade Wind*, of course, took the south channel.

The pilot book also warned of shark-fishing fleets' trailing lines, reefs, barely submerged rocks, tidal streams and oil rigs. King Island, I learnt, was first settled by sealers who turned to salvage as a more profitable and less exacting occupation. Many of the capes are named after some of the sixty ships wrecked on its coast.

Christmas Island and New Year Island struck a merrier note

until I read they were 'covered in mutton birds and infested with poisonous snakes'. So, if you were lucky enough to survive a shipwreck and swim ashore through shark-infested waters, you found yourself ankle deep in venomous serpents. And what were mutton birds? They sounded revolting. Were they sheep killers? I asked Mel.

'Don't talk to me about mutton birds,' he said grimacing. 'I'm a vegetarian.'

Mel, like many of the others, was enjoying the first day free from seasickness. To be seasick for one day is bad enough but to feel constant nausea for nearly two weeks is a very demoralising experience.

'It saps your will,' he said. 'By the third day I would've done anything, paid anything to get off the ship. And I still would. I didn't think it would be like this. The *Anna Kristina* is for young people.'

Mel was in his mid-fifties. I tried to console him by pointing out that Glen and Trish, both in their early twenties, had also been seasick for nearly two weeks.

'The sealers used to boil them down for oil.'

'What?'

'Mutton birds,' Mel said. 'Very fatty flesh.'

'The trouble with this sort of holiday is you're trapped,' Sam said. 'You can't get away if you don't like it. I haven't been seasick but I wouldn't do this again. If you're in a bad hotel you can leave.'

'And this won't last,' Mel said gloomily, looking up at the sky. 'Round here it can be flat as a bowling green one minute and the next forty-thousand-ton tankers are in trouble.'

That afternoon a diaphanous haze turned the sky into a tent of powdered blue silk. I watched a beautiful transformation take place. The haze hardened into delicate aqueous ribs to form the most exquisite herringbone pattern I've ever seen. It was quite eerie.

The next day the Bass Strait lived up to its reputation. It was a cloudless dawn. The sea was a muted celadon green under a sky of wet blue lacquer. The air glinted. The wind had a hard edge to it. The waves were closing up and rising as the ocean squeezed itself between Tasmania and the mainland. You didn't have to be an experienced sailor to sense that a dramatic change in the weather was imminent.

Then low on the horizon we saw an oily white cloud rolling up from astern like a colossal, foaming tidal wave. It seemed more a part of the sea than the sky. But just as it was about to envelop us, it rose and swept overhead accompanied by a blast of wind.

'Just what we need,' John said. 'We'll be through the strait in no time. Excellent sailing weather.' Those who'd enjoyed a brief respite from seasickness did not share his feelings.

We made good progress. By evening, after an exhilarating day of flying spray and vomit, we were approaching the eastern exit. Then the wind turned. Motoring against it would have wasted what little fuel we had. We learnt over the radio that some of the ships were heading for the shelter of Wilson's Promontory. The *Bounty* was 400 miles behind. The *Amorina* hove to. The *Søren Larsen* chose to batter on under power.

We reached Wilson's Promontory in the night. Dawn found us at anchor in Norman Cove with the *One and All*. The *Trade Wind*, *Our Svanen* and *Eye of the Wind* were anchored in adjoining coves. The *Tucker Thompson* had yet to arrive.

It was our first sight of land for two weeks. The scenery was magnificent. Bald granite hills, their lower slopes patched with scrub, formed a natural amphitheatre enclosing the cove and a forested plain. A cloud, like liquid alabaster, planed flat by the powerful easterly wind, was being gradually extruded between two peaks.

We didn't get ashore until the afternoon. The wind off the land prevented us from using the rowing-boat. We had to rely on lifts from the *One and All*'s rescue boat. This was one aspect of Hans's passion for authenticity that irritated me. An outboard motor would have saved us a lot of unnecessary hanging around.

Wilson's Promontory was a national park. Behind a sand dune a camp site lurked discreetly in the bush. Glen and I, followed reluctantly by Mons who wanted to get straight into the wild, headed for the shop. We hadn't had a cup of tea since Fremantle.

Katrina had, in her usual perverse approach to life, bought every kind of 'tea' but plain, unadulterated tea. There was plenty of jasmine tea, mint tea, garlic tea, curry tea but no ordinary, plain unadulterated tea. No wonder half the ship was spewing up.

Laden with bags of unperfumed tea, we set off to climb the nearest hill. We had to be back on the ship by six when, wind permitting, we were due to sail. It was hot and sultry. We saw lots of gaudy parrots and wombat holes.

About halfway up the weather changed. Inland the sky was a matchbox blue above tumescent white cumuli. Over the sea hung an evil-looking pewter cloud. It thundered like an artillery range. Forked lightning contused the sky.

'I'm going back,' I said.

'Why?' Mons asked. 'It's not far now.'

'The wind's veered. That cloud's coming right for this hill.'

'So what?'

'Lightning,' I said.

'How many people get struck by lightning?'

'I have and once is enough. I'm off.' Glen came with me. Mons continued alone, got drenched and returned to the ship otherwise unscathed. So ended our brief visit to Wilson's Promontory. As Larkin said, 'Nothing, like something, happens anywhere.'

We set sail for Eden. Above us wraith-like cirrus clouds feathered the sky. Inland, bulging, tumbling cumuli dwarfed the mountains. To the east a booming nimbus cloud trailed a grey skirt. To the west a sinking copper sun burnished the waves.

And, of course, a rainbow arched triumphantly over all. It must be a strain to be a weather forecaster in this part of the world.

Katrina rushed up, looking excited and coy at the same time.

'I've got a present for you,' she breathed, handing me a packet of tea. 'Tea!' she explained. 'Real English tea like they drink in England.'

I looked at the packet. She looked at me expectantly.

'Well?'

'Well . . . um . . . thank you very much.'

'You don't seem very pleased.' I suffer from the unfortunate social handicap of not being able to tell little lies to please people. I can tell big lies – 'Sorry, officer. I've got emphysema.'

'It's Earl Grey,' she trilled. 'The girl in the shop said the Queen drinks it.'

'It's perfumed,' I said, backing away.

We cleared the Bass Strait and sailed for Eden. On 12 January we came close inshore at Hicks Point where, coincidentally, Cook first sighted Australia. It was pleasant to sail in sight of the coast. We could feel the heat radiating from the 120-foot dunes and smell the heavy, musky scent of eucalyptus and gum nuts.

A twin-hulled speedboat propelled by twin 200-horsepower engines pulled alongside. They were abalone fishermen. They generously bombarded us with heavy oval shells. They shouted cooking instructions before roaring off in a spectacular welter of foam. There were enough for everyone but we each took care to cook our own.

We rounded Cape Howe. Twelve miles from Eden the wind turned. Johan estimated we had twenty litres of fuel left, probably less. It was not enough to batter us through the strong headwind. John solved the problem by motoring out to sea. This enabled us to tack in close to the wind.

Eden was an anticlimax. Evocative names always raise my

expectations. Bahía de Todos os Santos had, after all, lived up to its promise.

It was a small port at the foot of wooded hills. With the exception of the *Bounty* and the *Amorina*, the rest of the fleet was moored alongside a stubby mole. For a moment, but just for a moment, we seemed to enter a time warp. Masts and spars hid the concrete fishermen's co-operative and the old clapboard houses on the hillside took Eden back to the days when it was a whaling station. And what a fine sight the gaily coloured *Anna Kristina* must have presented as she curved across the bay.

The town itself was firmly fixed in the twentieth century. The whalers had given way to tourists who came for the fishing and fine beaches. On top of the hill there was a single wide main street of pubs, restaurants and shops. I shall always remember Eden for the best hamburger I've ever had – a tottering edifice of minced beef, bacon, onion, fried egg, slices of pineapple, lettuce, gherkins, tomato and Kraft cheese.

We sailed on northwards. The days passed in a pleasant lacuna of sunshine until the wind turned again, forcing us to take shelter in Wreck Bay. We and the *Tucker Thompson* dropped anchor nearest the shore opposite a glittering, white swathe of sand. A rocky promontory protected us from the north wind. We could hear the cicadas in the bush. A few aborigines pottered about on the rocks. The other ships dropped anchor further out.

We waited impatiently to go ashore. John was talking to the Commodore on the radio. He looked worried. He kept glancing at us.

'We can't go ashore,' he announced. 'It's an aborigine reservation. There's a village behind the hill.' We were enraged. We protested and threatened mutiny.

'The Commodore's in a difficult position.'

'The one on page twenty-three of the *Kama Sutra*,' Wayne shouted.

'Somebody, I don't know who, has informed him that we won't be welcome. There's even a rumour there could be violence. Something about eight hundred aborigine protesters armed with spears. He says it would be tactless to go ashore. We symbolise the invasion of their country.'

'What fuckwit started that rumour?' Wayne said. 'There must be a helluva lot of albino aborigines in this reservation. Look!'

We looked. A group of white Caucasians were strolling along the beach. (They were pink, actually.) I liked Wayne. He could spot bullshit before it hit the ground.

A rubber dinghy snarled round the promontory and headed towards us.

'Here they come. Prepare to repel boarders,' somebody yelled. The dinghy pulled alongside. Two portly aborigines clambered over the rail. They introduced themselves. William and George seemed very amiable. They admired the ship. They thought it was very pretty. I showed them round below. They were astonished.

'And this is the shower,' I said proudly, opening the door of the slimy, foetid cubicle. William sniffed. His broad nose twitched and wrinkled in disgust.

'We've got proper showers in the village,' he said. 'Why don't you come ashore? Have a good wash.'

'We thought there was going to be a reception committee.'

'Reception committee?' He looked puzzled. 'We didn't know you were coming. We can arrange a game of volleyball on the beach. Maybe knock up a barbecue for tonight.'

'We've been invited ashore,' I told John.

'Let's go,' Wayne shouted. He waved a fist in the general direction of the fleet. 'There's a fuckwit out there somewhere.'

We lowered the authentic dinghy. Mons, Johan, Helga and I piled in. Wayne rowed us ashore.

'Of course it's a trap,' he said. 'There's hundreds of 'em hiding in the bush. Can't you feel their eyes on you? We'll die under a hail of boomerangs.'

Mons rowed back to collect Katrina who was knocking up sandwiches for a picnic. I picked up his boomerang and slung it up the beach. It cartwheeled in a dead-straight line and stuck in the sand. Wayne retrieved it. He wandered back.

'This is how you do it,' he said, hurling it high in the sky. It described a long, looping arc and whirred back. It landed in the sand beside me. I moved away from Wayne. He launched it again. Again it returned. The trouble was it didn't return to him. It hummed over my head.

'Lay off, you silly bastard,' I said. Wayne was enjoying himself. He threw it again. I moved further away from him. It spun past my earhole.

'That does it,' I snarled, beating him to it. I hurled it out to sea.

'It's your bloody fault,' I told him. I was worried about Mons's reaction. Then I heard it coming back. Alcohol and nicotine have raised my nervous system to such a raw, irritable peak that I can hear somebody dot an 'i' at a hundred paces. I threw myself flat. The boomerang thrummed over my prostrate self.

'That's the best throw I've ever seen,' Wayne congratulated me.

Mons, Johan, Wayne, Helga and I set off for the village. The others stayed on the beach. After a ten-minute walk along a path through the bush we arrived. Mons looked disappointed. The village was a cluster of neat, white clapboard houses on brick bases. Lace curtains declared privacy. Lawnmowers ululated. Cars and pick-ups lined the shaved grass verges. We found the shop and bought ice-cream. It didn't sell alcohol. There was no pub. We could have been in the outer reaches of Dorking.

'What a dump,' I grumbled. Mons drifted away in search of

ethnic squalor. An orange VW camper pulled up. William and George offered assistance.

'We're out of red wine on the ship,' I said.

'We're going to Jervis Bay,' William replied. 'We can drop you off at a supermarket on the way.'

'How far?' I asked. I'd read a lot about the Australians' concept of distance. They thought nothing of driving 300 miles for a tube of Foster's with the lads.

'Ten minutes' walk,' William said. 'Hop in.' We hesitated. The sun blazed down. We hopped in. William drove as though he were delivering Black Magic chocolates to his girlfriend. We traversed a landscape of undulating bush exuding a rippling, oily rise of heat. About twenty minutes later they dropped us off at the supermarket. It was in the middle of nowhere. (It was strange how this trip kept revitalising clichés.) A red-brick, plate-glass emporium, stocked with all the decadent goodies of the West, stood in a wasteland of cacti, thorn and stunted scrub. You could buy anything from ear swabs to surfboards.

I bought two boxes of Château Sheepdip and a couple of cartons of Benson and Hedges because they came with free pens. I'm a sucker for that sort of gimmick. Wayne bought a block of ice big enough to sink the ship, half a gallon of rum and a clutch of the longest liquorice sticks I've ever seen.

'Ten minutes' bloody walk,' I fumed as we paused for a rest at the top of the first rise. The road snaked ahead into the shimmering horizon. 'How long was the drive here – twenty, thirty minutes? If I see them again I'll strangle them with your liquorice.'

'Abo's revenge,' Wayne said. A puddle was forming around his feet. We set off again. Johan had no shoes. The verge was shattered rock and thorn bushes. He hobbled along manfully. We tried thumbing a lift. Nobody stopped. We obviously looked like the Manson gang.

We stopped for a rest again. Johan's feet were in a bad way. Wayne's ice was shrinking.

'Take that fucking liquorice from round your neck,' I said. 'No wonder we can't get a lift. They look like dead snakes.'

A tiny two-door Honda pulled up. It was the woman from the village shop.

'I recognised you,' she said. Her daughter got out to let us in. I sat on Wayne and Johan on Helga. A quarter of an hour later we were straightening our joints at the edge of the village when the orange VW camper clattered up.

'Volleyball on the beach this afternoon,' William said. The sun pounded down. We made polite, noncommittal noises.

'I'm going back to the boat,' Wayne said, 'while I've still got some ice left.' Johan stayed to have a shower.

Back on the *Anna Kristina* we lay on the deck drinking rum cocktails and watching Helga varnishing the rail. She was always volunteering for deck work. Sanding, scraping, painting, oiling, plugging, caulking and sewing sails had the same effect on her as alcohol had on us. In Sydney John was to take her on as permanent crew.

Wayne was determined to finish the ice. We drank beneath the stars. He had an engineering firm in New Guinea. He regaled me with hair-raising stories of ex-patriate life there.

'Got this friend,' he said, handing me a rum cocktail and a vitamin B pill.

'Yeah!' I said with just the right tone of incredulity.

'Got this friend,' he continued. 'He's made a stack. He goes to England and buys small cargo ships – two or three thousand tons. Get's 'em for just above scrap value though they've got a bit of life left in 'em. He packs 'em full of high explosives, flies in a Filipino crew and sails 'em down to New Guinea and North Australia. The big shipping lines don't like carrying explosives or mixing 'em with general cargo. Puts up the insurance. Floating bombs. Anyhow, he gets good money from the mining companies for carrying the stuff. But here's the clever bit. He then sells the ship to the Indonesians for double what he paid. Then he does it again. One sank off the coast of Liberia. He was eighteen hours in the water before he got ashore. They won't let him take 'em through the Suez Canal. If one went up it'd blow a hole in Egypt as big as Ireland. Ready for another?'

A bonfire flickered on the beach. The sound of revelry drifted across the water.

'I don't think I can make it to the barbecue,' I said. There was no reply. Wayne was asleep.

By dawn the headwind had blown itself out. A blue ribbon of smoke curled lazily up from a black patch on the beach. I watched Mons ferry the last of the revellers back to the ship. They looked haggard and exhausted. They clambered wearily aboard and retired below.

One by one the ships weighed anchor and sailed around the point for the open sea. Nobody from the other ships had been ashore.

We sailed to Jervis Bay to fulfil a promise. The people and local council had made a substantial donation to the funds of the First Fleet Re-enactment Company. Our presence, anchored off shore for two days, drew thousands of sightseers, giving the local economy a brief but lucrative boost.

On 18 January we sailed into Botany Bay exactly 200 years after the original fleet. Nearly 1,000 yachts, cabin cruisers and wind surfers provided an escort. It was a grand reception. Champagne was served.

We had an eight-day wait ahead of us before we could sail for Sydney Harbour. Later that afternoon the fleet was ordered to an anchorage in a stretch of water near the runway of Sydney Airport protruding into the bay on reclaimed land. On the way we passed close by the *Trade Wind*. They bombarded us with water-filled condoms. We retaliated, using up our limited stocks. Somebody had been busy.

Monotonous Morris decided to bring into action the heavy artillery. He opened one of the storage chests near the bow and let fly with oranges, apples and grapefruit. This offended

Helga's sense of domestic economy. She protested. Morris ignored her. She protested again. Morris snapped. He hurled himself upon her. He seized her by the throat and, forcing her backwards over the chest, started to throttle her. Johan stormed to the rescue. He dragged Morris off and set about him. Johan was very strong. Morris was lucky. The 'reticent twins' taken on to replace Henrik, who had kept themselves to themselves to such an extent that I can't even remember their names let alone tell them apart, restrained Johan and saved Morris from serious injury. John radioed the harbour police. Morris got an early lift ashore. Charges were not preferred.

This ugly incident took the bubbles out of the champagne. We were shocked, not so much by the violence (I've seen better punch-ups outside Mothercare) but by the realisation that something had been festering inside Morris for all those weeks until finally the acid had eaten through the wire and released the spring.

Commodore Phillip and the officers of the First Fleet had found Botany Bay a disappointment. The sandy soil was not suitable for cultivation and the grass was too coarse for grazing. Phillip had taken three longboats slightly further north to explore the adjacent bay. They discovered what he described as 'one of the finest harbours in the world', capable of providing protection for 1,000 ships of line in its numerous coves and inlets. They also found a cove with a stream of fresh water. On 26 January 1788 Phillip moved the fleet there; and 200 years later to the day we sailed the last few miles of an eight-and-a-half-month voyage to the heads of Sydney Harbour to commemorate and celebrate the birth of a nation.

A colossal armada of yachts, launches, speedboats, cabin cruisers, water scooters and wind surfers surrounded the fleet as it sailed in line into one of the most impressive harbours in the world. We could hardly see the water for boats and champagne corks. An estimated 2,500,000 people crowded the shoreline, rooftops, balconies – in fact any vantage point that could offer a view. The 'old coathanger', as Sydney Harbour Bridge is affectionately known, and the controversial opera house, the huge interlocking shells of its roof echoing the sails in the harbour (and occasionally the odd shark's fin), embellished rather than detracted from nature's grand design.

The fleet dropped anchor in the lee of the opera house in Farm Cove opposite the Royal Botanic Gardens. There was no freshwater stream but green islands of trees rose above the dense crowds on the invisible grass. We were in an amphitheatre of eyes.

Prince Charles and Princess Di were attending a VIP reception in the opera house. On the radio we heard him declare that 'as history goes, two hundred years is barely a heartbeat. Yet look around you and see what has happened in that time. A whole new free people and the people of a whole new free country, Australia.'

Mons sniffed and pulled a face. Johan muttered darkly about aboriginal land rights. Glen, Mel and the other Australians aboard were profoundly affected by the occasion. Some of them had difficulty blinking back the tears. Formations of aircraft rumbled overhead.

'Military aircraft,' Johan muttered.

'What did you expect?' I asked. 'Boomerangs and kooka-burras?'

'Not *military* aircraft.'

'Oh, for Christ's sake, can't you let one day pass without exercising your conscience. Get some champagne down you.'

The harbour police launches cordoned off the mouth of Farm Cove. The focus of public and media attention moved to the 'Tall Ships' as they motored one by one on 'sail parade' out of the harbour. We resented them. What had they done? They'd sailed from Fremantle to Sydney and staged a race to Hobart, Tasmania. They'd spent the last two weeks moored in Sydney Harbour looking pretty. Sponsored by the Australian government, they had diverted public attention from our eight-and-a-half-month voyage.

'Get down, you ratbag,' Mel shouted. This was virulent abuse indeed from a man who rarely allowed himself the luxury of a 'damn'. Unnoticed, Mons had climbed the mast and unfurled the yellow sun of the aborigine flag. The crowd on the shore did not seem to notice. There were no howls of execration or cheers of support. In that now quiet and placid cove all I could hear was a contented murmur and the continuous popping of beer cans. John climbed wearily up to remonstrate with Mons. It took him over an hour to talk him down. Meanwhile the champagne flowed.

Hans was furious. It was, apparently, illegal to fly another flag, whatever the nation or significance, above the Australian flag in port. He sacked Mons. Mons declared that he was going to leave the ship anyway. Johan resigned as a gesture of solidarity with Mons. Suddenly I felt very tired. The champagne flowed on.

Then the sky exploded. Sydney Harbour Bridge became an incandescent arch over a Niagara of flame. Green stars studded the black dome. Livid contusions seared the night, effloresced and died in a pink haze of drifting pollen. A vast anemone of light and fire blossomed overhead. Golden tentacles reached down at us and, just when their probing, wavering tips seemed about to expire, they exploded into a multiplicity of smaller crimson anemones.

'Oh wunnerful, wunnerful,' Mons moaned. We'd arrived.

A NOTE ON THE AUTHOR

Marcus Mainwaring grew up in South Wales and Malaya.
He was educated at Stowe and graduated from London University with
a BA in English Literature after which he taught at a junior college in
Singapore for five years. He has travelled extensively in the Far East
and Europe. His poetry has been published in various journals,
magazines and anthologies. He collects rare books and lives
with his wife in Hampstead.